W9-BXX-652

THE IceBowl

Cheers for *The Ice Bowl*

"An insightful, bone-chilling replay of pro football's greatest game. *The Ice Bowl* recaptures all the chilling drama and finally gives Ken Bowman his share of pro football's most famous block."

—Gordon Forbes, pro football editor, *USA Today*

"A hundred myths and misconceptions about the Ice Bowl have been answered. This book captures the essence of Lombardi's finest hour."

—Bob McGinn, Packers beat, *Milwaukee Journal Sentinel*

"Kudos to Ed Gruver. Reading this terrific book brought back all the thrills and chills of being there. Now everyone can share the experience of arguably the greatest pro football game ever played."

—Chuck Mercein, #30, Green Bay Packers starting fullback, Ice Bowl Game

"A very accurate account of a major game in NFL history. Thanks for helping me remember the coldest day of my life!"

—Ralph Neely, #73, All-Pro offensive tackle, Dallas Cowboys, 1965–77

"It was a day I'll never forget and it was the highlight of my broadcast career with the Packers. Ed Gruver brings it back vividly."

—Ted Moore, Packer play-by-play announcer, 1960–69

"What a story. I've been away from that game for 30 years, and the manner in which it is presented here brought it right up to the 1990s. It's a story of two great teams, two great coaches, and great fans—all laboring over a game played in unbelievably cold conditions."

—Art Daley, former sports reporter, *Green Bay Press-Gazette*

THE IceBowl

The Cold Truth About Football's Most Unforgettable Game

by Ed Gruver

McBooks Press, Inc.
Ithaca, New York

Copyright © 1998 by Ed Gruver

All rights reserved, including the right to reproduce this book or any por-
tion thereof in any form or by any means, electronic or mechanical.
Requests for such permissions should be addressed to: McBooks Press, Inc.,
ID Booth Building, 520 North Meadow St., Ithaca, NY 14850.

Library of Congress Cataloging-in-Publication Data

Gruver, Ed, 1960-
    The Ice Bowl : the cold truth about football's most unforgettable game
/ by Ed Gruver.
        p.   cm.
    Includes index.
    ISBN 1-59013-080-4 (trade pbk. : alk. paper)
    1. National Football League—History. 2. Dallas Cowboys (Football
team) 3. Green Bay Packers (Football team)   I. Title.
    GV955.5.N35G78   1998
    796.332'64—DC21   97-13600
                                                         CIP

Excerpts from the radio broadcast play-by-play of the December 31, 1967
NFL championship game are used with permission of radio station WTMJ.

Additional copies of this book may be ordered from any bookstore or
directly from McBooks Press, Inc., ID Booth Building, 520 North Meadow
St., Ithaca, NY 14850. Please include $4.00 postage and handling with mail
orders. New York State residents must add sales tax. All McBooks Press
publications can also be ordered by calling toll-free 1-888-266-5711.

Visit our website at www. mcbooks.com.

Distributed to the trade by National Book Network, Inc.
15200 NBN Way, Blue Ridge Summit, PA 17214
800-462-6420

Printed in the United States of America

9 8 7 6 5 4 3 2 1

For Michael

Contents

Prologue
Cold Enough For You? 11

Chapter One
Lombardi: The Making of St. Vincent 25

Chapter Two
Landry: The Coach as Intellectual 40

Chapter Three
Fire and Ice: Apprenticeships in New York 52

Chapter Four
The Tactical Evolution 61

Chapter Five
New Regimes in Green Bay and Dallas 75

Chapter Six
The Struggles of '67 89

Chapter Seven
An "Appointment with Destiny" 103

Chapter Eight
The NFL Playoffs 116

Chapter Nine
Game Day in Green Bay 130

Chapter Ten
Wind Chill and the Will to Win 146

Photos 163

Chapter Eleven
"Doomsday" Dominates 171

Chapter Twelve
The Drive 187

Epilogue
The Cold Truth 217

Appendix
Statistics and Play-by-Play 231

Index 251

Acknowledgments

THIS BOOK COULD NOT HAVE BEEN WRITTEN without the cooperation and inspiration of the following people.

First and foremost, I have to acknowledge the influence of my late brother, Michael. It was Mike who first shared the Ice Bowl experience with me. I was just seven years old when this 1967 NFL championship was played. Being so young, I knew very little about football, but I can remember Mike, who was 12 at the time and a devoted Green Bay Packers fan, explaining this now-classic game to me into the early evening hours on that memorable New Year's Eve. The way in which he spoke of Vince Lombardi's legendary Packers and Tom Landry's up-and-coming Dallas Cowboys, struggling in the devastating cold, left me with an enthusiasm for this game that I carry to this day.

I have seen countless football games since then, and while a few qualify as great games, the Ice Bowl remains to me the greatest game in NFL history.

This book, then, was very much written for Mike.

I could not have accomplished this task without the love and inspiration provided by my family. My late father, John Gruver, remains a constant source of inspiration to me, as does my mother, Roberta, and my sisters, Kathie and Patrice.

Many thanks also to my wife, Michelle, for enduring a second book, and to my daughters, Patty and Katherine, for allowing their father enough free time to do a little writing.

Thanks also to my nephews and niece—David, Matt, Adam, and Lia—each of whom is special in their own right, as well as my late brother-in-law, Joe.

Thank you to my publisher, Alex Skutt, and his associate, S.K. List. Their enthusiastic belief in this project right from the start provided additional inspiration. A special thank you as well to Wendy Skinner, whose outstanding editing skills and editorial comments accounted for considerable improvements in the original manuscript. Throughout the ten-month process of pulling this book together, each of the above operated with a high degree of professionalism that was greatly appreciated.

A debt of gratitude is also owed Vernon Biever for his outstanding photos of the Ice Bowl. Thank you, too, to Michael Rider for the cover and page design and excellent play diagrams.

Thanks also to the coaches, players, and members of the media who shaped that cold day in Green Bay, and who took the time thirty years later to reflect warmly on their experiences. All were very gracious, and their candid recollections have provided a fresh, inside look at pro football's most memorable game.

Cold Enough for You?

I N HIS ROOM AT THE NORTHLAND HOTEL, Tom Brookshier awoke to the loud ringing of his bedside phone. Reaching out from beneath the covers, Brookshier picked up the receiver and heard the sweet voice of the hotel operator deliver a wake-up call he has never forgotten.

"Good morning, Mr. Brookshier. It's seven o'clock and it's *13 degrees below zero.*"

The same message was delivered over and over to the other hotel guests on the morning of Sunday, December 31, 1967. The day had dawned bright but cold in Green Bay, a small midwestern city that christened itself "Titletown, U.S.A." after the Packers beat the New York Giants 37–0 in the 1961 championship game. A mass of arctic air had settled over the region and temperatures held steady at minus-13 degrees Fahrenheit, while 15-mile-per-hour winds dropped the wind-chill factor to minus-38.

Brookshier was in Green Bay as a member of the CBS-TV broadcast crew covering the National Football League title game between the defending league-champion Packers and the Dallas Cowboys. The 1967 showdown marked the second straight year the two teams were meeting to decide the NFL title and a berth in the Super Bowl. Coached by Vince Lombardi, the veteran Packers owned an impressive roster. Dotted with future Hall of Fame players, it included Bart Starr, Ray Nitschke, and Willie Davis. The Packers had held off the

Cowboys the year before, stopping head coach Tom Landry's team with a goal-line stand in the final minute to clinch a 34–27 victory and a trip to Super Bowl I. Now a chance at Super Bowl II was within each team's reach.

The teams had not met in a meaningful game since then, and with both the Packers and Cowboys winning their respective divisions and advancing through the first round of the expanded playoffs, NFL fans eagerly anticipated the rematch.

When the CBS crew landed in Green Bay on Friday, the air was cold—temperatures hovered at 20 degrees under cloudy skies—but reasonable, considering it was Green Bay and it was late December. Brookshier and broadcast partners Frank Gifford and Jack Buck checked into The Northland, the downtown hotel serving as press headquarters for the game, then went to inspect the conditions at Lambeau Field. As Lombardi showed them around the turf, he boasted of the underground heating system installed the previous summer.

"We have these coils under the ground," Lombardi said in a husky voice tinged with a Brooklyn accent. "If the weather should turn colder we will just increase the power. There's no problem. The field will be in excellent shape as long as it doesn't snow. The forecast is for clear and dry. The field won't be frozen. The heating system will take care of that."

The three men stayed to watch the Packers and Cowboys work out. The Cowboys seemed almost giddy. Recent NFL title games in Green Bay had been played in equal parts snow and mud, and the Cowboys, whose offense was built on speed, worried about the Wisconsin weather. But when they worked out Friday, the field was dry and temperatures were in the high 20s. Saturday saw further improvement. The sun broke through the clouds, and afternoon temperatures climbed to 30 degrees. For Green Bay, this was downright balmy.

"We worked out the day before the game, and boy, it was a

good field," recalled Bob Lilly, Hall of Fame tackle and anchor of Dallas' "Doomsday" defense. "Maybe a little soft, actually. But the turf was good, and we felt real good about it."

The improving weather favored the Cowboys, since the Dallas offense was designed to deliver big plays. When Landry took over the team in its 1960 expansion season, he used an elaborate offensive style to camouflage a lack of talent. Yet even as the team acquired blue-chip players through the college draft, he continued to develop his offense, making it the most complex in the NFL.

While Dallas sought to deceive defenses with multiple plays and formations, Green Bay relied on power football, executing a minimum number of plays with maximum effort. Some NFL coaches liked the beauty of the passing game, but Lombardi favored the crunching feel of his power sweep, where the guards pulled and provided a convoy for the big running backs to follow.

Hank Stram, who had coached the American Football League champion Kansas City Chiefs against the Packers in Super Bowl I the previous January, had an up-close look at Lombardi-style football in a 35–10 loss. "They were pure vanilla," Stram said of Green Bay's grind-it-out style. "No nuts, no chocolate, just pure vanilla.

"Vince Lombardi's teams were like him—a sledgehammer. Nothing fancy. No frills, no gadgets, just a straight-ahead attack designed to run over you or through you."

Bad weather would negate Dallas' team speed and favor Green Bay's basic style, but players in both camps were confident the elements would not be a factor. After Saturday's practice, Dallas quarterback Don Meredith remarked on the weather in his Texas drawl, ". . . not bad. If it gets no worse, we'll be fine."

Lombardi told *Dallas-Fort Worth Press* reporters the forecast for Sunday was favorable. Even if it did get cold, he said, the heating blanket beneath the stadium floor would keep the bluegrass sod playable.

"Gentleman," he said, "the field will not be frozen." Later, he told *Green Bay Press-Gazette* sportswriter Len Wagner, "I guarantee it won't be the cold weather that beats the losing team."

Brookshier, Gifford, and Buck felt confident on the eve of the game that the title would be decided with no consideration for the weather. Even a slight shift in the wind and a drop in temperature to the 20-degree mark early in the evening left them unconcerned.

Cy Elsberger, however, was concerned. As resident forecaster for the U.S. Weather Bureau, Elsberger studied developing climate patterns and warned of a fast-moving cold front. Elsberger went on the air Saturday and forecast the following: "A cold air mass, moving down from Canada, will bring more fresh, cold air."

The cold air swooped in late Saturday night. Brookshier remembered the drop in temperature as being sudden and dramatic. "Saturday night, myself, Paul Hornung, and Gifford went out for dinner, and it was a normally cold evening," he said. "When we walked out of the restaurant around midnight, it was 15 below zero. When we woke up the next morning at The Northland, all the windows were iced up."

Radio personalities at WTMJ, which would later carry game announcer Ted Moore's play-by-play broadcast, interrupted their morning programming to advise church-goers to dress warmly. As they listened to the icy forecast, Packer fans studied the Sunday sports section of the *Green Bay Press-Gazette*. A banner headline on the front page read, "Packers Shoot for Historic Third Straight Title." Beneath a smaller headline that read, "Green Bay Pick To Stop Cowboys," sportswriter Lee Remmel offered one of three previews on the page:

"A date with destiny?

"At high noon on a sunny day in September, an optimistic Vince Lombardi told a fan luncheon, 'The 1967 Packers have the wherewithal to win a third straight National Football League championship.'

"This afternoon, at 1:05, they get a historic chance to validate his positive assessment in the chill of Lambeau Field, where the reigning world champions duel the explosive Dallas Cowboys for the NFL title—and a berth in the Super Bowl. . . ."

In his Green Bay apartment, Packers' fullback Chuck Mercein was awakened by the alarm on his bedside clock. Still half asleep, he switched on his radio.

"I heard them say it was minus-16 and thought I must have heard it wrong," Mercein recalled. "So I called the radio station and the guy said, 'It's minus-16, and it's going to get *colder.*'"

Staying at the Holiday Inn motel in nearby Appleton, the Cowboys greeted game day with tired eyes. Despite Landry's instructions to the hotel operator not to put any calls through to his players' rooms, the phones rang constantly all night, courtesy of overzealous Packer fans. Lilly and roommate George Andrie took their wake-up call at 8 A.M., were informed of the weather and looked outside their window where they saw nothing but ice, snow, and sliding cars. Andrie filled a glass with water from the bathroom tap and wordlessly splashed it on the window. "It froze," Lilly recalled, before it hit the sill.

In their room down the hall, Dallas offensive stars Lance Rentzel and Ralph Neely found their windows so iced up they couldn't even see outside.

"Holy . . ." Rentzel said.

"What's the matter?"

"Siberia," Rentzel said.

Neely, the team's all-pro left tackle, offered a comment on receivers being too delicate, then looked outside to see for himself.

"Holy . . ."

"At the hotel we were at, we had to walk outside to get to the restaurant to eat breakfast," Neely remembered. "I walked outside and almost died."

Packer guard Jerry Kramer awakened in his Green Bay home and kiddingly told his wife Barbara, "It must be ten below zero."

He was laughing, but then he heard on the radio it was actually 13 below. "I started to shiver," he said later.

In The Northland, referee Norm Schachter breakfasted with the officiating crew scheduled to work the game. The main topic of conversation was the weather. None of the officials had packed gloves or earmuffs; only three had brought thermal underwear. "We need more clothes," Schachter thought.

The referee got the owner of a local sporting goods store to sell him and the crew earmuffs, thermal underwear, and thermal socks. Schachter geared up for the game with thermal underwear, two pairs of thermal socks, a turtleneck nylon ski sweater, plastic baggies on his feet to keep the heat in, a large plastic bag under his black-and-white striped football shirt, gloves, and earmuffs.

Wearing heavy coats and thick gloves, the CBS crew left The Northland at 11 A.M. and made their way to Lambeau Field. Located on the southwest end of town, the stadium stands as a concrete-and-steel testimony to the love Packer fans have for their team.

Built in 1957, Lambeau Field was the fourth in a succession of Green Bay stadiums. With the growth of the NFL in the 1950s, it was apparent the Packers—the last survivor of the small-town teams that had first made up the league in the twenties—needed a new facility to compete with large-market clubs. Because the building of the new stadium was going to be the responsibility of both the city and the team, the $969,000 projected cost was going to have to be raised via a bond issue. When put to the voters, the bond issue passed by a 2–1 margin, insuring Packer fans their team would remain in Green Bay.

The new stadium was dedicated to Packers' founder Earl "Curly" Lambeau, and though its original seating capacity was 32,150, it was expanded three times—in 1960, '63, and '65—so that by 1967 the seating capacity was 50,861. Despite the expanded seating, to this day the stadium has remained practical and free of frills. It has cinder-block rest rooms and grandstands supported by metal frames, but its single-level, bowl-shaped layout provides a sweeping view of the field. Lambeau's top row of seats—Row 60—is said to be closer to the field than the first row in the Los Angeles Coliseum, and this closeness lends an intimate feel to home games.

By late morning, Lambeau Field resembled the surface of a glacier, snow-covered and gleaming in the frozen sun-light. Helicopters hovered above the stadium, blowing snow off rows of spectator seats. A sign at field level warned, "CAUTION—FIELD ELECTRIFIED." It was a reference to the 14 miles of plastic-coated heating cable installed at 12-inch intervals $6\frac{1}{2}$ inches below the surface. Technicians put a control panel in a utility room under the stadium from which the staff could power 780,000 watts of electricity to the system as soon as the air temperature fell below 45 degrees. Once the coils were turned on, control panel lights showed which sections of the surface were warm and which needed defrosting.

The "electric blanket" was not unique to Green Bay; the Air Force Academy in Colorado had a similarly heated field, as did several other college teams. Yet while the universities used their heating units to induce grass growth in cold climates, Lombardi installed his system believing the $80,000 gridwork of coils would prevent Lambeau's bluegrass field from freezing.

With kickoff scheduled for 1:10 P.M., long lines of traffic grew outside the stadium as the hour of noon approached. Fans wearing parkas and ski masks, and packing lap robes and Sterno-heaters drove across the bridge at De Pere, to Oneida Avenue and into the parking areas, where attendants in yellow caps collected fees. Packer fans lacking tickets gathered at Speed's Bar, the Lyric Lounge, the Picadilly, or one of the town's other favorite clubs to watch the game on TV or listen to Moore's radio broadcast. Many who lived close to Lambeau and were walking to the game stopped to warm up at Kroll's Restaurant, a cafe that locals describe as being "a short punt" from the stadium.

Mark Thurston, the 10-year-old son of Packer guard Fred "Fuzzy" Thurston, was among those walking to the game. Fuzzy had called his house after arriving at the stadium and told his wife, "Don't let him go. It's too cold." Despite his father's warning, Mark slipped his coat on, left the house and headed to the stadium. He had only gone a block when his grandmother picked him up and took him to the game, where he stayed, wrapped in a sleeping bag, for the next three hours.

Arriving at the stadium, the CBS crew examined the playing surface. The tundra crackled underfoot, then turned slippery as frost gave way to moisture. The field was hard, but not completely frozen. Lombardi's underground system seemed to be working. The reality, however, was that the electric blanket was making matters worse. The turf was moist because the combination of tarpaulin covers and heat from the electric coils had dampened the surface. But when Johnny Proski's 40-man grounds crew began the two-hour task of removing the tarp at 8 A.M., thus exposing the field to the cold air, the moisture froze. By noon, the field was hard and slick as glazed pavement.

NFL commissioner Pete Rozelle was in Oakland for the AFL championship game between the Raiders and Houston Oilers, which was scheduled for a 4 P.M. Eastern Standard Time start. Rozelle spoke with his assistants in Green Bay that morning, and listened as they debated whether the game should be postponed. The commissioner told Jim Kensil, his right-hand man, to seek out Lombardi.

"We're concerned whether you can play or not," Kensil told the Packers' coach.

"What do you mean? The weather's beautiful. The sun is shining."

Lombardi showed him the control panel for the underground heating system, and told Kensil the field was playable. Rozelle's main concern was the health of the players and fans, but when a doctor told him the cold would not be injurious, the NFL commissioner made his decision. "Okay," he said. "Let's play."

Later that morning, however, Packers' public relations director Chuck Lane told Lombardi the system wasn't going to be operational for long. Because of the intensity of the cold, the decision was made by John Harrington, the engineer who installed the heating unit, to turn it off. "If we tried to increase the electricity to warm up a field this cold," one member of the grounds crew said, "we would increase the power just enough to blow up the ball park."

The Packers' boss frowned. "It's going to be known as 'Lombardi's Folly,'" he said.

Harrington told reporters his system just couldn't handle the cold. "It will do a good job down to zero, but it was 18 below, and then that wind," Harrington said. "We had it up as high as we dare go. We can't go any more."

To provide the players with protection from the elements, Proski's crew built makeshift pipe-frame shelters around each bench. Heavy plastic was draped over the back and sides of the frame, leaving the front open. A canvas tarp was placed over the plastic, then anchored with concrete blocks.

Fans pushing through the turnstiles and walking into the stadium encountered a number of unfamiliar sights and sounds. Some of the normal trappings were evident—golden "G's" decorated the interior walls of the stadium, along with the red, white, and blue bunting customary for championship games. The NFL emblem was painted in rich red, white, and blue colors at midfield, and the hash marks and yardline numerals were painted gold. Each end zone carried a team name painted against a white backdrop—PACKERS in bright yellow in the north end of the field; COWBOYS in royal blue in the south.

In place of a pregame show, fans watched workers breathing clouds of steam as they pushed brooms across ice patches. The Wisconsin State University of La Crosse Marching Chiefs, scheduled to play before the game, were silent. After a field practice that morning, 11 members of their unit had to be rushed to the Brown County Veterans Memorial Arena for treatment for cold exposure. Instead the fans heard the hollow-throated roar of eight Hunter space heaters, blasting out 320,000 BTUs an hour. Stationed at each bench, the units had worm-hose attachments which funneled the heat into the players' shelters.

"What can you do?" Proski sighed to a reporter. "You do all you can, but the man upstairs gives us this weather for some reason."

An hour before kickoff, the Packers shouted, "Let's go!" and began filing out of their locker room. To Lombardi, their cleats sounded like hailstones hitting concrete. A roar flooded down from the stands, which were by then about two-thirds full, when the Packers emerged from the stadium tunnel at the north end zone for warm-ups. Sun glinted off their bright yellow-gold helmets, marked on the sides with the "G" that was the most famous monogram in football.

The Lombardi dynasty was now in its eighth season, and the Packer uniforms—forest green jerseys with yellow-and-white piping on the sleeves and bright yellow pants with green-and-white trim on the sides—were a national symbol of excellence, like Yankee pinstripes and Boston Celtic green.

Since Lombardi felt that excessive clothing restricted movement, the Packers picked up thermal underwear from equipment manager Dad Braisher, then cut the sleeves off at the elbows and the pants at the knees. Kramer debated whether to wear gloves, thinking he could psyche the Cowboys into believing the cold didn't bother him. But then he remembered it was 13 below zero. "Who the hell am I kidding?" he thought, and picked up a second pair of gloves.

Packer defensive tackle Henry Jordan felt the sting of the icy wind. He quipped later that Lombardi had gotten down on his hands and knees to pray for cold, and had stayed too long.

Lombardi and his chief lieutenant, defensive coordinator Phil Bengston, followed the team onto the field, and Bengston noticed that the sights, sounds, and sensations of the day were different than any he had experienced in his long career. The thousands of brightly-colored hunting and skiing outfits in the stands gave the stadium a reddish tinge. Bengston described it as a "red halo surrounding the playing field" and said it remained a vivid image in his memory.

Green Bay middle linebacker Ray Nitschke squinted as he stared up at the stands. "You could hardly see any faces," he recalled. "Everyone was bundled up so much."

Following the Packers down the ramp was Brookshier. The former Philadelphia Eagles' defensive back joined CBS in 1962 following his retirement as a player. After two years as a color commentator on CBS Radio, he was named to the network's television broadcast crew. The 1967 championship was his first chance to work a title game, and he handled the pregame, halftime, and postgame reports.

"I went down the ramp with Boyd Dowler, Carroll Dale, and Bart Starr," he remembered, "and Lombardi's walking down with us. Dowler and those guys had cleats on, and they came down off the ramp and they skated. They looked like Sonja Henie. I thought, 'Oh, man.' They looked around, and Lombardi put his heel into the ground and said, 'It's perfect.' They looked at him like, 'The old man is really nuts.' But that was Lombardi's attitude."

Wearing a black fur hat, beige woolen overcoat, and tan leather gloves, Lombardi watched his team go through drills. When he heard the roar of the crowd behind him, he turned to see the Cowboys coming down the ramp.

Dallas had celebrated its sixth season in the NFL the year before by ordering new uniforms. Their white jerseys bore blue satin numbers, and the TV numerals, usually found on the sleeves, were on top of the shoulders. Their pants were a metallic silver-blue poly-urethane knit, and their helmets were silver with blue-and-white striping down the middle and a blue-and-white star on the profile.

The Cowboys immediately tested the playing surface. "Pure ice," thought Rentzel. Landry took the field wearing a long fur coat, fur hunter's cap, and hooded sweater. He felt so heavily bundled up he joked to an assistant that he moved "like a polar bear with arthritis." Sitting with a contingent of Cowboy fans on the west side of the field was Landry's wife, Alicia. Before long, her eyelashes froze together, and she had to wrap her feet in plastic bags to prevent them from freezing.

Dallas players tried to go through their normal pregame drills, but the weather wouldn't allow it. Rentzel was so cold he could barely breathe. Backs and receivers skated when they tried to cut. Neely walked to the Dallas sideline and was struck by the strong scent of peppermint schnapps. He looked up, and saw fans swigging from small silver flasks. "Wish I had some," he thought.

Some of the Cowboys pointed to a spot in the stands where a Packer fan was holding a sign that read, "COLD ENOUGH FOR YOU?"

Landry looked across the field and saw Lombardi, his former coaching companion, grinning and holding his hands near the surface as if to warm them with his heating system. The frozen field favored the Packers, and both sides knew it. Defensive tackle Jethro Pugh kicked at the icy field with his metal cleats and muttered, "That . . . Lombardi. He turned off his machine."

On top of the press box, an NFL cameraman was disgustedly stripping unusable film from a magazine. "(The cold) slows down the drag in the camera," he told *Press-Gazette* writer Bob Woessner. "It makes the film brittle."

Sportswriter Frank Luksa of the Fort Worth *Star-Telegram* slipped and fell on a snow bank outside the stadium and rolled into a ditch. Two onlookers had to form a human rope to pull Luksa out.

Fans scraped ice off the seats and lit small fires around the stadium to keep warm. Most people's faces were hidden behind mufflers, ski masks, even surgical masks. *Green Bay Press-Gazette* sportswriter Jim Zima discovered the ultimate in layering when he came across a fan who was wearing six pairs of socks, three pairs of pants, three coats and muffler. *Press-Gazette* photographers Ken Behrend, Russ Kriwanek, and Orvell Peterson snapped photos of fans cooking hot soup in the parking lot, carrying banners that read, "PACKERBACKERS FROM BEAR LAND!" and huddling in front of warm-air blowers. Hundreds of fans wrapped in mackinaws, sleeping bags, and blankets stood under the stands eating charcoaled chicken and sipping from coffee cups and brandy flasks. Marie Johnson of Wassau told *Press-Gazette* reporter Dave Devenport she hadn't missed a Packer game in eight years. "We just had to come today," Johnson said, smiling. "This is history, you know."

When Devenport asked William Putnam of Milwaukee why he was willing to venture out in the arctic cold, Putnam laughed. "I'm nuts, that's why. Just like 50,000 other people."

A heated stove was placed inside the press box, but it did little to blunt the cold. One writer wondered aloud, "When does ballpoint ink freeze?" A press box attendant placed a cup of hot coffee on a ledge, and it froze solid within minutes. Long lines formed in front of the coffee urn, and the combination of the writers' breathing and steam from the hot coffee clouded the windows with ice.

Packers' business manager Tom Miller and press box attendant Joe Melotte tried scraping the ice off the windows, but it was futile. Finally, Melotte told reporters, "You've got a choice of opening the windows and freezing to death, or not seeing anything." Some of the writers began chipping away at the ice with credit cards and the edges of their empty coffee cups.

Baltimore Sun reporter Cameron Snyder thought playing conditions were "atrocious," and said so in his story the next day. Sportswriter Bob St. John of the *Dallas Morning News* felt the game should have been postponed, but national television was ready, and St. John knew the NFL had to keep its commitments. Down on the field, CBS technicians were wrapping electric blankets and pads around the TV cameras to keep them from freezing.

Inside the 40-foot CBS mobile unit located beneath the stadium, directors Tony Verna and Bob Dailey, and producer Bill Creasy sat with their crew as the network prepared to start its national telecast. An associate director began the countdown: "Ten seconds to air . . . nine . . . eight . . ."

Inside the mobile unit, crew members alternately studied their monitors and the ticking clock. One producer compared a television crew in the seconds before a broadcast to tourists aboard an ocean liner helplessly watching a tidal wave approach. The crew barely breathed as the count for the historic broadcast reached its climax.

"Three . . . two . . . one . . . We're on!"

Gifford took a deep breath and let the rest of the country in on the startling conditions at Lambeau Field by announcing:

"Good afternoon, ladies and gentlemen, and welcome to the National Football League championship at Green Bay, Wisconsin . . .

"The temperature is thirteen degrees below zero . . ."

When Dallas won the coin toss and the Packers chose to defend the north goal, a writer joked, "Was that goal or *pole?*"

As Packer placekicker Don Chandler prepared to kick off to Cowboy rookie return man Sims Stokes, it was apparent the record cold would brand this game unique in pro football annals.

What followed over the next three hours was one of pro football's greatest games, an epic struggle that has come to be surrounded by more myths and legends than any in NFL history. To many, it remains a game shrouded as much in wonder today as it was shrouded in ice on New Year's Eve, 1967. It is a game forever immortalized in NFL lore as the "Ice Bowl."

Chapter One

Lombardi
The Making of St. Vincent

"**C**'MON, LIFT THOSE LEGS, LIFT 'EM. HIGHER, HIGHER. Move those damn legs. This is the worst-looking thing I ever saw. C'mon, Caffey, move your legs. C'mon, keep them moving. C'mon, Willie Davis, you told me you were in shape. Faster. Crenshaw, you're fat. Ten bucks a day for every pound you can't lose. Move those legs. Dammit, what the hell's the matter with you guys. Let's move. LIFT THOSE LEGS!"

Vince Lombardi's voice reverberated across the two practice fields on Oneida Avenue, opposite Lambeau Field, the site of Packer home games in Green Bay, Wisconsin. The mid-July sun burned the steamy bluegrass turf, and brought small rivers of sweat from the 70 men who, clad in white shorts and T-shirts, were competing for the 33 roster spots on pro football's defending world championship team, the 1967 Green Bay Packers.

At the height of the Lombardi years, cars and trucks carrying spectators routinely arrived half an hour before the ten A.M. workout. Mothers with station wagons crammed full of wide-eyed children would pull to the curb and ask the policeman at the gate, "When do the Packers start to practice?" As many as two thousand fans, some from out of state, flocked to the sideline viewing areas and filled the low green bleachers. Children in the crowd wore youth-size Packer jerseys, the most popular being Bart Starr's number 15. They stood behind the railing near the spectator benches, where some of the famous players like Starr, Ray Nitschke, Herb Adderley, or Willie Wood usually stopped after practice to autograph scrapbooks and footballs.

Most of the fans' attention however, was focused on Lombardi, who after arriving in Green Bay in 1959, had in just two years lifted the Packers off the bottom of the NFL standings to championship status. Lombardi directed the practices in a starched white T-shirt, forest green baseball-style cap with an interlocking "G" and "B" in gold on the front panel, beige football pants rolled up on his calves, thick white athletic socks, and black ripple-soled coaching shoes. The exposed skin on his neck, face, and arms, normally a Mediterranean, olive-colored tone, was tanned walnut brown by the summer sun. His hair was graying at the temples, and he had long arms and big, hard hands. He studied the proceedings from behind black-framed sunglasses, his face occasionally breaking into a gap-toothed grimace.

As Lombardi moved around the practice field, his was a presence people could *feel*. Bill Curry, who played center for the Packers in 1965–66, said it's difficult to articulate how forceful Lombardi's aura was. "It was unique," Curry said. "When Lombardi came around, everybody got afraid, but highly active. The voice, like the personality, had just the most indescribable intensity."

Between the two practice fields stood a 15-foot-high steel camera-tower, with signs posted on either side reading: "KEEP OFF—POLICE ORDERS." At the top of the tower, a cameraman recorded the day's practices on film. Like almost everything else connected with the Packers, the camera tower has special significance in Green Bay. On a windswept July afternoon in 1960, one year after Lombardi came to town as head coach and general manager, a strong gust toppled the tower and landed it on Nitschke's helmeted head, knocking him to the wet ground. The hard plastic shell absorbed the blow, and although the helmet's web suspension was punctured by a tower bolt, it protected the future Hall of Fame player from serious injury.

By 1967, the tower had added significance. At the base of the structure was a chalk-drawn square, where members of the print media were sent to watch daily practices. The chalked territory was referred to in Green Bay as "the magic square." By Lombardi's orders, local newspapermen like Glenn Miller of the *Wisconsin State Journal,* Lee Remmel and Art Daley of the *Green Bay Press-Gazette,* Chuck Johnson and Oliver Kuechle of *The Milwaukee Journal,* and Bud Lea of the *Milwaukee Sentinel* were told to stand there when observing Packer workouts. Visiting members of the media, like Leonard Shecter, who was in Green Bay in July of 1967 to interview Lombardi for *Esquire* magazine, were also assigned to the restricted area. Lombardi got away with such indignities because his word in Green Bay was absolute. When one of his assistants, Norb Hecker, tried to install a similar area after taking over as head coach of the expansion Atlanta Falcons in 1966, members of *The Atlanta Constitution* stalked off the field in protest. Hecker caved in; he didn't have Lombardi's clout.

Lombardi was distrustful of the press, and preferred to keep the media at a safe distance. Miller felt the Green Bay boss met each question like it was "a stab in Packer territory and must be defended against." Lombardi almost visibly flinched whenever a sportswriter asked him a question, and he occasionally lashed out at them. "Gee, that's a stupid question," he would say, or "Why in the hell would you ask a question like that?"

Once in awhile, a reporter would lash back. Jerry Izenberg of the Newark (N.J.) *Star-Ledger* engaged in a memorable verbal sparring session with Lombardi on September 26, 1965. The Packers had just defeated their Western Conference rivals, the Baltimore Colts, 20–17, and this without Starr, halfback Paul Hornung, and fullback Jim Taylor, all of whom were on the injured list.

At the postgame press conference, Izenberg asked Lombardi, "Did you ever think you could win a game without Starr, Hornung, and Taylor?"

"Certainly."

"You mean you never had any doubts?"

"I told you, certainly!"

Izenberg could see Lombardi getting angry, and he said, "Look, I'm not trying to badger you. Let me ask you this in a different way. Did you ever think you'd have to coach a game without them?"

Getting red in the face, Lombardi snapped, "That's a very stupid question, mister!"

Insulted, Izenberg snapped back. "I don't think you coached such a brilliant game, mister!"

"How dare you say that! You don't know a damn thing about football!"

"Agreed," Izenberg said. "And how dare you tell me my question was stupid. You don't know a damn thing about journalism. You stick to football and I'll stick to journalism. If you don't want to answer, don't answer!"

Smart enough to know when he was wrong, Lombardi settled down. "What do you want to know?" he calmly asked Izenberg.

Off-the-cuff statements were not Lombardi's strong point. "My game is football," he gruffly told one reporter. "Not 'Twenty Questions.'"

"I have seen too many seemingly sound statements blow up in the faces of too many sound coaches," Lombardi told writer W.C. Heinz in the 1963 book, *Run To Daylight,* "and I'm not at my best when I'm walking off the practice field, honestly feeling that my whole future will depend upon my discovery of some way to rearrange our blocking on our 49-Sweep . . . and a sportswriter comes up to me and says, 'Well, coach, what do you think today?'"

Lombardi maintained a guarded persona, and was selective in granting interviews. He at first refused the *Esquire* request, but relented. Though the reasons behind his change of heart are unclear, it may have had something to do with Shecter being a native New Yorker like himself. Born in New York City, Shecter attended New York University and started his career in journalism as a copy boy with the *New York Post.* Over the next 20 years, he was a reporter, night editor, and sports columnist for the *Post,* then left the paper to become a freelance writer. Gifted with an impassioned, descriptive writing style, Shecter's work appeared in numerous national magazines, and it was with these credentials he arrived in Green Bay in the summer of '67 to interview Lombardi.

To Shecter, the 54-year-old Lombardi looked less like the "toughest man in football," as the *Esquire* article later proclaimed, and more like an Italian papa. "He has a bit of a weight problem," Shecter noted, "and walks with his belly sucked in and chest expanded, like a pigeon's."

Lombardi's loud instructions to his team were delivered in what Shecter described as an odd New York accent, a product of Vince's upbringing in the 1930s in Sheepshead Bay, then a tough, Italian-immigrant section of Brooklyn. Each Lombardi edict was accompanied by the sounds of large men drawing increasingly short breaths and the pounding of cleats and bodies on ground baked hard by the sun. When Lombardi yelled "Front!" the players threw themselves face down in the grass. No sooner had they touched the turf when the call would be "Up!" and they would jump to their feet and resume running in place.

The Packers survived Lombardi's grass drills because of their dedication to year-round physical conditioning. Bill Curry, who played for three NFL teams in his career, including the 1968 and 1970 Baltimore Colts Super Bowl teams, said the Packers were the most impressive physical specimens he had seen. "Standing in the Packer locker room," Curry said, "gave you the strong feeling that everyone in there could push over a wall."

While most NFL teams in the 1960s began practices with 15 side-straddle hops; the Packers started with *a hundred.* At the conclusion of the calisthenics, which were led by an assistant coach, Lombardi would walk to the front of the group, and with what Curry remembered as a "sadistic grin," would begin the grass drills.

Players ran in place, pulling their knees high up to their chests, then at Lombardi's command diving to the ground and bouncing up again. Sometimes Lombardi would have the Packers repeat this drill 70 or more times. Curry, who along with fellow center Ken Bowman, kept track as a way to distract themselves from the pain, once counted 78 sets of "Front!" and "Up!" Unsuspecting rookies and out-of-shape veterans were particularly vulnerable to the drill. After awhile, they would begin vomiting; some would sink to their knees, unable to rise; one literally passed out.

Shecter described the grass drill as an exercise that turned grown men, most of them in their 30s with families to support, into "groveling, gasping, sweat-soaked, foamy-mouthed animals without breath enough left to complain."

It was a drill, he wrote, "best conducted in the summer sun at brain-frying temperatures because sane men will not do it. The crazy men run in place, double time, as hard as they can, while Lombardi shouts at them in his irritating, nasal, steel-wool-rubbing-over-grate voice. . . . As the drill goes on, the noises they make breathing almost drown out the sound of Lombardi's voice. The breathing becomes louder and somewhat wetter, until it sounds like the ocean when the last waves roll up into the sucking sand. Finally, when they are beyond the point of humanity or sanity, Lombardi lets up. 'All right!' he shouts. 'Around the goalpost and back. Now RUN!'"

Shecter, perhaps insulted by being held at bay by the chalk line, found Lombardi abrasive and repulsive, animal-like in appearance, and unsophisticated in his views on football and society. When his article appeared in the December, 1967 issue of *Esquire*, it shaped to some degree the public image of Lombardi as a callous man with a win-at-all-costs attitude. It's a cardboard image that lingers as part of the Lombardi legend, and for better or worse, remains one of the ornaments of the NFL's modern era.

That a non-sports magazine like *Esquire* even pursued Lombardi as the subject of a feature was indicative of the media's growing fascination with the sport. By the mid-sixties, pro football was in the process of passing major league baseball as the nation's foremost spectator sport.

The advent of television in the fifties had brought the drama and excitement of an NFL Sunday into living rooms across the country. As Americans turned on their sets, they were captivated by the precision of Otto Graham and the Cleveland Browns, by the riverboat gambling style of Johnny Unitas and the Baltimore Colts, and by the sophisticated play of Frank Gifford and the New York Giants. By the late 1950s, television had replaced radio as the electronic medium of the nation, and football, more than baseball, is a television sport. Television and the NFL was a near-perfect union, developing what the authors of the 1972 book, *The National Football League: The First Fifty Years* described as "a viewer's medium that was unexcelled for excitement, clarity, and sustained interest."

The marriage of pro football and television was performed, quite suitably, in the cathedral-like surroundings of Yankee Stadium on Sunday, December 28, 1958. In the cold, gray dusk of that winter afternoon, the Baltimore Colts defeated the Giants, 23–17, in sudden-death overtime. This NFL championship game has been called the greatest ever played. Certainly it was the most important played to that point. The image of Unitas, in his white Colts' uniform, dropping, wheeling, and dissecting the famous Giants' defense of Sam Huff, Andy Robustelli, and Rosey Grier on two late-game drives gripped the imagination of the public.

Sportswriter Louis Effrat wrote in *The New York Times* the next day, "the excitement of pro football's longest game left most of the 64,185 spectators limp." If the world had by then become the global village Marshall McLuhan believed it had—a community where people overcame great distances and shared a common experience via television—then the excitement was felt not just by the crowd in Yankee Stadium but by ten million viewers across the nation.

Pro football's visual images—the simultaneous movements of 22 men on a rectangular field—fit perfectly into the confines of a television screen, and technological innovations such as slow motion replays and isolated camera close-ups gave viewers a fascinating new insight into the violent world of pro football.

NFL Films was organized in the early sixties, and helped popularize the sport with weekly highlight films described by one observer as "beautiful essays on the sport, fast- and slow-motion tributes to the art and courage of the ballplayers."

By the mid-sixties, polls revealed pro football had become the "most followed" sport among American males aged 18 to 49. Modern society was complex and turbulent, and pro football reflected the new culture more than any other sport. The game became a symbolic combat for a nation torn by an unpopular foreign war, and an outlet for a people whose home front was unsettled by demonstrations and rioting. In an urban, middle class society in which control was expected of one's emotional and physical states, pro football offered a cathartic discharge, a purging of pent-up frustrations.

"I've always considered myself a group therapist for 60,000 people," said Sonny Jurgensen, a Hall of Fame quarterback for the Washington Redskins in the sixties and seventies. "Every Sunday I hold group therapy and the people come and take out their frustrations on me. If I fail, it magnifies their failures, and if I succeed, it minimizes them. The fans actually add to the game itself, because if you are playing at home, they are pulling for you, and if you are on the road, you are fighting 60,000 people."

America embraced pro football, and NFL attendance rose steadily throughout the sixties, averaging 54,430 per game by 1969. The television audience was also expanding, reaching an estimated 21 million by 1964. When the New York Jets pulled off their historic upset of the Baltimore Colts in the 1969 Super Bowl, giving the American Football League its first-ever victory over the established NFL, the TV audience was estimated at a then-record 60 million.

Television revenue helped the NFL and AFL sign talented athletes away from other major sports, notably baseball. In 1964, the AFL secured its existence by signing a five-year, $36 million television contract. Within a week, the NFL countered with a two-year $14.1 million deal with CBS. Thus, in the space of seven days in late January, 1964, TV committed more than $64 million to the pro game.

"Sunday, the day of rest, will undergo a transformation in the American home," wrote William N. Wallace in the February 2, 1964 edition of *The New York Times*. "C.B.S., with a lot of football to sell, proposed to telecast double-headers, meaning an East Coast game followed by a West Coast one, for instance. This can mean five hours of televiewing for the pro football buff on 14 Sunday afternoons of the year. Mrs. Buff and all the little Buffs had best learn up on blitzes, drops, influences, down-and-outs and keys. The blend of the game and television has become too potent to oppose. Pull up a chair."

Television helped popularize pro football, and made household names of stars like Lombardi, Huff, Unitas, Dawson, Alworth, and Namath. The media exposure put faces on the game, but it came at a cost. Although newspaper and magazine stories were generally favorable, a new breed of journalism was emerging, one that viewed things with a sharper—sometimes more cynical—but ultimately more realistic eye.

The era of "house" journalism, in which reporters protected athletes by not writing about their excesses away from the field, was ending, and its demise brought on clashes between those who played the game and those who reported it. When Lombardi objected to the content of a *Look* magazine article on the bachelor lifestyle of Hornung in October 1962, sports editor Tim Cohane exploded.

"You're getting just like all the rest of them," Cohane shouted. "All you people, you coaches and athletes, are all alike. Everything is fine as long as we write a lot of pandering pap extolling you as heroes and publicizing your game, but the moment we write something that doesn't make you look like tin gods you get your backs up."

Taken aback, Lombardi relented. He won minor concessions from Cohane on several points in the article, but for the most part the story ran as written. What emerged was an honest, human look at one of the NFL's most famous players, and even Lombardi referred to it as "a forthright and fascinating article."

There were no such platitudes in the Packer camp for Shecter's *Esquire* piece, even though it won the "Best Sports Stories–1968" magazine award. Dining out with friends shortly after the article was published in early December, Lombardi read portions of it to his companions at the table. His face reddened and he blinked furiously behind his clear glasses as he read a description of himself bawling out an injured player:

"There is a pileup and out of the bottom of the pile comes a cry that has been torn out of a man's throat, a shriek of agony. It's Jerry Moore, a rookie guard, who hasn't learned he is not supposed to cry in pain. The pile untangles and Moore is left writhing on the ground, his hands grabbing at a knee which is swelling so fast that in another minute the doctor will have to cut his pants leg to get at it. 'Get up!' Lombardi bawls, the thick cords on his heavy, sun-browned neck standing out with the effort. 'Get up! Get up off the *ground.*' The sight has insulted him. He is outraged. 'You're not hurt. *You're not hurt.*'"

Lombardi looked up at his dinner companions. "Am I like this?" he asked. "Am I really like this?"

Before anyone could answer, he hurled the magazine to the floor and pounded his fist on the table. The story hurt Lombardi, and the members of his family; his mother, Matilda, cried when she read it. Still upset by the article days later, Lombardi sought the counsel of legendary coach Paul Brown, who founded the Cleveland Browns franchise in 1946. He complained to Brown that Shecter had portrayed him as "Mussolini," a "Mafia man." He told Izenberg,

"If you don't talk to people you're damned. If you do, you're damned."

Green Bay guard Jerry Kramer thought the article made Lombardi look "like nothing but a cruel, vicious man . . . I thought the story gave a distorted picture of the man; it showed only one of his many sides."

The coach drove his players, Kramer said, but he drove himself and his staff even harder. During the season, the Packer coaching staff worked every night except Thursday, and routinely put in 15-hour workdays. Said Kramer, "Someone once figured out, on an hourly basis during the season, a Green Bay coach earns less than a Green Bay garbage man."

In time, Lombardi dismissed the article as a hatchet job, and other members of the media, including Red Smith, Jim Murray, and Howard Cosell, went on record to defend him.

Murray, the respected syndicated columnist of the *Los Angeles Times*, acknowledged Lombardi's rough exterior, but noted the human side as well. To Murray, the Packer coach was a "a man of intellect in a body of a caveman, a soft heart in a cage of granite."

Lombardi's impulsive reaction to Moore's practice injury was the by-product of a code of living instilled in him by his father, Harry. The oldest of five children, young Vince inherited his mother's dark looks and softer qualities, but was more heavily influenced by his father's belief in mental toughness.

"They have written about the mental toughness with which I have supposedly instilled this team and, when they ask me what it is, I have difficulty explaining it," Lombardi said in *Run To Daylight*. "I think it is singleness of purpose and, once you have agreed upon the price that you and your family must pay for success, it enables you to forget that price. It enables you to forget the minor hurts, the opponent's pressure and the temporary failures."

Harry Lombardi drummed into young Vince the notion of playing with minor pains. "Hurt," Harry said, "is in your mind."

Vince's own willingness to play with pain was put to the test in 1936, when as a right guard on Fordham's famous "Seven Blocks of Granite" line, the 172-pound Lombardi was called on to block University of Pittsburgh's Tony Matisi, a 215-pound All-America tackle. This was the era of leather helmets and 60-minute players, and early in the game Matisi came up out of his stance and slammed his elbow into Lombardi's mouth, knocking out several teeth. In addition to losing his teeth, Lombardi received deep cuts in his mouth, to the extent that he played almost the entire game with a mouth full of blood.

"I think the point in that," said writer Cohane, then Fordham's public relations director, "is when I say the player is father of the coach, there is nothing that Lombardi has demanded of the Packers that he didn't demand of himself in full measure in his own playing days."

After the Fordham game, as he was being attended to by Dr. Gerry Carroll, Vince remembered his father's edict that "hurt is in the mind."

Years later, Lombardi recalled the 30 stitches that were put in his mouth that day, and said, "I certainly was hurting in my mind."

Vince's wife, Marie, said that despite his insistence that his players play with minor pain, he did not ask them to risk serious injury. "He has complete compassion for these players," she said in 1968. "But you can't harp on (injuries) every day. If you do, they become big problems. Live with it, in other words."

Lombardi's philosophy that "hurt is in the mind" extended to his family life as well. "I have done so much talking about the necessity of ignoring the small hurts that it has pervaded our own household and she refuses to go to the doctor," he said on one occasion when Marie was ill with the flu. A day later, however, he told her that "this Spartan business of ignoring the small hurts has gone far enough," and he called the doctor. Occasionally, Marie would turn the tables on her husband. When Vince complained once of pain in his leg, Marie looked at him and said, "Hurt is in the mind."

Asked once to characterize her husband, Marie Lombardi said

she couldn't. "He's a mystery," she said. "He eludes you. All I know is that to me he's the most wonderful man in the world."

Vince was a teacher-coach at a tiny New Jersey high school when he married his college sweetheart, Marie Planitz. He was 27 years old and just getting started in the occupation that would dominate his life.

After graduating from New York City's Fordham University in 1936, the Jesuit-trained Lombardi studied for awhile for the priesthood, then aimed briefly at a law degree. Times were hard and jobs scarce, and Vince intermittently earned pocket money playing football for a minor-league team called the Brooklyn Eagles. He also worked for a time as an insurance adjuster.

The summer of 1939 found him working at DuPont in Wilmington, Delaware for $20 a week when a former teammate from Fordham, Leo Paquin, told Lombardi of an opening for an assistant football coach at St. Cecilia High School in Englewood, New Jersey. Another ex-teammate, Andy Palau, offered Lombardi the job. His salary jumped to $22 a week in return for which St. Cecilia, a coed high school with about 200 boys, got not only an assistant football coach, but a head basketball coach, a baseball coach, and a teacher of chemistry, physics, and Latin.

Lombardi stayed at St. Cecilia for eight years. He excelled as a coach, leading the basketball team to a state championship and an overall record of 105-57 under his direction. In 1942, when Palau entered the armed services, Vince took over the school's football program and instituted the new T-formation offense popularized by the 1940 NFL champion Chicago Bears. His first year as head football coach produced a 6-1-2 record, and in 1943, little St. Cecilia embarked on a 25-game winning streak and set a state record by being unbeaten in 31 straight games.

As relentless with the high-schoolers as he would later be with professional players, Lombardi drove his teams to perform by putting them through rigorous practice sessions, often getting into the trenches to demonstrate blocking techniques. His innovative offenses and demanding practices produced powerhouse squads at St. Cecilia. His mastery of the high school game was such that one year his undersized team outscored the competition 267–19.

In 1947 Lombardi returned to Fordham, this time as head coach of the freshman football team. He led the young Rams to an unbeaten season his first year, then was named assistant varsity coach in charge of offense. In one year, under Lombardi's command, an offensive team that had averaged just under 6.3 points per game improved to 20.2 points per game.

At first, Lombardi harbored hopes of becoming head coach at Fordham but the Jesuits were planning to de-emphasize football, and he began to look elsewhere. After just two years at his alma mater, Lombardi went to West Point where as an offensive line coach for Army, he came under the tutelage of head coach Colonel Earl "Red" Blaik.

Blaik was a close personal friend of General Douglas MacArthur, and the colonel had adopted the general's "There is no substitute for victory" attitude and applied it to the football field. Being exposed to Blaik's precision practices and intense, disciplined film study helped to refine Lombardi's coaching style, and he dovetailed many of Blaik's habits with his own. He took comfortably to addressing the cadets as "Mister," as military protocol demanded, and the custom followed him to New York and Green Bay. More than one future Giant or Packer had heard the withering remark, "You are really something, you are, *Mister.*" Lombardi also took to repeating one of Blaik's pet phrases, "You've got to pay the price."

Change again came for Lombardi when Blaik turned down an offer to succeed Steve Owen as head coach of the New York Giants. In his stead, he recommended Lombardi, but Vince's dream of being a head coach was not yet to be. Except for Wellington Mara, a classmate of Lombardi's at Fordham, the team's ownership decided they needed a "name" coach and chose Jim Lee Howell. Mara then put Lombardi's name forward as an assistant, and Howell agreed. Lombardi was named Giants' offensive coach in 1953, a post he held until Green Bay hired him to regenerate the ailing Packers.

Lombardi offered no mysteries in his approach to football and life; he was a fundamentalist in both areas. A devout family man and practicing Catholic, he went to Mass every morning and was a daily communicant. But morning Mass was followed by practice, and he blistered the field with the language of a longshoreman.

Many writers wrestled with the persona of Vince Lombardi. Joe Donnelly of *Sport* magazine wrote an article titled, "Whipcracker of the Packers." Tom Dowling, in an article for *The Washingtonian,* referred to Lombardi as "St. Vincent."

Red Smith, the legendary columnist for *The New York Times,* in a piece following Lombardi's death from cancer in 1970, thought this paradox—"a deeply religious man who worshipped the God of peace and taught a game of cruel violence, with total dedication to both"—was the very essence of Vince Lombardi.

"He was emotional, mercurial, sentimental, quick-tempered, profoundly loyal, fiercely honest," wrote Smith. "A perfectionist, he made harsh demands on his players to prepare them for the harsher demands of combat. . . . In short, he was a good man who was supremely good at what he did."

Chapter Two

Landry
The Coach as Intellectual

TOM LANDRY STOOD WITH FOLDED ARMS AND A FIXED STARE in the press box high above the playing field in Thousand Oaks, California, the site of the Dallas Cowboys' preseason training complex. The Cowboys' head coach squinted through the glare of the afternoon sun, his gray-green eyes following the intricate and patterned movements of the 22 players taking part in the scrimmage below.

Under Landry, Cowboy scrimmages utilized a scoring system in which the defense received points for creating turnovers and stopping the offense on downs. By the mid-sixties, the Dallas defense was one of the most dominant units of the decade, and like the "Fearsome Foursome" in Los Angeles and the "Purple People Eaters" in Minnesota, the Cowboys' soon picked up a colorful nickname. When *Dallas Morning News* sportswriter Gary Cartwright wrote that "it takes until doomsday to score on them," the Dallas defenders gained a nickname that remained with the team through the early part of the eighties. On this July day in 1967, "Doomsday" was proving its worth, leading the offense by the startling score of 40–0 at halftime.

Satisfied with his first-team defensive unit and realizing his offense wasn't getting any useful work done, Landry left the press box and headed to the field. Wearing a white T-shirt with DALLAS COWBOYS spelled out in dark blue letters, matching blue shorts,

white socks, and black coaching shoes, the 6 ft 1 in., 200-pound
Landry cut a solid, powerful figure as he strode towards his coaches
and players. A whistle hung from a leather strap around his tanned
neck, and his balding head was covered by a white baseball-style
cap that featured a blue "D" on the front panel and a blue bill. He
was ruggedly handsome, with a strong, square jaw and high cheekbones. Landry's exposed arms and legs were tan and muscular, and
only the gray hairs that flecked his short brown sideburns gave any
indication the head coach of the Cowboys was 43 years old.

Landry had a quiet, dignified air about him, and as he walked
toward assistant head coach and defensive coordinator Dick Nolan,
he waited until he was just a few feet away before he spoke.

"Okay, Dick. Now play just a straight 4-3 and give the offense
a chance to get in some work against it."

Landry's words were delivered in a calm voice tinged with an
unmistakable Texas twang. It was the voice of a man who had spent
his youth in Mission, Texas. He had returned to his home state in
1960 to take over as head coach of the expansion Cowboys.

Nolan answered Landry with a "Yessir," then began sending his
second-team defensive unit in.

Landry blinked, his computer-like brain taking a moment to
comprehend Nolan's action. "Hey, Dick," he said in a slightly irritated tone, "do what I said. Put the first team back in there and let
the offense run against them in the standard 4-3. We need the
work, to move the ball."

Nolan's back stiffened at the sudden upbraiding. At 6-ft. 1-in.,
185 pounds, the 45-year old Nolan was just a shade smaller than
Landry, a man he had been friends with since the mid-fifties when
both were members of the New York Giants' defensive secondary.
Nolan played for Landry after the latter was named player-coach in
1954 and fulltime defensive coordinator in 1956. Retiring as a 30-
year-old player in 1962, Nolan was hired by Landry as the Cowboys'
defensive backfield coach. When injuries decimated the Dallas secondary that year, Landry named Nolan player-coach, a position he

held until retiring as a player for good at the end of the season.

Nolan's experience with Landry's defensive system was instrumental in the development of cornerback Cornell Green and safety Mel Renfro, each of whom became all-pros for the Cowboys. Renfro has since been elected to the Pro Football Hall of Fame.

The end of the 1967 season would see Nolan take his expertise to San Francisco, where as 49ers head coach he opposed Landry in the 1970 and '71 NFC title games. On this day, Nolan's pride in his defense led him to oppose his head coach even sooner.

"Tom, you can run on the second team all you want," Nolan said, "but nobody is going to use my first-team defense as a bunch of dummies. When they go on the field, they're in there to win."

Throughout his career as head coach of the Cowboys, Landry was famous for his unruffled cool. Autumn Sundays found him standing on the sidelines, on the fringe of organized mayhem, wearing his felt fedora, starched white shirt, patterned necktie, and solid light-blue sports jacket. Regardless of the situation on the field, Landry maintained a posture of poise. He was the center of calm amid turbulent surroundings, the eye of every NFL Sunday's storm.

Rather than respond to Nolan's comments, Landry relaxed his jaw muscles, shrugged his shoulders, and without uttering a word, headed back to the press box. More than anything, Landry knew when to pick his battles, and raging at a highly-capable assistant over a camp scrimmage would be detrimental to his goal for 1967, which was to end the title run of his coaching rival to the north, Vince Lombardi.

It was situations such as these that led Dallas sportswriter Sam Blair to say that while Landry felt emotional inside, outwardly he handled situations in the manner of a Methodist Sunday School teacher, which Landry was in the off-season. It was an approach that didn't always work with his players.

"It seems like athletes always want something that someone else has," Dallas Hall of Fame defensive tackle Bob Lilly said, looking back. "Coach Landry wasn't as emotional maybe as we would have liked as players, because I do think coaches can motivate you sometimes. And that was maybe the one flaw that he did have, not coming in and kicking our rear ends. But that just wasn't Coach Landry, and I don't think we would have received it very well if he had forced himself to do it.

"Whereas with Vince Lombardi, that was his nature. He was certainly in character doing that, and I don't think he would have been in character being silent and aloof.

"But Coach Landry did have a lot of emotion in him. He just kind of buried it. It came out one time. We were playing in Pittsburgh in 1965. We were close to a division title, but we started the season with two wins and four losses, and then we lost in Pittsburgh. After the game was over, Coach Landry ordered everyone out of the locker room except the players and coaches.

"He told us he thought we'd given 110 percent. He said when he came to Dallas he thought the flex defense and multiple offense would carry the Cowboys into the next decade. And he said maybe he was wrong, and then he broke down and cried. He cried for some time, maybe two, three minutes. It seemed like two, three hours.

"As a team, we became more serious after that talk. Because we did see that he was very emotional and that he loved us and cared for us. We won six of the next seven games, went to a playoff game the next year, and from then on, we were in the play-offs every year. So I guess he was right about the flex and the multiple offense."

Thomas Wade Landry was born September 11, 1924 in Mission, Texas, and few people have so personified the name of their home-town as the middle son of Ray and Ruth Landry. From a three-year tour as a copilot of a B-17 "Flying Fortress" bomber in World War II to becoming a player, assistant coach, and ultimately head coach in the NFL, Landry lived his life as if he were on a mission.

He developed his coaching career with the Giants, where his

intelligent planning allowed him to become the architect of modern NFL defenses. While working under legendary Giants' head coach Steve Owen, Landry invented the modern 4-3-4 defense (*See Diagram 1*), which he first introduced in 1955. Owen had popularized the 6-1-4 "umbrella" defense, so named because it employed six down linemen and four defensive backs, giving it the look of an umbrella opening up. Owen's scheme was effective against the run-oriented offenses in Philadelphia and Chicago because it crowded the line of scrimmage with defenders and shut off the ground game before it could get started.

When the Cleveland Browns joined the NFL in 1950 after winning four straight All-America Football Conference championships, head coach Paul Brown unleashed precision passer Otto Graham and receivers Mac Speedie and Dante Lavelli on the NFL, and the league's run-oriented defenses were caught flat-footed. Owen studied the Browns' artistic aerial attack before their mid-season showdown and decided to counter it by taking his defensive ends out of their three-point, down lineman stance and putting them in a standing position three yards behind the line of scrimmage. Released from their responsibilities to cover the run first, the ends dropped into coverage of the short pass patterns run by Speedie and Lavelli.

The idea for this new 4-3-4 defense belonged to Owen, but it was left to his defensive back, Landry, to teach it. The Giants' 4-3 defense stymied the high-powered Browns' offense in 1950, allowing New York to become the first NFL team to beat Cleveland. Landry continued to coordinate concepts for the 4-3, and by 1958, the Giants had enough veterans on their team to employ a "key" defense, an advanced system which allowed intelligent players like Sam Huff, Rosey Grier, and Andy Robustelli to read the offensive formation and focus on clues or "keys" which would tip off the play.

Landry improved the key defense when he took over the fledgling Cowboys in 1960, instituting a scheme known as the "flex," in which he offset two of his four down linemen in a staggered formation and taught them to fill their assigned area, or "gap" in the line, and slow down the ground infantries that were carrying the day in Green Bay and Cleveland.

Yet just as Landry worked to develop his defense as an assistant coach with the Giants, he also sought ways to defeat it once he became head coach of the Cowboys. The success of the Giants' defense led other NFL coaches to imitate it, and Landry found himself trying to destroy the very monster he created. He outfitted his

---

DIAGRAM 1

Landry's 4-3-4 Defense
1956 New York Giants

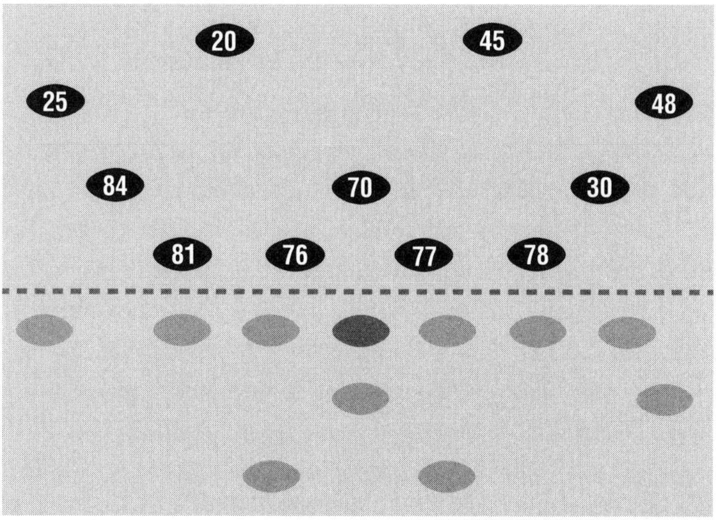

81 Andy Robustelli, *RDE*	**84** Harland Svare, *RLB*	**25** Dick Nolan, *RCB*
76 Rosey Grier, *RDT*	**70** Sam Huff, *MLB*	**20** Jimmy Patton, *RS*
77 Dick Modzelewski, *LDT*	**30** Bill Svoboda, *LLB*	**45** Emlen Tunnell, *LS*
78 Walt Yowarsky, *LDE*		**48** Ed Hughes, *LCB*

Cowboy offense with computer-complex strategies, putting men in motion, shifting formations before the snap of the ball, and employing false keys designed to confuse opposing defenses.

At a time when most NFL teams were running the standard "pro-set" offense in which the halfback and fullback lined up behind and on either side of the quarterback, the Cowboys ran a shifting I-formation, in which both backs lined up directly behind the quarterback and then shifted just before the snap.

Despite his attention to the offense, Landry remained a defense-minded coach. He felt drawn to that aspect of the game because of the intellectual challenges it presented. Offenses have their plays diagrammed for them ahead of time, so they know exactly what they're supposed to do. Defenses however, must constantly anticipate the action, and then react to it. Landry was fascinated by the challenge of studying an opposing offense and then anticipating what they were going to do and thinking along with them.

"I always have had an analytical mind," Landry said at the time, "and this (challenge) was most intriguing to me."

Landry's intellectual pursuits reached far beyond football. He earned an engineering degree at the University of Texas, and continued his studies in the off-season by attending classes in Houston. He also undertook a study of the New Testament. He had been raised a Christian, but by his own admission, was experiencing a strange emptiness in his life in the late 1950s, despite the fact he was happily married and the head of a growing family.

He attended church regularly, but admitted it was a "half-hearted" effort. "I thought of myself as a Christian," he said, "but found out I wasn't. I was just a church-goer, which is a lot different."

Landry researched the life of Christ with the same scientific approach he used in his engineering studies and in coaching football. Gradually, he reached a point where his intellectual questions were resolved. "I simply believed that Christ wanted me to bring him into my daily life, including football," he said.

Landry's football life began at Mission High School, where as a senior he quarterbacked the team to an undefeated championship season. He received a scholarship to play at the University of Texas, where he was a teammate of future Pro Football Hall of Fame quarterback Bobby Layne. With his fiery leadership and fun-loving lifestyle, Layne was a sharp contrast to Landry. Still, the two men got along well, respecting each other's personal beliefs. One resident of Landry's dorm said that while Tom did not take part in all pranks, he was not a prude. He didn't criticize those whose dorm life was diametrically opposed to his own, and seemed at times to enjoy some of the college shenanigans.

Landry's mature attitude toward college life was shaped by his experiences as a bomber pilot in World War II. He had survived where other men, including his brother Robert, had not. Three years older than Tom, Robert joined the Air Force shortly after the Japanese attack on Pearl Harbor. He had completed his flight training and was ferrying a plane to England in 1942 when he was reported missing. Several months passed, during which the Landrys maintained hope. The family finally learned that Robert's plane had exploded in midair over Iceland.

Tom had joined the reserves the year his brother died, and he was called to active duty in the spring of 1943. He took his preflight training in San Antonio, and by the fall of 1944, was based in Epwich, England, not far from London. Over the course of the next year, Landry flew 30 missions over German-occupied territory. He volunteered for extra missions and later told his aunt, Viola Bourgeois, he did it in memory of Robert.

Landry's first mission found him in one of two thousand planes whose objective was to bomb the oil fields at Mersburg, Germany. Landry had been told about the flak from Nazi guns, but like all first-time pilots, he was unprepared for the experience. "It was really a scary feeling," he told biographer Bob St. John in his book, *Landry*. The toughest mission, however, was still to come. On a return flight to England following a bombing run over Germany, the four engines in Landry's plane lost power over Belgium, and the craft began losing altitude, dropping to barely a thousand feet off the ground. Believing the plane had run out of gas, Landry shouted, "Let's get out of here!" As the crew prepared to parachute out, Landry paused and checked the instrument panel one more time. Showing remarkable presence of mind for a 20-year-old, he reached over and flicked a switch that adjusted the engine's fuel mixture. The engines suddenly regained power, allowing the crew to return to their seats and guide the plane safely back to England. Had they bailed out in enemy territory as intended, they probably would have been captured and made prisoners of war.

The war touched Landry deeply, and changed forever his attitude towards football. As he put his priorities in order, such things as won-lost records and championships carried little lasting meaning for him. While he still appreciated success and praise, winning and losing football games paled in comparison with the events of the war.

Discharged from the service in November, 1945, Landry returned to college life with a deeper, more mature outlook on life. Clean-cut, with wavy brown hair, he was very much a man among boys at the University of Texas. Bill Wiggins, who was Landry's fraternity brother at Delta Kappa Epsilon, recalled Landry as being serious but not overly serious. Tom would joke around, but he never made a fool of himself. "He stayed in control," Wiggins said.

The war years had dulled Landry's football skills, but he followed head coach Dana X. Bible's advice that if players were willing to work hard, they could be successful. Pay the premiums, Bible told his team, and reap the dividends.

"Tom paid them," said Bible, who named Landry starting halfback. Texas went 8-2 in 1946, 10-1 in 1947, and 7-4-1 in 1948. The team capped the latter two seasons with victories in the Sugar and Orange Bowl games, respectively. Following the Longhorns' upset of Georgia in the 1948 Orange Bowl, Landry was approached by Jack White, an assistant coach with the New York Yankees' football team of the All-America Football Conference. Begun in 1946 by *Chicago Tribune* sports editor Arch Ward, the upstart AAFC was engaged in a signing war with the established National Football League for top collegiate talent.

Landry was drafted his sophomore season by both the Yankees and the NFL's New York Giants, and White met with Landry immediately after the game to secure his services for the AAFC before the Giants could sign him. White had with him a contract calling for Landry to receive $7,500 a year, pocket change for NFL players today but good money at that time. Because the money was substantially more than the Giants had offered, Landry signed with White on the spot. Together with his young wife, the former Alicia Wiggs, a UT classmate whom he had married in January of 1948 after two years of dating, Landry was about to enter a world that would occupy his life for the next four decades.

The AAFC opened its first season in 1946, and fielded teams in nine cities across the country—Baltimore, Brooklyn, Buffalo, Chicago, Cleveland, Los Angeles, Miami, New York, and San Francisco. Unlike earlier challengers to the NFL, the AAFC had an abundance of talent, evident in coaches like Paul Brown, Jimmy Crowley, and Buck Shaw; and players like Otto Graham, Marion Motley, Y. A. Tittle, and Buddy Young.

Landry's rookie campaign with the Yankees saw him used in a number of roles—punter, offensive and defensive back, kickoff and punt returner. He performed capably in each, and ranked among the league leaders in punting. But it didn't take long for him to realize his limitations, which were underscored when the Yankees hosted Cleveland. New York had lost starting cornerback Harmon Rowe to injury, and Landry was sent in to replace him. The untested rookie, whose fastest time in the 100-yard dash was 10.3, lined up against Speedie. The whippet-lean Speedie was aptly named, since he ranked among the quickest receivers in the league. When Speedie and Graham spotted Landry at cornerback, they tested him immediately with an assortment of turn-ins, quick outs, and deep posts.

By game's end, Speedie had set an AAFC record by hauling in 11 passes for 228 yards in a 31–0 win.

"I've never seen so many passes in my life," Landry said later. "Otto Graham went crazy when he saw me (trying to cover Speedie)."

Though the game was a disaster for Landry, it marked the turning point in his professional career. "I was too slow to play cornerback," he said, "so in order to keep my job I had to study a lot. I had to try and figure out what the other team was trying to do."

The 1949 season was the AAFC's last. Financial difficulties doomed the young league, and a merger was announced with the NFL prior to the 1950 season, though it was less a merger than a corporate takeover. The NFL absorbed three AAFC teams—the Browns, Colts, and 49ers—and the remaining AAFC teams were forced to disband. Players exiled from defunct teams were drafted into the NFL. With hostilities at an end, the New York Giants welcomed five ex-Yankees into their 1950 camp, Landry among them.

As a cornerback with the Giants, Landry found himself under the tutelage of Steve Owen, one of the most innovative defensive minds in pro football history. An all-league tackle before beginning his 23-year tenure as Giants' coach, Owen played in the NFL for nine years. He captained the 1927 Giants to the NFL title, anchoring a defense that allowed a record-low 20 points in 13 games. Owen was named player-coach of the team in 1931, and over the next 22 years, directed New York to two NFL championships and six division titles.

The cornerstone of the Giants' dynasty under Owen was its defense. Five times New York led the league in fewest points allowed, and Owen came to be regarded among football observers as the finest defensive mind the league had produced to that time. His defensive planning helped the Giants stop Chicago's explosive offense in the 1934 NFL title game, and Green Bay in the '38 championship.

By 1952, Landry was an unofficial player-coach for Owen, coordinating the movements of the Giants' defensive backfield. Two years later, under new head coach Jim Lee Howell, Landry was named assistant coach in charge of the defense. That same year, Howell also hired an assistant to run the offense, an obscure college coach named Vince Lombardi.

Guided by Howell and triggered by Landry and Lombardi, the Giants won the Eastern Division title in 1956 and defeated the Bears 47–7 in the NFL championship game. Later, the modest Howell lauded the work of his chief assistants.

"The way our offense and defense played," Howell said, "was a tribute to two men, Landry and Lombardi."

It was a coaching relationship whose dynamics would shape and forge the future of pro football for years to come.

Chapter Three

Fire and Ice
Apprenticeships in New York

IRED IN 1954 TO REPLACE STEVE OWEN as the New York Giants' head coach, Jim Lee Howell was a soft-spoken, self-effacing native son of Arkansas. He played offensive end for the Giants before becoming a head coach at Wagner College in Staten Island. While coaching at Wagner, Howell also served as an assistant to Owen, showing up at noon on weekdays to coach the Giants' offensive ends. At 6-5, 240 pounds, Howell was a big man physically, and game days found him standing on the sidelines, hands stuffed deep into the pockets of his dark overcoat, his silver-white hair covered by a tan felt fedora. It was a look strikingly similar to the game-day wardrobe Tom Landry adopted as head coach of the Dallas Cowboys in the 1960s.

Quietly intelligent, Howell spoke in a deep, southwestern drawl common to Ozark country. He had dark, penetrating eyes, prominent cheekbones, and a wide mouth that seemed forever curved in the hint of a toothy smile. Giants' players used to laugh at Howell's pants, which he wore so high they appeared to be buttoned at his chest.

For reasons unknown, Howell was prejudiced against rookies and players from California. He told Giants' flanker Kyle Rote that "West Coasters" played with their sleeves rolled up to "show off their suntans." Yet as much as Howell mistrusted California athletes, he mistrusted rookies even more. He yelled at them constantly, "bellerin'" he called it, and was nearly responsible for running two of the Giants' best rookies out of camp.

"He liked to pick on rookies," said Hall of Fame linebacker Sam Huff, who along with roommate Don Chandler was a first-year man in the Giants' training camp at St. Michael's College in Winooski, Vermont in 1955. Huff recalled running and hustling and "busting a gut" as a rookie, and then hearing Howell holler across the field in his Arkansas drawl, "Huff, you're not running!"

The week after the Giants played their first exhibition game of 1955 against the Baltimore Colts, a game in which Huff took a blindside hit as a member of the kickoff team and suffered a painful knee injury, Huff and Chandler were in their room feeling homesick as they listened to the radio. A mournful song called "Detroit City," that contained the lyrics "I wanna go home, oh, how I wannnnna go home" was getting frequent play. After hearing the song for the second or third time, Huff turned to Chandler and said, "That's it. Let's go."

They grabbed their playbooks, and with Huff balancing his 235 pounds uncomfortably on a pair of crutches, they headed to the coaches' rooms. Howell wasn't there, but Vince Lombardi was, taking a nap between practices. Huff and Chandler walked into the room and shook Lombardi awake.

Blinking the sleep from his eyes, the gruff coach looked at the two rookies. "What the hell do you want?"

"We're handing in our playbooks," Huff spat out. "We quit!"

Lombardi leapt from the bed, and began blistering Huff and Chandler with a verbal tirade. "Listen!" he shouted. "You might not make this club, but nobody runs out on me. Nobody!"

It was the first time Huff and Chandler had ever seen Lombardi angry. They froze. As Lombardi berated them, Chandler backed out of the room and escaped down the hall. Huff was stuck there, teetering on his crutches. Lombardi eventually calmed down and, with help from offensive line coach Ed Kolman, talked Huff into staying by promising to get Howell off his back. Chandler meanwhile, was headed for the nearest airport. Lombardi pursued him in the team station wagon. He found Chandler in the airport lounge and persuaded him to return to camp. Huff eventually went on to become the linchpin of the Giants' great defense. Chandler excelled as a kicker and punter for the Giants and, later, Lombardi's Green Bay teams of the mid-1960s.

Howell went out of his way to praise Lombardi and Landry to the influential New York media. He told reporters he had "the two smartest assistant coaches in football." When someone asked him what his duties were as head coach, Howell smiled and said, "I just pump up the footballs and keep curfew. With those two around I have very little to do."

Howell handled his staff in a firm and even-handed manner. Lombardi shouted, screamed, kicked, ranted, jumped up and down. "But," Howell said once, "he knew how far he could he go." Howell said once that Lombardi was up and down emotionally, but "very brilliant, very smart. Vince knew what he could do with players. He was very basic in his thinking. He was just a fine coach."

A fine *assistant* coach who was forever looking for an opportunity to become a head coach. Believing time was rapidly passing him by, Lombardi's search to create his own coaching identity bordered on being frantic.

"He was older by this time," Howell said. "He'd been kicking around. What would he get low about? Mostly, he thought he should have been somewhere else. He should have been a head coach somewhere, but he wasn't."

Howell used to sit and listen while Lombardi worried aloud about whether he would ever run his own team. He had applied at several colleges, including Notre Dame, but nothing ever materialized. Lombardi's eyes welled up with tears when he revealed that Notre Dame never even acknowledged his application.

Suffering the obscurity of being an assistant coach rankled Lombardi. He decided to write a book about football techniques, but after composing several chapters, was told by an agent that publishers weren't interested in a book written by an unknown coach. Howell wrote countless letters of recommendation for Lombardi, each aimed at helping him land a head coaching job.

While Lombardi was almost desperate in his desire to become a head coach, Landry wasn't sure how long he wanted to remain in football. During each off-season, he and his wife Alicia returned home to Texas, where he worked in real estate and insurance in Houston. Landry never thought of himself as a career coach, even when he was an assistant in New York. He had a degree in industrial management and leaned towards a career in business. To him, coaching was temporary. Yet his evolution from player to coach was so smooth that Don Smith, the Giants' publicity director, said it felt as if Landry had been coaching for years. "There was no sense of time passing," Smith said.

In his playing days, Landry had been a coach on the field. When the Giants huddled, he called the defensive play, then told teammates what to expect on the next play. "If they put the flanker out in front of you," he would say, "then you key the fullback, and if the fullback swings out, the flanker will run a down-and-in, so be ready."

Landry was usually correct in his assessments, and his knack of being in the right place at the right time frustrated opponents. The Los Angeles Rams had a sprinter-fast receiver named Bob Boyd who used his speed to simply outrun defenders to the ball. Landry gave Boyd fits because he studied the Rams' game films, and knew from reading their offensive formations when they were going to send Boyd deep. Despite being much slower than Boyd, Landry always read the play, adjusted, and was in position to defend him.

Landry's approach to the game was different than that of most players in that era. Most men relied on their football instincts, but not Landry. He studied the game, and in time knew not only his assignments, but the assignments of everyone else on the defense as well. In the days of single-platoon football, Giants' halfback Frank Gifford also played defensive back. During a 1952 game, Gifford left his coverage area and intercepted a pass. Instead of complimenting Gifford on his interception, Landry simply said, "Frank, you know you were out of position on that play."

When he became defensive coordinator two years later, Landry handled the Giants' players much the same way, quietly pointing out mistakes they made even when they stopped the runner. Rosey Grier starred at right defensive tackle for the Giants from 1954–62. By his own admission, Grier was a stubborn player who resisted change. When Landry installed his coordinated 4-3 defense, in which every player adhered to his area of coverage, Grier looked upon it as "another new-fangled idea I did not have much use for."

Grier preferred playing defense the way other teams did, which was a furious, all-out rush for the ball. The big tackle's attitude was that Landry would have to prove the worth of his new ideas. During one scrimmage, Grier stuffed the ball carrier for no gain, and left the field feeling smug about what he regarded as a sensational play. Landry stood waiting for him on the sideline, his face expressionless as always.

"If you hadn't made that play," Landry said quietly, "the linebacker would have. The defense was designed for him to make it."

When the offense ran the same play again, Grier held up, and waited to see if what Landry said would prove true. He was testing his coach, but when Grier turned around, he saw right linebacker Harland Svare stop the runner just as Landry predicted he would. "That was all I needed to become a believer," Grier said.

Landry's football mind, his ability to analyze a situation and find the solution, impressed Howell. "Tom was extremely talented at analyzing films," he said. "It would take him maybe 20 minutes to dissect a team's performance, whereas it might take somebody else hours."

With his subdued manner and quiet nature, Landry was the ice to Lombardi's fire. Despite their diverse personalities, they were equally competitive. As often as Lombardi was in Howell's office seeking more practice time for his offense, Landry was just as diligent seeking extra practice time for his defense. Howell eventually solved the problem by organizing separate offensive and defensive staff meetings, a first among NFL teams. Howell's willingness to let Lombardi and Landry each run his own unit stemmed from an incident when he was a first-year assistant coach at the University of Arkansas. Expressing his opinion about a football situation, Howell was told by the head coach, "When I'm talking, don't open your mouth."

"Some of these head coaches think they're God, that they're the only ones who know anything," said Howell. "And I said to myself that if I ever got to be head coach the one thing I wouldn't do was that. If I had assistants I'd want them to run their departments. I want their ideas; I want the benefits of their experience—not just me calling all the shots."

Howell's easy-going manner fed the Giants' team chemistry. There was an ever-present friction between the offensive and defensive units under the respective commands of Lombardi and Landry. Howell was aware of it and didn't disapprove.

"I knew the players had a rivalry," Howell said once, "but I didn't do anything about it. It was healthy as far as I was concerned, an incentive for each of them to do as well as they could."

At times, the rivalry between the Giants' offense and defense matched the intensity of a league game. Each squad had its own dressing room in preseason camp, and the defensive players went so far as to psyche themselves up with pre-scrimmage pep talks. "That Frank Gifford," someone would say. "He walks around here like he's making a movie, like he's in Hollywood, and he's making all that money."

A defensive star like Huff, who was making $9,000 and fighting management to make it $10,000, resented the $20,000 Gifford was making. Yet the animosity extended far beyond salaries. Despite the fact they were part of a unit that brought defensive play to the forefront, players like Huff and Grier still envied their offensive counterparts because it was stars like Gifford and Rote who were adored by the sporting public. "There is no shout louder," Grier said, "no cheer more joyous, no applause more glorious than for the man who carries the ball for a touchdown."

Before 1956, defensive players weren't even introduced to the crowd before the game. That honor was reserved for the offense alone, and in New York, the biggest cheers were heard when Yankee Stadium's public address announcer, Bob Sheppard, intoned, *"Ladies and gentlemen, Number 16, from Southern California, Frank Gifford."*

The Giants' defense resented the glamour boy images and high salaries of stars like Rote and Gifford. Huff, the tough son of a West Virginia coal miner, referred to Gifford as "the Golden Boy from Southern Cal." Huff and his defensive mates felt underpaid and unappreciated by Giant management, and it galled them, particularly since they felt responsible for the club's success. During one three-game stretch, New York's offense failed to score a touchdown, but the defense scored off forced turnovers and the Giants won two of the three games. Backup quarterback Don Heinrich recalled Huff at one point walking past the offense and sneering, "See if you can hold 'em. We'll try and score on defense the next time around."

During one close game, the Giants' offense faced a fourth-down, short-yardage situation. Howell turned to Landry and asked, "What should we do?"

Without blinking an eye, Landry said, "Punt. Give them the ball." The implication was clear. The defense would bail the team out again. As the defense began winning games on its own, media attention shifted its focus from Gifford and Rote to Huff and Grier. And the loudest cheers were now coming when Sheppard's baritone voice reverberated through Yankee Stadium: *"Brown tackled by Huff, Number 70 . . ."*

"We really did have a great defensive unit," Rote admitted. "It won most of the games for us, and it bailed us out of trouble most of the time. We'd cough up the ball, lose it after not gaining much yardage, and the defense would get it back for us."

For the first time in NFL history, a defensive unit had come into prominence and overshadowed its offensive unit. "This (media) treatment did not sit well with all the members of our squad," kicker Pat Summerall remarked.

The competition between the offensive and defensive units became so fierce that the toughest competition either faced was when it scrimmaged the other. The scrimmages were controlled, but Landry's defense invariably controlled Lombardi's offense. "That used to get the offensive guys ticked off," said Huff, who used to see an angry Lombardi still drilling his troops on the darkened practice field long after Landry had sent his men to the showers.

"He hated to look bad," Landry said of Lombardi. "If his offense didn't perform well, it could be two or three days before you could talk to him. But that was Vince. We understood him. And I got along with him very well. We were good friends. If he was successful, he was very outgoing, very emotional. If he was unsuccessful he wasn't speaking to anybody."

Landry called Lombardi "Mr. High-Low" because of his moody personality. Landry kept a more even keel, but the two were more alike than most observers believed. Both had dominating personalities, and both were highly-motivated men whose precise organizational skills, teaching abilities, and extensive knowledge of their sport made them excellent coaches. They were equally strong at dissecting film and evaluating talent. Landry was more innovative, but Lombardi was a better teacher.

Giants' owner Wellington Mara said once that while Landry lectured the upper 10 percent of his defense, Lombardi tutored the lower 10 percent of his offense.

The biggest difference between the two men however, was in their personality. Dallas sportswriter Gary Cartwright observed the two men up close and described Lombardi as "a gurgling volcano, blistering everyone in his path." Landry, Cartwright noted, was "placid as a mountain lake."

Mara agreed. "You could hear Vince laughing or shouting for five blocks," he said. "You couldn't hear Landry from the next chair."

Giants' players thought it was hard to imagine two more differing personalities than Landry, the reserved Texan, and Lombardi, the volatile Italian. Landry was the picture of quiet confidence; Lombardi wore his emotions like a badge of honor.

Different as they were, Landry and Lombardi liked and respected each other, and remained on good terms despite the rivalry between their players. Howell described them as competitive friends, each owning "a fire in him to win."

By his own definition, Lombardi's inner fire was "a burning incandescence," and it was evident in his stormy surface as he raged at defeat. Landry kept his fires well-banked.

Yet each man's will to win spurred him to excellence, and sparked creative, and contrasting, coaching methods that dominated pro football into the next decade.

Chapter Four

The Tactical Evolution

PRO FOOTBALL AT THE DAWN OF THE 1950s offered a wide-open, offensive showcase. Superstars like Elroy "Crazy Legs" Hirsch and Otto Graham filled the stands of NFL stadiums with weaving runs and precision passes, and scoreboards began posting numbers that resembled set-shot era NBA games.

Coaches looked to counter the point-producing machines in L.A. and Cleveland by putting many of their better athletes on defense. Defensive players gradually shed their status as nameless brutes, and gained attention alongside the offensive stars. Detroit's secondary, led by Jack Christiansen, was known as "Chris's Crew," and it brought fans out to Briggs Stadium. Two-platoon football had arrived, bringing with it a sharp dividing line between a team's offense and defense.

Nowhere were these lines more sharply drawn than in New York, where assistant coaches Vince Lombardi and Tom Landry were developing their strategies to a fine point. No longer an outsider to the NFL, Lombardi had gone from a coach who leaned on his players to one who could lead them.

"He was so dynamic that he made you feel like you had a hell of a unit," flanker Kyle Rote said. "His voice had a booming quality in the locker room, and when he made a point, you knew he'd made a point."

Diagramming a play, Lombardi sometimes made his point with such emphasis he snapped the chalk in two. He punctuated his X's and O's with a strong, punching motion. He issued simple instructions to his players, repeating himself as he drove his point home:

"All right, this is the 26 Power play, 26 Power play, do you have that? Two-six, 26 Power play. Now, the right guard MUST pull back, MUST pull back, the right guard MUST pull back, and he HAS TO PULL BACK to avoid the center, who will be stepping to the onside. So the first step is back. Got that? The FIRST step is back."

"He drove us mad," Frank Gifford said, "but when we went out on the field, we had it."

Lombardi's coaching suffered at first because of his unfamiliarity with the pro game. He wasn't assertive, and preferred a deferential attitude toward the team's established stars. He called quarterback Charlie Conerly "The Pro," relying on Conerly's observations because he wasn't sure what he knew about football was enough for the NFL.

At first, the veteran Giants looked at Lombardi as just another college coach. "He knew football," Gifford said, "but he didn't know pro football."

Lombardi's lack of knowledge of the pro game was evident from the start. The first play he gave the Giants in the summer of 1954 was "Stutter Dive Lateral and Rollout," which called for Conerly to carry the ball around the end. After getting smashed to the turf several times, Conerly flung the ball at Lombardi in disgust and shouted, "You like the damn play so much, you run it!"

Though the play remained in the Giants' playbook for three more years, Conerly never called it in a game. "There was no way it would work," Gifford said.

Conerly was also troubled by Lombardi's unsophisticated passing attack. During training camp, Giants' safety Emlen Tunnell quickly diagnosed the rudimentary patterns Lombardi gave his receivers and deflected the passes. Perceptive enough to recognize his own inadequacies, Lombardi accepted the help of others, most notably offensive end coach Bill Swiacki. A former receiver at Columbia University, Swiacki was instrumental in teaching Lombardi key elements of the pro passing game.

Lombardi made a number of coaching mistakes his first year with the Giants. He put in a college-style running play in which the quarterback sends the fullback off tackle, then depending on the reaction of the defensive end, either lets the fullback run the ball, keeps it himself, or pitches to a trailing halfback. The play was designated "47 Belly" in the Giants' system and was similar to the triple-option play colleges still use.

Conerly hated the play, but called it on occasion during non-contact scrimmages. The sight of his quarterback running "47 Belly" elated Lombardi. "That's it, that's *it!*" he would shout excitedly. "You've got it." But Conerly never called the play during contact scrimmages, despite the fact Lombardi would stand behind the offensive huddle and say, "Let's see that '47 Belly' now."

Engaging in a cat-and-mouse game with his coach, Conerly would say, "I think we better work some more on the '26 Power.'" Lombardi would relent, then tell Conerly on the next play, "Let's see that '47 Belly' *now.*"

"Coach, I think we should work on the '49 Sweep.'"

It wasn't until Conerly took a breather that the Giants ran "47 Belly," with Conerly's backup, Don Heinrich, getting drilled by the defensive end time and time again.

The play that became number one in the Giants' system was the sweep, a play Lombardi later made famous at Green Bay. The Giants' version of the sweep (*See Diagram 2*) differed from the Packers' power sweep because it was a sweep away from the tight end. Gifford would take Conerly's pitchout and follow the blocking of Rosey Brown, who pulled and ran interference from his left tackle position.

The sweep predated Lombardi's arrival in New York; Giants'

offensive line coach Ed Kolman and end coach Ken Kavanaugh had installed it years before. But Lombardi refined it by recognizing the unusual talents of the 250-pound Brown.

Brown's forte was speed and quickness, and his responsibilities on the sweep were to cut off the inside defender. In practice, Brown would pull out from the line of scrimmage and cut off any defender that got through the line. Brown's speed however, allowed him to get outside quicker than the pulling guard, thus providing an additional blocker as the play turned upfield.

DIAGRAM 2

Lombardi's Halfback Sweep

1956 New York Giants

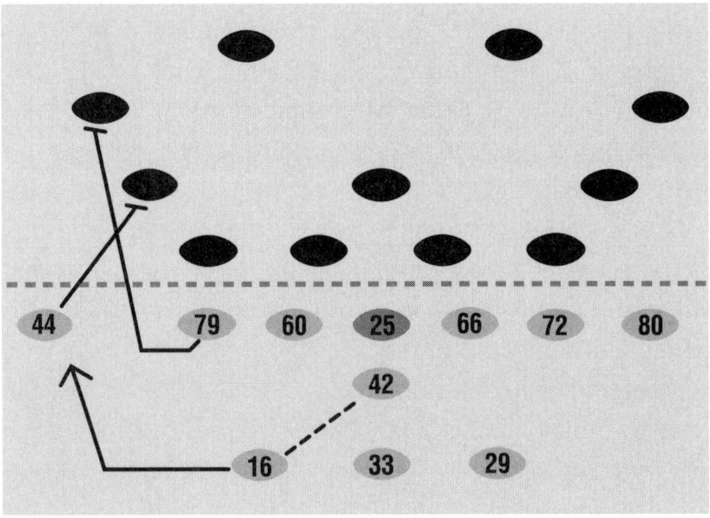

44 Kyle Rote, *LE*	**66** Jack Stroud, *RG*	**42** Charlie Conerly, *QB*
79 Rosey Brown, *LT*	**72** Dick Yelvington, *RT*	**16** Frank Gifford, *LH*
60 Bill Austin, *LG*	**80** Ken MacAfee, *RE*	**33** Mel Triplett, *FB*
25 Ray Wietecha, *C*		**29** Alex Webster, *RH*

Brown was passing the guards so regularly that Lombardi took him aside one day in practice and said, "Okay, Rosey, you pull, and if you can get around the corner, just keep going."

Scripting the game's first offensive series became a Giant trademark, and it usually resulted in a big play. Though he favored a fundamental approach, Lombardi relished an occasional deception. Before a game with the Pittsburgh Steelers, he designed two plays to take advantage of cornerback Dick Albans' aggressive style. On the first play from scrimmage, Gifford was flanked left and the Giants faked a sweep by halfback Alex Webster. As Gifford simulated a block, Albans raced in to stop the run. Gifford stepped around Albans, then raced upfield and Conerly hit him for a 67-yard touchdown.

When New York got the ball back, Conerly called for the same formation, and the Giants ran a fake off-tackle play to fullback Mel Triplett. Conerly faked to Triplett, hid the ball on his hip as Albans charged, then lofted another long scoring pass to Gifford.

Against the Washington Redskins in 1956, Lombardi took advantage of a young cornerback named Don Shula by mapping out an option play from Gifford to end Bob Schnelker that went for a 68-yard touchdown. When the Giants played the Philadelphia Eagles, whose defense was now headed by Steve Owen, the former Giants' coach, Lombardi frustrated Owen with his end sweeps. Against the Cleveland Browns, he put in a play that called for Gifford to get the ball on a double reverse and then lateral it to a trailing Conerly. The play resulted in the Giants' only score in a 10–0 win in their 1958 playoff game. The call stunned Cleveland coach Paul Brown, who asked a reporter after the game, "The lateral to Conerly? What the hell was he doing there?"

One week later, Lombardi mapped out a strategy that disrupted the Baltimore defense in the historic championship game at Yankee Stadium. The Colts had heard about Lombardi, but they weren't prepared for what defensive tackle Artie Donovan called a "pretty damn good strategy."

Since the strength of the Colts' pass rush was concentrated on the left side, where future Hall of Famers Donovan and end Gino Marchetti played next to one another, Lombardi instructed Conerly to fake a pitch to his right and roll left, away from Donovan and Marchetti. By inducing the Baltimore defense to flow one way and having Conerly go in the opposite direction, Lombardi was giving his quarterback precious seconds to scan the field.

"That was a hell of a strategy," Donovan said later, "because they did manage to neutralize our rush to an extent."

Lombardi's biggest contribution to the Giants however, was his work with the running game. He was a lineman at heart, having played the position as a guard on Fordham's famous line in the 1930s, and then coaching the line at Army under Red Blaik. Lombardi was heavily influenced at Fordham by head coach Jim Crowley, who was a member of the "Four Horsemen" backfield that played under Knute Rockne at Notre Dame. Crowley taught Lombardi the same blocking concepts he had learned from Rockne, and in the same fashion, getting down in the dirt opposite his players to show them proper technique.

Having played in the era of single-wing power football, Lombardi was a product of a time when, as he said once, "everybody ran, nobody threw the ball." When he arrived in New York to coach the Giants' offense, Lombardi was dismayed to find pro coaches de-emphasizing the running game. NFL offenses were relying on misdirection running plays, and linemen were being taught to simply nudge faked-out defenders from the path of the runners. Lombardi frowned at this free-and-easy style of offense because it seemed to him an abject admission of surrender.

"They just felt that they couldn't run," he said once in reference to NFL coaches in the mid-1950s. "They couldn't run because the people were too big or because of the defenses and so forth and so on."

Lombardi and Kolman came up with ways to counter the defensive strategies and took their ideas to head coach Jim Lee Howell.

"Ed and I thought if we put double-team blocking into our running game, we'd catch a lot of teams by surprise," Lombardi told Howell. "I don't think there's a lineman in the game today who can handle a double-team block."

With Howell's approval, Lombardi and Kolman put together a series of plays that reemphasized power running. By combining the quick-hitting features of the modern game with old-style power blocking, the offense could double-team the defense at the point of attack.

Two offensive plays emphasized this new approach—"26 Power" and "47 Power." The terms came from the numbering system that all football teams use to simplify play calling. In the Giants' system, the holes between the linemen were even-numbered (2,4,6,8) to the left side of the offensive line and odd-numbered (1,3,5,7,9) to the right. The backfield positions were also numbered, with "2" being to the right of the quarterback, "3" directly behind the quarterback, and "4" to the quarterback's left.

On "26 Power," the "2" back, halfback Alex Webster, carried the ball through the "6" hole between Brown and left guard Bill Austin. On "47 Power," Gifford, the "4" back, ran through the "7" hole, accompanied by double-team blocks from right tackle Dick Yelvington and right end Ken McAfee.

To give his blockers better angles, Lombardi widened the gaps in the line, spacing his guards and tackles an extra foot or two apart to isolate defenders at the point of attack. Lombardi called it "putting the other fellow on an island," and with distance on either side of the defenders, the runner was free to follow his blocks and cut inside or outside.

Blaik told Lombardi once that football's strategies were complex enough to occupy a man's mind for a lifetime. Like his mentor, Lombardi was a student of the game, and he took his studies seriously. It was said at the time that when the other coaches left the Giants' offices at night, there was always one light still burning, the light in Lombardi's office. From July through December, he worked

15-hour days and rarely took a day off. He stuffed reels of film in his briefcase to take home to study, and he was constantly updating a notebook full of play diagrams. He spent his daily 50-minute train ride from his house in New Jersey to his Yankee Stadium office diagramming strategies.

"When he came into pro football with us it was his first time in the (professional) game," Landry said, "so he was not only doing the job but also learning. But it was pretty obvious to all of us that Vince one day would be a really great coach. He was very basic in his approach and was a master of knowing how to utilize, to get the most out of personnel."

Lombardi motivated the Giants' offense to perform, but his unit remained in the shadows of Landry's defense. The success of the Giants' defense was unique to pro football in the 1950s. The first three decades of the NFL had seen an emphasis on the offensive aspects of the game. Strategies focused on the drive to the goal line.

Defensive specialists like Owen and Neale were lone voices drowned out by the choruses of offense-minded coaches like Paul Brown, Weeb Ewbank, and Sid Gillman. NFL teams concentrated on drafting offensive stars out of college, and it was players like Red Grange, Bronko Nagurski, and Otto Graham who made headlines.

The NFL's move to two-platoon football in 1953 gave each team separate offensive and defensive units. Landry's creation of the coordinated defense and its success in leading the Giants to the 1956 NFL championship ignited interest in defensive strategies and the men who carried them out.

By raising the public's awareness and appreciation of defensive play, the Giants paved the way for the celebrated units that followed in the 1960s and 1970s—the Los Angeles Rams' "Fearsome Foursome," the Dallas "Doomsday" defense, Minnesota's "Purple People Eaters," Pittsburgh's "Steel Curtain," and Denver's "Orange Crush."

At the heart of New York's great defense lay Landry's powers of observation. He studied NFL offenses and discovered team tendencies based on pre-snap formations. During the week he would watch the films of Cleveland for instance, then stand on the sidelines during Sunday's game and accurately predict which play the Browns were going to run next. When team owner Mara asked him what would happen if he guessed wrong, Landry steadied a looked at Mara and said, "There is no way I can be wrong."

Recalling the incident later, Mara called Landry "the cockiest quiet man I ever met."

Before Landry, defensive players had to rely mainly on their own experience. They attempted to read the play by the movement of the offensive linemen, and then guess where the ball was going.

Landry removed guesswork from defense. He would take a young defender aside and say, "Son, this is what's going to happen. You do it the way I tell you and if you get in any trouble, don't worry. That's my responsibility."

Knowing that every offense had a weakness, Landry became one of the first coaches to set his defense against the strength of the formation. The Giants gave the defense the same look every down by lining up in a standard 4-3 alignment, but they studied the offense before the snap, taking note of where the backs lined up, which side of the field the tight end was on, and then reacting at the snap according to their prearranged keys.

Over time, the 4-3 evolved into the "4-3 Inside" and "4-3 Outside." In the 4-3 Inside, the defensive tackles shut off the middle by charging inside while the linebackers pursued to the outside. Their charge was reversed in the 4-3 Outside, where the tackles rushed to the outside shoulders of the guards and the middle linebacker headed inside.

The Giants practiced their responsibilities endlessly. "We worked until we were ready to drop," Landry said, "and then we'd work some more."

No detail was too small for Landry's attention. He put his tackles, Grier and Dick Modzelewski, in a four-point stance with both hands on the ground, rather than the traditional three-point stance.

Landry felt a four-point stance gave the linemen greater flexibility to push off to either side.

Grier found the four-point stance awkward at first, but he realized it allowed him to get off the ball quicker. "Tom was always thinking about football and how to play it better to win games," Grier said. "His insistence on the four-point stance shows that no detail was too small or insignificant to escape his attention."

Landry's game-planning was coordinated but flexible. In a 1959 game against the Washington Redskins, the Giants planned to stop the Redskins' strong running game by having Modzelewski hit and slide off his block while Grier fired out from his tackle position. Redskins runners foiled the strategy by hesitating a split second after the handoff, then cutting inside or outside of Grier's charge.

Landry adapted in the second half by having Grier and Modzelewski hit and slide, thus forcing the runner to declare his intentions much quicker. It was the start of the flex defense he refined later in Dallas.

In a game against the pass-happy Pittsburgh Steelers, Landry came up with a defense that introduced a new name into the pro football lexicon—the "Red Dog." With no great runners at his disposal, Pittsburgh head coach Buddy Parker decided in 1957 to rely on his passing game. The Steelers scored 69 points over their first three games, and Landry looked to counter Pittsburgh's passing game by pressuring quarterback Earl Morrall. The result was the "Red Dog," an all-out linebacker blitz by Sam Huff, Harland Svare and Bill Svoboda. The maneuver caught the Steelers by surprise, and the Giants rolled to a 35–0 win.

By the late 1950s, Landry was proving himself a defensive mind equal to that of his forerunners, Neale and Owen. His 4-3 was a combination of Neale's 5-2-4 Eagle defense and Owen's 6-1-4 scheme. Landry incorporated Neale's idea for a dominant middle man, and improved upon it by putting him in a standing position off the line and dropping him into pass coverage. Landry made the middle linebacker the focus of his defense, giving him freedom to act as a "rover" in order to find his way to the ball carrier.

Landry utilized Owen's concepts of an umbrella-style pass defense and upgraded them with zone coverages and surprise blitzes. His concepts were advanced for their time, carried out by men whose intense play proved equal to intelligent planning. Landry's approach was almost artistic, and Huff remembers watching film of the Giants' defense and coming away impressed with his team's sophisticated style. "It was a thing of beauty," he said.

No man benefited more from the 4-3 than Huff. The Giants' defense was designed to funnel the action in the direction of the middle linebacker, and Huff played with a flair that captured the imagination of New York's media and fans. When the Yankee Stadium public address announcer intoned, "Tackle by Huff . . ." fans would stand and yell, *"Huff . . . Huff . . . Huff."* Hearing the breathless chant, one observer said the stadium sounded liked a giant locomotive.

Huff gained fame for his fierce battles with the premier fullbacks of his day, Cleveland's Jim Brown and Green Bay's Jimmy Taylor. He became the focus of a television program, "The Violent World of Sam Huff," as well as cover stories in national magazines like *Time.* But the media's high-gloss treatment of Huff did not obscure the fact that the middle linebacker was one piece of a coordinated puzzle, one man among eleven.

"Our defense was not designed specifically for Sam Huff to follow Jim Brown," Landry said. "Our defense was designed to stop the offense we were working against. Our defense was based on coordination . . . Sam was just one of eleven people who were coordinated."

The Giant defense became equal parts grit and glitz, and behind it all stood Landry, unflappable beneath the brim of his fedora as he signaled in plays from the sideline—hand on hip for a 4-3 Inside; hand over the stomach for a Red Dog. Yet while Landry displayed his desired plays through body language, he never exposed his emotions. Lombardi ranted and raved on game days, but Landry maintained his cool. Defensive end Andy Robustelli said that as great a coach as Lombardi was, he was lost on game days. "Tom Landry," Robustelli said, "was the only coach I knew who knew what he was doing all the time."

By 1958, Landry's defense was the driving force in New York's run at another Eastern Division title. As the team band played in the background, Yankee Stadium announcer Bob Sheppard introduced one by one the members of a defensive unit that had captured the hearts of the big city:

"From the University of Iowa, left safety Emlen Tunnell . . .

"From Arnold College, right end Andy Robustelli . . .

"And from the University of West Virginia, middle linebacker Sam Huff . . ."

Late in the season, when the enemy offense was driving deep into New York territory, a chant would echo down from the cavernous rafters of Yankee Stadium, building to a crescendo as it cut through the gathering cold and darkness:

"Dee-fense . . . Dee-fense . . ."

The chant became a tribal custom in New York, and it struck a responsive chord. Grier called it "music to our ears," adding, "When the crowd would start chanting, it felt great. We were heroes."

New York's defense became celebrated members of the city's sports scene, the subject of conversation in clubs like Toots Shor's and P.J. Clarke's. Huff, Jim Katcavage, Jimmy Patton, and company carried the team down the stretch as the Giants clung to second place in the division, one game behind the rival Browns.

NFL schedule makers indulged their sense of drama by matching the Giants and Browns in the season finale in Yankee Stadium. Between them, New York and Cleveland had split the previous two division titles. These were two dynasties at their peaks. Combined, they had won three of the past four NFL championships, and they owned the Eastern Division in the 1950s. From 1950 through 1959, no team other than the Browns or Giants wore the Eastern crown.

In 1958, Cleveland entered the final regular season game of

their 12-game schedule with a 9-2 record; the Giants were 8-3. A victory would give the Browns their second straight division title and eighth of the decade. A win by the Giants would force a one-game playoff to decide who would host the Baltimore Colts in the NFL championship game.

Playing in a blinding blizzard, the Giants defeated the Browns 13–10, with Summerall supplying a 49-yard field goal in overtime. One week later, the two rivals met again in Yankee Stadium. In what ranks as arguably the greatest clutch defensive performance in NFL history, the Giants held Jim Brown to just eight yards on seven carries and shut out Cleveland, 10–0.

"Only one man could have done this to us," Browns' kicker and offensive tackle Lou Groza told reporters after the game. "Tom Landry."

In the December 28 championship against Baltimore, the Giants gained momentum from a third quarter goal-line stand and clawed past the Colts to take a 17-14 lead late in the game. But thanks to the two-minute magic of crew-cut quarterback John Unitas, Baltimore broke back, tying the game on a field goal by Steve Myhra with 20 seconds showing on the stadium clock.

Exhausted by a late-season run that included back-to-back, must-win games with the Browns and now this late charge by Baltimore, the great Giants defense finally gave way. Operating in the cold, floodlit surroundings of Yankee Stadium, Unitas displayed the guile of a gambler—dropping, wheeling, finding the open receiver—as he marched the Colts to the Giants' one-yard line.

With the New York defense breathing steam and standing in the shadows of its own goal post, Unitas called "16 Power," a fullback blast over the right side, and handed off to fullback Alan "The Horse" Ameche, who churned over the goal line and into history.

The 1958 title game marked the end of an era. Exactly one month later, Lombardi signed a five-year contract to become head coach and general manager of the Green Bay Packers.

Landry left New York a year later; the man from Mission

returned to Texas to take over as head coach of the new Dallas franchise. Howell retired at the end of the 1960 season, thus ending the storied relationship of one of pro football's greatest coaching staffs.

But while an old era was fading in New York, new eras were dawning in Green Bay and Dallas. The past was serving as prologue, and Lombardi and Landry were about to lead the tactical evolution that marked the NFL in the 1960s.

Chapter Five

New Regimes in Green Bay and Dallas

FEBRUARY 1959 FOUND VINCE LOMBARDI visibly squirming in his office chair as he watched game films of the Green Bay Packers from their previous season.

The once-proud Packers had won just one of their twelve games in 1958, hitting rock bottom with a humiliating 56–0 loss late in the season to their Western Division rivals, the Baltimore Colts. Green Bay's 1-10-1 record was the worst in franchise history dating back to 1919, and with 11 straight non-winning seasons, this small Wisconsin town, known for its cold climate and cheese products, also became known for the worst team in the NFL.

"It was the Siberia of pro football," said Packers' halfback Paul Hornung, a former Heisman Trophy winner from Notre Dame who had been drafted in 1956. "Any player who did something wrong was threatened to be sent to Green Bay."

Hornung was the Packers' star player, but years of losing had taken the luster off Green Bay's "Golden Boy." By 1958, he was known more for his playboy image and love of the nightlife, which earned him a new nickname, "Picadilly Paul," for his frequent visits to a local club. By 1959, Hornung's goal mirrored that of the majority of his teammates. "I wanted to get the hell out of Green Bay," he said.

A foot of snow filled the streets outside Lombardi's window in the Packers' offices as the new head coach studied the flickering black-and-white images on the screen. He drummed his thick fingers impatiently on the tabletop, and squinted at the sight of a Green Bay receiver running under a long pass and barely making an effort to catch the ball. The Packers were a team blessed with raw potential but cursed by ragged play. They lacked discipline and direction. As guard Jerry Kramer said, the club's attitude was, "If you did something, you did it, and if you didn't, don't worry about it; there were more important things to do after the game."

Suddenly, Lombardi leaned forward in his chair. "Let's see that again!" he shouted. A staff assistant rewound the film, then set it in motion again. Lombardi watched the play unfold, and as he watched Hornung take the handoff from quarterback Bart Starr, head right and cut back for a good gain, the new coach flashed his toothy grin.

"Hornung," he said later, "is the guy who can make us go."

Beginning with his days in New York as an assistant coach with the Giants, Lombardi had made the left halfback position the key to his attack. In his run-oriented offense, the left halfback was expected to function like an old-style single-wing tailback—making his cuts over tackle behind the double-pull of the two guards; diving through the line on quick openers; blocking; decoying; catching passes; and on occasion, throwing the ball on the option play.

The halfback was not only the runner on his number-one play, the sweep, he blocked for the fullback on running plays away from the tight end. Gifford had excelled in that multi-purpose role in New York, and Lombardi saw Hornung as a bigger, stronger version of Gifford. Watching Hornung on film, he discovered that his new halfback had many of the same talents Gifford had—namely, the ability to run under control on the sweep and follow the lead of his blockers. Like Gifford, Hornung was a former quarterback, and his passing ability made him a natural for the option, a play that starts out like the sweep but gives the back the choice of running or throwing.

When he met with Hornung in training camp five months later, Lombardi pulled him aside and said, "You're going to be my left halfback. Either you play left half or you don't play. You're going to sink or swim at that position."

Lombardi sized up Hornung—6-2 and movie-star handsome at 220 pounds, with curly blond hair and clear blue eyes—and said, "I know about your reputation. You've done some things you shouldn't have done, but I don't think you've done as many things as people say you've done."

Looking his new boss straight in the eye, Hornung shrugged. "If that's the way they want to think, that's the way they'll think."

Lombardi grinned. There was something in Hornung's roguish manner that appealed to him. In much the same manner a loving father would speak to a rebellious son, Lombardi told Hornung, "I trust you, and don't forget that. I just don't want you to let me down. If you do, it'll be your ass."

Said Hornung later, "I got the message."

Lombardi was not long in delivering his message to the rest of the squad. In his first team meeting, he stood in front of his players and said, "Gentlemen, I have never been associated with a losing team, and I don't intend to start now."

He spoke slowly, in a deep, gruff voice that Hornung thought sounded like authority itself. "There is nobody big enough to think he's got the team made or can do what he wants. Trains and planes are going out and coming into Green Bay every day, and he'll be on one of them. I won't. I'm going to find thirty-six men who have the pride to make any sacrifice to win. If they're not here, I'll get them."

Players used to the easy-going manner of former coach Ray "Scooter" McLean were transfixed by Lombardi's forceful tone. Starr listened to his new coach and thought, "Where have you been all my life?"

Blinking behind his glasses, Lombardi raised his voice as he said, "If you don't want to pay the price, if you don't want to sacrifice, if you don't want to work and do the things you have to do to win, then GET THE HELL OUT!"

No one moved, and as wide receiver Max McGee said later, "He knew he had us." Kramer said Lombardi had "a very clear, precise image" in his mind of what he wanted to do and where he wanted to go. Inside him was a drive, a great fire to achieve, to accomplish, to excel, and he brought the team along with him. "He *demanded* that you go along with him," said Kramer, "*demanded* that you perform."

Lombardi's internal image was of a team that was an extension of himself, a team that reflected his personality. He was dictatorial and demanding, but also a man of compassion, warmth, and understanding. He treated his players as individuals, pushing one, prodding another, giving a pat on the back to a third. He would call Kramer "a fat cow" during practice, then drape his arm around the discouraged guard's shoulders later and tell him, "Son, someday you're going to be the greatest guard in the National Football League."

Having been impressed by his father on the values of hard work and mental toughness, Lombardi instilled the Packers with the same principles. Arriving in Green Bay, he felt the team's passive attitude was "a disease" that infected the whole squad. When he walked into the training room the first day of practice and found some 20 players waiting for the whirlpool, he was so frustrated he felt like crying. Instead, he blew his stack.

"What is this?" he roared. "An emergency casualty ward? Get this straight! When you're hurt, you have every right to be here. But this is disgraceful. I have no patience with the small hurts that are bothering most of you. You're going to have to live with small hurts if you're going to play for me."

When he returned to the trainer's room the next day, he found only two players waiting for treatment. He believed that by making his team mentally tough, they could keep going in games that looked impossible to win.

Lombardi cured the Packers of their "passive disease" that first summer by riding them through rigorous workouts and repetitive drills. The first play he installed was the power sweep, (*See Diagram 3*) identified as "49 Sweep" in the Packer playbook. It was similar to the Giants' end run with its pulling guard and halfback cut-backs, but it gained added muscle with the pull of the off-guard and the drive block by the fullback. "Gentlemen," declared Lombardi, "if we can make this play work, we can run the football."

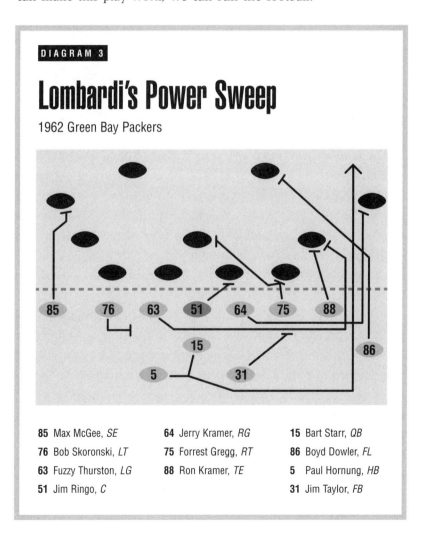

DIAGRAM 3

Lombardi's Power Sweep

1962 Green Bay Packers

85 Max McGee, *SE*	**64** Jerry Kramer, *RG*	**15** Bart Starr, *QB*
76 Bob Skoronski, *LT*	**75** Forrest Gregg, *RT*	**86** Boyd Dowler, *FL*
63 Fuzzy Thurston, *LG*	**88** Ron Kramer, *TE*	**5** Paul Hornung, *HB*
51 Jim Ringo, *C*		**31** Jim Taylor, *FB*

Lombardi broke the sweep down step-by-step, going over it so often his players could hear the coach's instructions, delivered as they were in his Brooklyn accent, in their sleep:

"We ask our lead *guahd* to pull *hahd* to the outside and kick out on the halfback, who is forcing on the play. Our off *guahd* pulls *hahd* as the left *guahd* did, and he finds the first opening. . . . What we're trying to get is a seal *heah,* and a seal *heah,* and run this play IN THE ALLEY."

The sweep was a teaching aid for Lombardi because it involved every player on the offense and a variety of techniques: the pulling action of the guards, down-blocking by the tackles and ends, drive-blocking by the fullback. "In this play," he wrote once, "we can teach most every block we want."

The Packers began and ended every practice with the power sweep, and Lombardi would shout, "Good timing, *good timing!*" as the back followed the guards around end. "That's the way! Real good!"

The Lombardi Sweep, as the play came to be known, was a variation of the single-wing off-tackle play run from a T-formation set. When he was at Fordham as a member of the "Seven Blocks of Granite" line, Lombardi took note of the play as it was run by squads at the University of Pittsburgh under the direction of Jock Sutherland.

The Packers adopted the same techniques that Sutherland had used 30 years earlier. Lombardi learned the coaching techniques for the play from his head coach at Fordham, Jim Crowley, who in turn had learned the play from Notre Dame's Knute Rockne.

Lombardi made the most of the sweep's versatility in adapting it to the modern game. The sweep was three plays in one, since it could be run outside, off-tackle, and inside. It became the most feared play in an offense that featured a ferocious running game based on precision and power. With Hornung sweeping the flanks at a hard sprint, and bruising fullback Jim Taylor bucking up the middle, the Packers pounded out yards the tough, old-fashioned way.

Lombardi called his offense "grinding meat," and his main objective was to run simple plays and wear down the opponent with superior desire and execution. Taylor was the prime mover in the Packer attack, an iron man who grunted and growled his way to becoming just the second back in NFL history at the time to rush for over a thousand yards three straight years.

The Packers popularized an alternate way of gaining ground with their use of option blocking. Defenses in the fifties and sixties read offenses so well and reacted so quickly they clogged running lanes before the ball carrier could get through. Lombardi ordered his blockers to ride the defender in the direction they wanted to go, and taught Hornung and Taylor to "read" the blocking on the run and cut inside or outside. If a play was designed to go over right guard for instance, Hornung keyed Kramer's block. If the defender moved inside, Kramer rode his man in, and Hornung headed outside. If the defender's move was outside, Hornung veered back and cut inside.

A Packer team that had won just one game in 1958 won seven games Lombardi's first year, then followed with three straight Western Division titles and consecutive NFL championships in 1961–62. The '62 team finished 14–1 overall and is considered one of the greatest teams in NFL history. The Packers missed the championship game in 1963–64, but returned to the top in '65, claiming their third league championship in five years.

Lombardi's success spawned a host of imitators, and it wasn't long before other NFL coaches were espousing the merits of running to daylight and option blocking. For years, they had given up on rushing the ball because of the increased size and strength of defensive linemen. But Lombardi, the former physics teacher, realized that size and speed were relative, and if defenses could be manned with quick, intelligent linemen, so too could offenses. He emphasized the run, becoming in effect, the great doctrinaire of the ground game. Others followed Lombardi's lead, and by the mid-sixties, small backs like the Rams' Dick Bass and the Eagles' Timmy Brown were veering to daylight, and big backs like the 49ers' Ken Willard and the Giants' Tucker Frederickson were cutting against the grain rather than running headlong into a pileup.

In Dallas, Tom Landry watched the development of Lombardi's power sweep and run-to-daylight theories. He saw his old friend dominating the league with his running game, a phenomenon that required a response. Landry studied the perfect synchronization of the Packers' power sweep, broke down its option blocking and cut-back running, and devised a defense to defeat it.

"The primary philosophy (behind run to daylight)," Landry said, "was big linemen blocking for big backs." Recognizing that there were eight gaps along the line of scrimmage, six between the line-men and one in each flat, Landry assigned a defender to each of the gaps. "If the play comes in a defender's direction," Landry said, "he covers his gap, rather than go directly for the ball."

The result was the creation in 1964 of the gapping flex defense (*See Diagram 4*) in which each defender was taught to refrain from over-reacting and chasing the play too soon, thus preventing the opening of a running lane behind him. Dallas defensive linemen took staggered positions along the line of scrimmage, and were taught to hit and hold, play their coverage areas, and not respond to false keys and pressure from their offensive counterparts.

In a conventional defense, linemen reacted to the flow of the offense and fought through the blocks to get to the runner. Each man was an island, and thus became easy prey for the advanced blocking schemes unleashed on the league by Lombardi. Packer linemen were taught to ride a defender in the direction of his own momentum. As they blocked the defense in one direction, the backs followed at a controlled trot and headed for the open gaps.

"That's all (Lombardi) was talking about," Landry said, "running to daylight. That was his concept, and it worked."

Landry had designed the "umbrella" defense to stop the aerial artistry of Paul Brown's Cleveland Browns in 1950, and created the coordinated 4-3 to slow down Jim Brown in 1958. His response to Lombardi's cut-back features was to take away the gaps in the line. The gapping defense coordinated the arrival of three or four defenders at the point of attack. It was a defense, said Landry, "designed to stop every play on the line of scrimmage."

Ernie Stautner, a Hall of Fame defensive tackle for the Pittsburgh Steelers in the fifties and assistant coach with the Cowboys, said at

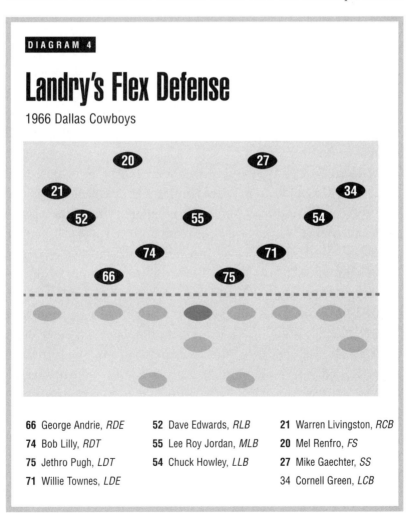

DIAGRAM 4

Landry's Flex Defense
1966 Dallas Cowboys

66 George Andrie, *RDE*	**52** Dave Edwards, *RLB*	**21** Warren Livingston, *RCB*
74 Bob Lilly, *RDT*	**55** Lee Roy Jordan, *MLB*	**20** Mel Renfro, *FS*
75 Jethro Pugh, *LDT*	**54** Chuck Howley, *LLB*	**27** Mike Gaechter, *SS*
71 Willie Townes, *LDE*		**34** Cornell Green, *LCB*

the time that the Dallas staff believed they had "the only defense that can cover every running play."

Yet the initial problem with the gapping defense was that the delay in reaction restricted the football instincts of the defensive players, most of whom preferred to be high-speed destroyers. "If the ball carrier is going inside," Stautner said, "it isn't easy for a lineman to learn to go outside." Stautner called Landry's defensive scheme "a damned work of art" but acknowledged that it took several years to learn to play it. The gapping defense was difficult because linemen had to wait before they committed to the play.

The second problem in the gapping defense was lack of a pass rush. By holding their ground first and then reacting, Dallas defenders found it difficult to pressure the quarterback. "We were waiting too much," Lilly said. It wasn't until 1966 that players like Lilly, George Andrie, and linebackers Lee Roy Jordan and Chuck Howley felt comfortable playing this style of defense, but when they did, it became second-nature.

"I started out at defensive end (with Dallas in 1961)," Lilly remembered, "and (Landry) was putting his flex defense in very slowly. I think the reason for that was he didn't have the players he really wanted to have. By the time I moved to tackle in the middle of my third season, he had put the flex in, but we really didn't know how to run it. By 1964, we were starting to understand it pretty well.

"He knew what he wanted to do, and he had players in New York that ran something similar to the flex defense. But I don't think he got it all together until he came to Dallas. Maybe he had it in mind what he wanted to do, but none of us had ever experienced a defense like that, where you had to key, and watch people, and move after they move.

"It was difficult to learn, because it was totally opposite to a defensive player's nature. I think it was about '65 or '66 before we had it down. But our entire goal with the flex defense was to stop the run on first down and put them in a passing situation on second and third down. It worked pretty well."

The flex worked well enough that it allowed the "Doomsday" defense to hold opponents to a 3.2 yards-per-carry average from 1965–74.

The Cowboys ran the flex in two forms. When opposing offenses placed their tight end next to the right tackle, Dallas staggered its defensive formation so that Lilly and right end Willie Townes crowded the line of scrimmage, while left end Andrie and right tackle Jethro Pugh played off the ball. When offenses put the tight end next to the left tackle, the Cowboys changed as well, putting Andrie and Pugh close to the scrimmage line and dropping Lilly and Townes back.

"Our whole defense was basically a 'gap' defense," Lilly said. "Each one of us had responsibility for a gap even though we were lined head-up on a lineman, and the linebackers also had their own gap responsibilities. When I was up on the ball, I was just basically keying on the guard. When I was off the ball, I keyed the guard and center. It was complicated, because it all had to do with certain formations, and we had to learn a lot because teams were starting to be multi-formations. But it was an interesting defense, and it became even more interesting when I finally grasped its concepts."

Landry's inspired strategies and the infusion of young talent helped the Cowboys grow into a contender. The signing of players like Lilly, Don Meredith, Ralph Neely, Mel Renfro, and Bob Hayes helped the Cowboys claim their first non-losing season in 1965 when they finished 7-7. Meredith proved prophetic when he told a reporter, "Landry knows just what kind of personnel he wants at each position, and he knows precisely what he wants to do with them. . . . When he gets it, the Cowboys and the Packers will be playing for the championship."

By 1966, the Cowboys were fully stocked with star players, and their breakout season saw them score an NFL-high 445 points en route to a 10-3-1 record. In winning the Eastern Division title, Landry and his young team earned the right to play Lombardi's Packers for the NFL title on New Year's Day in the Dallas Cotton Bowl.

The coaching version of point-counterpoint between Landry and Lombardi was taking center stage in the Texas sun. The stakes were enormous, since the winner would for the first time advance to meet the champion of the rival American Football League in a game billed as the "Super Bowl."

The CBS Radio announcer calling the game noted the unique coaching relationship between the Packers and Cowboys when he told his listening audience:

"I think it can certainly be said that both teams have a pretty strong line on the coaching philosophy of the other. They were both on the coaching staff of the New York Giants when Vince Lombardi was the offensive coach and Tom Landry the defensive coach, and they've moved from there to their respective head coaching positions. That long-time common employment is serving them in good stead right now."

Amid the festive atmosphere in Dallas, Lombardi and Landry rose to the occasion with game plans that demonstrated each man's brilliance. Recognizing that the Cowboys' gapping defense was geared to stop cut-back running, Lombardi shelved his lead play, the power sweep. In its place, the Packer boss put in crossing motion for his backs and altered blocking assignments. He also emphasized Starr's passing game in order to exploit weaknesses in the Cowboy secondary. Lombardi pared the Packer game plan down to eight running plays and six passing plays. "A game plan is nothing without execution," Starr said, "but this was a great plan."

The Cowboys were no less impressed with Landry's planning. Dallas sought to confuse Green Bay middle linebacker Ray Nitschke with a flamboyant attack featuring speed and shifting formations. Said Meredith, "By the time of the game we were brain-washed. We knew we could run and move on the Packers."

New Year's Day dawned sunny and warm, with temperatures in the low 70s, and 75,504 spectators crammed into the Cotton Bowl for the classic showdown. The Packers sprang their new offensive strategy on the game's first play, crossing the backs and sending halfback Elijah Pitts off right tackle for a 32-yard gain. Starr methodically moved Green Bay deep into Dallas territory, then hit Pitts for a 17-yard touchdown.

Green Bay made it 14–0 when Renfro fumbled the ensuing kickoff and Jim Grabowski recovered the ball and ran it in for the score. Undaunted by the Packers' lightning-quick lead, the Cowboy offense clicked into gear. Their shifting formations nudged Nitschke out of position, and backs Perkins and Dan Reeves twisted and turned through the Packer defense like two Texas tornadoes. Eventually, they each touched down in the end zone, Reeves romping for a 3-yard TD and Perkins skipping to a 23-yard score that tied the game at 14.

Starr gave the Packers back the lead with long touchdown passes to ends Carroll Dale and Boyd Dowler. The latter offered an illustration of how Lombardi set up Landry's defense. In order to hit Dowler over the middle, Starr first had to clear Jordan from his middle linebacker position. He did so with a play-fake to Taylor, who then ran a pattern into Howley's area at left linebacker, pulling Jordan and Howley with him. With both linebackers out of the way, Dowler cut over from his split end position and Starr hit him in the vacated area for a touchdown.

Down by 14, the Cowboys responded with a big play of their own in the fourth quarter. Landry manipulated Lombardi's secondary by sending split end Hayes sprinting deep on a flag pattern. Hayes drew double coverage from cornerback Bob Jeter and free safety Willie Wood, leaving Meredith the middle of the field to work with. When strong safety Tom Brown slipped, tight end Frank Clarke was wide open for a 68-yard TD.

The sudden score cut the Cowboys' deficit to 34–27 late in the game and left Lombardi frowning on the sideline. "That's Landry," he told reporters later. "We had everything covered and he springs that on us."

In the end, it was a surprising mental lapse by Landry and his staff that helped defeat Dallas. Facing a fourth-and-goal at the Green Bay two, Landry called "Fire 90," a roll-out play for Meredith. In the Cowboys' goal-line offense, Clarke was supposed to replace Hayes at flanker, with Pettis Norman playing tight end. By playing the stronger Clarke at flanker, the Cowboys were looking for better blocking on the right side, the side Meredith rolled to.

Inexplicably, Dallas kept Hayes in the game in the crucial fourth-down play against the Packers, and it cost them.

In the CBS-TV broadcast booth, Ray Scott called the game's decisive play in his famous, clipped tones:

"Dallas out of the huddle, Meredith over center . . . Meredith keeps it, rolls out . . . under pressure . . . throws . . . intercepted by Tom Brown at the goal line!

"Green Bay has the ball. They have held off the Cowboys."

Packers' left linebacker Dave Robinson forced the interception by reading Hayes' first step and diagnosing a Dallas pass. Making a strong inside move, Robinson pressured Meredith into heaving a weak floater. The pass hung illuminated in the glare of the Cotton Bowl lights for what seemed like an eternity, before being intercepted by Brown in the back of the painted turf of the end zone.

The Packers had earned a second straight NFL championship, and they carried a grinning Lombardi off the field on their shoulders. Two weeks later, they defeated Kansas City, 35–10, in Super Bowl I. Yet while Green Bay gained glory in victory, Dallas claimed distinction in defeat. As their general manager Tex Schramm said, the Cowboys were the "heroes of the country." Young and inexperienced as they were, they had played the poised Packers to a standstill.

Despite Green Bay's aging star players, the Cowboys believed the Packers would be the team to beat in 1967.

Chapter Six

The Struggles of '67

E VEN BEFORE IT BEGAN, THE 1967 SEASON was branded unique in the history of the National Football League because it was the year the league instituted divisional play.

The NFL had been expanding steadily throughout the sixties, largely in response to meeting the challenge presented by the American Football League, which was showing itself to be ambitious and competitive. The AFL was breaking ground by bringing the pro game to cities like San Diego, Oakland, and Houston. NFL owners who had resisted expansion throughout the fifties embraced it as a way of preventing the AFL from fielding teams in new territories.

In 1960, the NFL hastily awarded the Cowboys franchise to Dallas to provide direct competition against the AFL's Dallas Texans, coached by Hank Stram and blessed with the new league's best runner, halfback Abner Haynes.

That same year, the NFL persuaded the owners of the AFL's Minneapolis team to jump leagues and field an NFL team to start the 1961 season. The AFL lost Atlanta to the NFL in 1966, and New Orleans completed the older league's expansion picture when it was granted a team for the '67 season.

The addition of the Saints' franchise swelled league membership to 16 teams, and brought about a revamped divisional alignment and playoff format. Dating back to 1933, when Chicago Bears' owner George Halas pushed for the idea at a July league meeting, the NFL had been divided into two conferences, Eastern and Western. For the next 32 years, the NFL postseason consisted of a one-game playoff between the conference champions.

The merger of the AFL and NFL in 1966 added a new postseason game—a showdown between the champions of the two leagues. The contest was originally called the AFL-NFL World Championship Game. It wasn't until 1969 that the name "Super Bowl," coined by AFL founder Lamar Hunt, was used. The moniker was enthusiasically adopted and applied to the first two games in retrospect, complete with Roman numerals.

Prior to the 1967 season, NFL commissioner Pete Rozelle met with league owners and instituted a realignment of the 16 teams that made up the Eastern and Western Conferences. Rather than have two unwieldy divisions of eight teams each, the NFL streamlined the league into four divisions of four teams each. Traditional rivalries were maintained under the realignment, which took the following form:

EASTERN CONFERENCE

Capitol Division

Dallas Cowboys
New Orleans Saints
Philadelphia Eagles
Washington Redskins

Century Division

Cleveland Browns
New York Giants
Pittsburgh Steelers
St. Louis Cardinals

WESTERN CONFERENCE

Central Division

Chicago Bears
Detroit Lions
Green Bay Packers
Minnesota Vikings

Coastal Division

Atlanta Falcons
Baltimore Colts
Los Angeles Rams
San Francisco 49ERS

For the first time in NFL history, a semifinal round of playoffs was added, making for a three-week tier of postseason games. The team that looked to be most affected by the expanded playoff format was Vince Lombardi's Green Bay Packers. Having won NFL titles in 1965 and '66, Lombardi was seeking a third straight title, an accomplishment unprecedented in the modern history of the sport.

To reach their goal, the aging Packers would have to remain healthy through a rigorous schedule that included six preseason games, 14 regular-season games, and three playoff games. That meant sustaining themselves through 23 games, and in every one they would be branded the team to beat. It was a lot to ask of a team on which 13 of its 40 players were 30 years old or more.

Tired and concerned about his health following Super Bowl I, Lombardi contemplated stepping down as head coach to concentrate on his general manager duties. But the lure of a record-setting third straight title and the task of rebuilding a backfield depleted by the loss of Paul Hornung to retirement and Jim Taylor to the expansion Saints energized him. Realizing that winning the league championship would give the Packers a special place in NFL history, he prepared his veterans to make one final run at the record book. The 1967 season would mark Lombardi's last stand in Green Bay.

Most NFL observers picked the Packers to win again in 1967. In his book *Pro Football 1967*, Jack Zanger, a veteran writer who had been covering pro sports for 15 years, predicted the Packers could win any of the NFL's four new divisions and "surely should win in the Central Division." Zanger called Green Bay the best-balanced team in the league, with individual standouts in Bart Starr, Forrest Gregg, Ray Nitschke, and Willie Davis.

The editors of *Pro Football Illustrated* said there was "no reason to believe that Green Bay won't continue to dominate pro football," remarking that "extra incentive" would come from the desire to win the title again.

The team most observers figured to stand in the way of Green Bay was their 1966 championship opponent, the Dallas Cowboys. The Cowboys had captured the imagination of the football public with their near victory over the Packers the previous January, and NFL experts picked Dallas to waltz through the Capitol Division.

Pro Football Illustrated wrote, "the Cowboys won so impressively last year, and seemed not yet at their maximum potential, that it's difficult not to stick with them this year."

Said Zanger, "Tom Landry, acknowledged as one of pro football's sharpest defensive tacticians, tooled an offense that was the most productive in the league. With all the parts back in place, the Cowboys should do it again in 1967."

Key parts in the Dallas offense consisted of all-pro tackle Ralph Neely, wide receiver "Bullet" Bob Hayes, the fastest man in pro football, and a solid backfield that started Dan Reeves at halfback and Don Perkins at fullback. Dallas added depth to its squad by drafting flanker and kickoff returner Sims Stokes and tackle Rayfield Wright, and trading for wide receiver Lance Rentzel.

Landry's multiple offense had jumped from seventh in the NFL in scoring in 1965 to first in 1966, and by 1967, the Cowboys had wedded skill with strategy in a near-perfect union. Orchestrating the Dallas offense was Joe Don Meredith, a colorful character from Mt. Vernon, Texas. Partial to cowboy boots and blue jeans, he spoke in a down-home drawl that made words like "oil" come out "awl," as in *awl* money. His sometimes indifferent personality made him unpredictable both on the field and off, and writer Elinor Kaine labeled him "a complex nut," who had married, divorced, remarried, and redivorced his college sweetheart.

The brown-haired, green-eyed Meredith was a graduate of Southern Methodist University, and it was as a member of the Mustangs football team that he added to his assortment of names: Dandy, Dandy Don, Joe Don, Joe Jim Dandy, Jim, and Jimmy. The 6 ft. 3 in., 210-pound Meredith was also called Slim because of his thin legs. Teammates and opponents teased him about his build, and Rentzel remembered him sitting in front of his locker saying, "The Lord gave me a pitiful body, but I'll just have to do the best I can with it." He was regarded as having the skinniest legs in pro football during the 1960s, and he eventually took to wearing foam rubber "falsies" in his football pants and pulling extra-thick socks up over his calves.

Meredith was good at taking a joke, and he could deliver one as well. His green eyes were always flecked with a sense of bemusement. As a quarterback, he was unpredictable and entertaining. Following the dramatic last-second loss to Green Bay in the 1966 NFL championship game, Meredith explained to a reporter that he threw against the Packers because "you have to put a little intrigue into it."

Meredith mixed an "aw shucks" country-boy personality with a street-wise common sense, and carried himself in a way that even opponents admired. "Meredith has this charisma around him," Los Angeles Rams' defensive tackle Merlin Olsen said. "He's like (Bobby) Layne . . . a great player and exciting to be around."

By his own admission, Landry preferred a studious quarterback more in the mold of Starr rather then a rebel like Layne. Meredith provided a sharp contrast to the serious-minded Landry, and throughout their nine years together, they struggled to understand each other's ways and moods.

Before an exhibition game with the Chicago Bears, Meredith was sitting in a quarterbacks meeting, smoking a cigar and watching Landry draw diagrams on the blackboard. As Landry talked about ways of beating the Bears' defense, Meredith began playing with his lit cigar, gesturing grandly with it, taking exaggerated puffs, and twirling it between his fingers like a baton.

Suddenly, Landry turned to ask Meredith a question, and Don mistakenly stuck the lit end of the cigar into his mouth. Coughing smoke and spitting ash, Meredith looked up to see Landry staring down at him, his face a stony, stoic mask.

"You understand what I'm telling you, Don?" A shaken Meredith nodded as fellow quarterbacks Craig Morton and Jerry Rhome covered their mouths to keep from laughing.

Landry's attitude was that nothing funny ever happens on the football field, but Dandy Don found humor in almost every situation. He sang in huddles during timeouts, doing country ditties like "God Made Me a Black Land Farmer."

Against Washington, he called a play at the line of scrimmage, only to have Redskins' middle linebacker Sam Huff shout the perfect defense to stop it. Meredith looked across the center at Huff and saw him grinning back at him. Meredith called an audible, and Huff countered with another perfect defensive call. A flustered Meredith began stammering as he searched his mind for another audible. Finally, Meredith yelled, "Aw . . . time out . . . time out," to a chorus of jeers from the Redskin defenders.

When blitzing linebackers put Meredith on his back, he would look up and wonder why he allowed his "poor thin body" to be pounded as it was. "I tell myself, 'Dandy, why did you ever take this up as a career? You're too nice a person for this to be happening to, Dandy. Why don't you go back to East Texas, where you belong?'"

Frustrated Cowboy fans often wondered the same thing. From the time he was drafted number-one by Dallas in 1960 following an All-America career at SMU, Meredith had been expected to be something he was not. He chafed under comparisons to other quarterbacks, telling Cowboys' general manager Tex Schramm at one point, "I'm not Bart Starr! I'm Don Meredith!"

Schramm, who felt the future of the Cowboys was riding on their quarterback, would preach to Meredith, "You have to be dedicated, you have to pay the price," and would point to Starr as the "epitome of a hard-working dedicated athlete." While Schramm didn't expect Meredith to adopt Starr's regimented personality, he did hope his quarterback could be a little more serious, a little less flippant. When Schramm heatedly told him to "join the adult world," Meredith stormed out of the Cowboy offices. Dandy Don returned the next day, walked up to Schramm and drawled, "I'm not gonna join your adult word. I'll live in my world and you live in yours."

During his first six years with the Cowboys, Meredith's world in Dallas was a complex one. He had left SMU as an All-America quarterback, but one who had divided the Mustangs' fans, half of whom considered him the best thing to happen to SMU since football great Doak Walker, the other half who considered him the worst thing to happen since the bleachers collapsed at SMU's old Ownby Stadium.

Upon arriving in Dallas, Meredith succeeded in dividing Cowboy loyalists the same way. He was the highly-touted rookie quarterback of an expansion franchise, and he preferred to rely on what had worked in college rather than learn Landry's complex offense. "Instead of trying to learn," he said, "I fought it. I became lax in things."

Dandy Don drew a reputation as lazy, overconfident, and spoiled. Both his skinny body and blithe spirit suffered after he replaced aging Eddie LeBaron at starting quarterback in 1962. He became the target of linebacker blitzes and loud booing, but he refused to quit on himself. To Meredith, it wasn't so much a matter of courage, but one of determination. As he picked himself up off the ground from yet another blitz and heard the Cotton Bowl crowd deride him, he would think, "Nobody is going to beat me." For the man known as Dandy, these instances of painful defeat became defining moments in his career.

"I knew if I didn't get up they would have beaten me," he said. "I couldn't stand the thought of that."

Meredith played through multiple injuries, and while Landry never doubted his quarterback's ability, he did question whether he would ever be physically healthy enough to lead Dallas to a championship. The turning point for both Meredith and the Cowboys came in Week Seven of the 1965 season. The Cowboys began the season with easy wins over the Giants and Redskins, then hit a slump where they lost four straight games. Dallas expected a turnaround to come in Week Seven when they traveled to Pittsburgh to play the struggling Steelers. Instead, Meredith played poorly, completing just 12 of 34 passes in a shocking 22–13 loss. Meredith later called it "the worst game I ever played in my life."

The postgame found both quarterback and coach in tears, and over the weekend rumors circulated that Meredith's career hung in the balance as Landry decided whether or not to bench him. Landry, who was involved in numerous quarterback controversies during his years in Dallas, called the Meredith decision the "most difficult I've ever had to make." Meredith had become the fans' scapegoat for all that was wrong with the Cowboys, a team that had rashly been picked by some preseason publications to win their conference title that season.

According to Landry, Meredith was getting booed "something awful." The popular choice would have been to bench Meredith in favor of promising 22-year-old backup Craig Morton. But Landry knew that those booing Meredith had forgotten how he had played through injuries. Meredith, Landry said, had "quarterbacked us when no other man could have stood on the field with the injuries he had." Landry wasn't foolish enough to favor personal sentiment over reality, and he wouldn't run a quarterback out there who could not do the job. But he had no doubt Meredith could lead the Cowboys, and told him so the Tuesday morning following the loss to the Steelers.

"Don, you're my quarterback. I believe in you."

Meredith, who had headed to Landry's office expecting the worst, began crying again, and Landry wept as well. Landry then told the Dallas media, "We need a quarterback to lift us to our potential . . . and that's why Don Meredith will start the next seven games this season."

The process proved to be a turning point for the Cowboys, who rallied around Meredith and won five of their next seven games to finish 7–7 and secure their first non-losing season. Dallas receiver Frank Clarke said Landry's decision pleased a lot of players. "We knew sticking with one (quarterback) would remove a lot of uncertainty," Clarke said. "Meredith had to be our leader."

By 1967, Meredith was the unquestioned leader of the Dallas offense, a take-charge type who was not afraid to call one of his offensive linemen "a yellow dog" for failing to block a defensive end and ordering him off the field.

Neely, who was a teammate of both Meredith and Roger Staubach, said Meredith was just as much a field general as Staubach, but in a different way.

"In '66, we were a young team playing in our first championship when the Packers came to town," Neely said. "We kicked off and Bart Starr took them in for a score. They kicked off to us, we fumbled the ball and they ran it in for a score.

"Now it's 14–0 and we have not yet run an offensive play. We're in the huddle, and Meredith came up next to where I was standing and I heard him singing, 'I didn't know God made Honky-Tonk.' He got in the huddle, kneels down, looked up at all of us and says, 'Folks, we're in a heap of shit.' That got us to laugh, which is what he wanted us to do.

"I think to this day Don is still a little bitter about (the fan abuse). The guy played with pneumonia, broken ribs, and everything else. By the time I got to Dallas in '65, he was almost a physical wreck. He was a helluva quarterback, and a tremendous leader.

"You'd go through a brick wall if he asked you to. He was a player's quarterback, he wasn't a coach's quarterback. He and Landry didn't get along at all. But there was no doubt that Don could win for you.

"He had that thing you couldn't teach, charisma, but he was loose about it. One time during a Washington Redskins game, Sam Huff was doing a lot of blitzing. Don told him, 'Sam, if you don't start playing by the rules, I'm going to take my ball and go home.'"

Meredith began the '67 season with high expectations, but the campaign took a downward turn when he injured his arm in the preseason, then suffered a twisted knee and broken nose. Still,

Dallas won two of its first three games, then trailed the rival Redskins in Week Four, 14–10, with 10 seconds left in what had been a bruising game. Reeves said later Meredith was so battered he could hardly stand as the Cowboys huddled for the final play. Mustering an inner resolve, Meredith found Reeves for a 36-yard score. The Cowboys won, and Meredith displayed great courage in quarter-backing his team throughout the long afternoon. But it almost turned to tragedy when his wife Cheryl called an ambulance to their home that night and he was rushed to the hospital with pneumonia. He lost 20 pounds, and few people realized how serious his situation was. While most men would have been off their feet for months, Meredith returned three weeks later and helped the Cowboys carry a division-leading 5-2 record into the season's midpoint.

"Courage is what did it," Landry said of Meredith. "It was February before he ever felt good."

The Cowboys' inconsistent first half of the season was mirrored by Green Bay, which opened the season with a 17–17 tie against the Detroit Lions. A hard preseason schedule left Starr nursing an assortment of injuries. With Hornung's retirement hastened by a pinched nerve in his neck and Taylor playing out his option and returning to his home state of Louisiana to play for the Saints, the Green Bay ground game was suddenly suspect.

Responsibility for the success of the Packers' precision offense fell on the slight shoulders of Starr, but he began the season with his ribs encased in foam rubber padding, surgical tape wrapped around a pulled thigh muscle, and a sprained thumb on his throwing hand. He was further battered by Detroit Lions' left tackle Alex Karras in the season opener, then threw five interceptions against the rival Chicago Bears in Week Two.

With the Packer offense riddled by injuries and inconsistencies, Lombardi looked to his defense and its fierce ring-leader, Ray Nitschke, to carry the team through the early weeks of the '67 season. Nitschke was the heart and soul of a unit in which eight of its eleven players had been named to various all-pro teams during their careers, and he presented a picture of pure menace as he leaned over center from his middle linebacker position.

In many ways, Nitschke as a player was an internal contradiction, a split personality. Away from the field, he wore horn-rimmed glasses and business suits, and his receding blond hair and articulate speech made him seem more like a middle-aged professor than a middle linebacker. After being named Most Valuable Player of the 1962 NFL championship game, Nitschke was the mystery guest on the television show "What's My Line?" His mild manners stumped the panel for several minutes.

Sunday afternoons, however, saw the balding, bespectacled Nitschke undergo a personality transformation. He stuck his false teeth on the top shelf of his locker, trading them in for a gummy piece that gave his wide mouth a cruel, downward curve. His glasses were replaced by a battle-scraped gold helmet pulled down low on his forehead and eye-black was smeared high on his cheekbones to cut the sun's glare. He wrapped his thick forearms in pads and tape, and he pushed through blockers and punished ball carriers with an aggressive fury that struck fear into opponents.

When Kansas City Chiefs quarterback Len Dawson faced Green Bay for the first time in Super Bowl I the previous January, he looked across the line and was momentarily shaken at the sight of the 6 ft. 3 in., 240-pound Nitschke, with his hawkish features, staring back at him. Said Dawson, "I thought to myself, 'This is the ugliest, meanest man I have ever seen.'"

Nitschke played tough but clean, and he treasures his reputation as one of the hardest hitters in NFL history. "You want them to respect you when they run a play," he said. "You want them to remember that you're there."

Former Baltimore Colts and Pittsburgh Steelers running back Preston Pearson remembers. Pearson recalled a play in which a missed block allowed Nitschke to draw a bead on him.

"I saw this monster only a moment before he hit," Pearson said. "It felt like he was tearing my head off. It was the kind of hit that can break a man's back. I saw Nitschke as I was going down, and he had a wild look in his eyes."

While he played in an era dominated by great middle linebackers like Sam Huff, Dick Butkus, Joe Schmidt, and Tommy Nobis, Nitschke's fearsome appearance allowed him to carve his own special niche.

"He was toothless, ugly," said Bill Bergey, who played middle linebacker for the Cincinnati Bengals and the Philadelphia Eagles.

"He looked the part (of middle linebacker)," said Nobis, an all-pro with the Atlanta Falcons. "He was so damn ugly with his helmet and the mask. He ran like a football player, and sounded like one."

Nitschke, who talks in a voice that sounds like crunching gravel, kept up an incessant chatter on the field. He was loud and noisy, and his non-stop talking irritated Lombardi.

"Hey, Nitschke," the Packer coach would yell.

"Yes, coach?"

"*Shaddup.*"

Nitschke overcame an adverse childhood to forge a life as a football great and father of three adopted sons. His father was killed in a car accident when Ray was three, and his mother died when he was 13. He and his 18-year-old brother Richard were raised by their oldest brother, Bob, who was 21. "My brother was wonderful to me, but I never had any discipline," Ray said. "I felt I was somebody who didn't have anything and I took it out on everybody else."

By his own admission, Nitschke grew up "belting the other kids in the neighborhood." He channeled his aggression into sports, and became an all-state quarterback and star baseball player. He accepted a football scholarship from the University of Illinois, playing fullback on offense and linebacker on defense. Refusing at first to wear a facemask, his teeth were knocked out his sophomore season in a game against Ohio State.

Drafted as a linebacker by the Packers in 1958, Nitschke spent his first three seasons as a backup to Tom Bettis. Being benched did not sit well with Nitschke, who goaded Lombardi with comments like, "Just call me the judge, 'cause I'm always on the bench."

Nitschke sometimes took his frustration out in barroom brawls, and his trouble-making nearly caused the Packers to trade him. But he excelled in practice against the team's established stars. Nitschke survived by adhering to what he called "the two B's: Be ready and Beware."

Packer center Bill Curry remarked that Nitschke didn't care if it was Starr or Paul Hornung carrying the ball in practice, they were going to get hit if they ran by Nitschke. All-pro tackle Forrest Gregg added, "When you scrimmage Nitschke, you have to be ready or you'll get one of those big forearms in your teeth."

By 1962, Nitschke was an established star, and his intelligent play and cool professionalism epitomized the Green Bay defense run as it was coached by Phil Bengston. Bengston told his tackles to pinch, or slant, inside to keep blockers occupied and off his middle linebacker. Nitschke credits much of his success to Bengston, who has long been underrated as a defensive tactician, largely because the quiet, chain-smoking Swede was overshadowed by Lombardi's personality.

"It was Bengston who ran the defense," Nitschke said. "He was the same kind of student of the game as (Lombardi)."

Bengston's tactics and teachings inspired players like Nitschke, Davis, Henry Jordan, Herb Adderley, and Willie Wood to Hall of Fame careers, and molded the Green Bay defense into arguably the greatest unit ever.

"I'd put the Packer defense ahead of anyone," the Cowboys' Neely said upon reflection. An offensive tackle with Dallas from 1964–77, Neely played against the great defenses of the sixties and seventies, including Minnesota's "Purple People Eaters," Miami's "No-Name" unit, and Pittsburgh's "Steel Curtain" squad.

"Pittsburgh had a great defense in the seventies, and Miami did too," said Neely. "But Green Bay had nine all-pros on their defense. For complete defense, from linemen to linebackers to defensive backs, the Packers of the sixties were the best. It'll be a long time before we see a defense like that again."

With Starr sidelined and the offense sputtering, the Packer defense took center stage for the first half of the '67 season. In Week Two, they held the Bears to ten points and a total of six first downs in a 13–10 win. One week later, they limited Atlanta to 58 yards on 50 plays in a 23–0 shutout. In a return match against the Lions in the season's fourth week, Nitschke ignored an injured left thigh to make a game-breaking interception off a deflected pass and then limp in for a score in a 27–17 win.

Through the first four games, the defense had been the determining factor in Green Bay going 3-0-1. But when Minnesota handed them their first loss with a 10–7 upset in Week Five, doubts arose as to whether the Packer offense could overcome its injuries and forge a championship season.

Circling the wagons, Lombardi called his team together. He made an emotional appeal to his veterans for a renewal of Packer pride. "Gentlemen," he said, "this week we begin 'The Big Push.'"

Wounded and bloodied, the Packers picked up "The Big Push" as their rallying cry as they prepared for the second half of the season.

Chapter Seven

An "Appointment with Destiny"

A THIN LAYER OF INDUSTRIAL SMOG hung like gauze over northern New Jersey as the chartered 727 jet carrying the Green Bay Packers taxied to a stop at Newark Airport. Air traffic during the early afternoon hours of Saturday, October 21, 1967 was heavy, and the mix of jet stream and industrial fumes created a low ceiling of smog that all but eclipsed the skyline view of Manhattan, which sat just a half-hour's ride to the north.

The Packers arrived in New York for a Week Six date with the Giants. Despite being two-time defending champions of the National Football League and current leaders of the Central Division with a 3-1-1 record, they found themselves under attack by the New York media. Suffering from a number of crucial injuries and critical mistakes, the offense began the season in an inconsistent fashion, and articles previewing the Packers–Giants game at Yankee Stadium the following Sunday afternoon asked, "What's wrong with Green Bay?"

Green Bay right guard Jerry Kramer read a number of stories that week in which the Packers were written off as a team of "old men" who were "over the hill." One reporter noted the number of balding heads and receding hairlines on the league champions and thought they resembled a reunion of the class of 1940.

It seemed symbolic then, that as the Packers disembarked from their 727 they were informed that one of the chartered buses that was to take them to the Waldorf-Astoria Hotel in New York had broken down.

To many NFL observers, Green Bay's chances of repeating as NFL champions were as dead as the engine of their bus.

Fielding questions from reporters who wanted to know what was wrong with the Packers, Kramer felt as if he were surrounded by vultures who were circling overhead and hoping the carcass wouldn't suddenly climb to its feet. Yet despite his resentment of the media, Kramer too had doubts as to how good the Packers really were. At the beginning of the season, he felt this Green Bay team might be Lombardi's best, but five weeks into the season there was a sense of doubt lingering in the world champions' locker room.

Though nothing was said out loud, other Packer players shared Kramer's doubts. Even Vince Lombardi, who had carried himself with confidence, worried. To his players, Lombardi appeared confused and frustrated, almost powerless in his attempt to gauge the abilities of his team. His trademark tongue-lashings and tirades had been replaced by a restless attitude. Finally, on Tuesday, October 17, two days after the upset loss to the Vikings, Lombardi called a meeting of the 14 veteran players who had been with the team since their championship run began back in 1961. "Frankly," he said, "I'm worried. I just don't know what the hell to do."

He told his veterans it would be up to them to provide clubhouse leadership and bring the young players along. Asking for help in motivating the team was a radically new and different approach for the Green Bay boss, who in past seasons had always known when to pick his players up psychologically and when to drive them down.

The Packers' problems during the first half of the season were threefold. The team had grown so accustomed to winning they had a difficult time motivating themselves against lesser teams; they had suffered a number of debilitating injuries; and they were the target of every club in the NFL.

Lombardi warned his players that the '67 season would be their most challenging season ever, simply because every team on their schedule was going to be primed for the Packers. "Everybody we're going to play this year," Lombardi said, "has read all this stuff in the papers about who's going to beat the Green Bay Packers, who can do it, who can beat them, can anybody beat them. So everybody says, 'By gosh, we can, we can do it.' This is the price of winning. This is the price of the last two championships. You're paying for it now because everybody in the league wants to beat you. They're giving it their maximum supreme effort. There's no loafing, no halfway, against the Green Bay Packers."

The price proved to be a steep one, as evidenced by the injuries sustained by several key Packers. Kramer was nursing a sore right ankle suffered in the previous week's loss to Minnesota, and middle linebacker Ray Nitschke had a torn muscle and internal hemorrhaging in his left leg. The injury left the back of Nitschke's leg, from the middle of the thigh down to the middle of the calf, a bright purple mass bordered by patches of skin that were olive, yellow, and blue in color. Tight end Marvin Fleming had a severed Achilles tendon, and defensive tackle Henry Jordan a chronic sore back. Running backs Jim Grabowski and Elijah Pitts were also sidelined by injuries, forcing Lombardi to go to second-stringers Donny Anderson and Ben Wilson. Before the season was out, the Packers went to their third string, utilizing rookie halfback Travis Williams and fullback Chuck Mercein, who had been released by the New York Giants and was chosen off the waiver wire.

Heading the list of the Packers' walking wounded was quarterback Bart Starr. A blow to the right armpit by blitzing middle linebacker Tommy Nobis of Atlanta in the season's third week numbed Starr's passing arm and forced him to the sideline, where he spent the following two weeks watching backup Zeke Bratkowski.

Starr's shoulder pain was so intense he was taking two Emperin-codeine compound pills per day just to get through practice. With his passing motion hampered by a sore shoulder and rib injury,

Starr wasn't able to throw with the accuracy and velocity that had made him the league's leading passer and Most Valuable Player in 1966, when he led the NFL with a 62.2 pass completion percentage and a league-low three interceptions. A sprained right thumb prevented him from gripping the ball properly, and a pulled thigh muscle prevented him from setting up correctly in the pocket. Yet his courage in playing with pain was such that it brought tears from Lombardi during an emotional team meeting.

"I don't know if you guys know it or not," the coach said, "but this guy's been hurt and he's been in pain, and he's been playing hurt, and . . ."

Unable to finish his sentence because his voice was breaking up, Lombardi sat down and motioned to an assistant to start the film session. It wasn't until two days before the Giants game that Lombardi entertained the thought of playing Starr. He approached his linemen during practice and said, "Look, I'm thinking about starting Bart. Do you think you can protect him? We can't let anybody get close to him."

By 1967, the 33-year-old Starr had become one of the top two or three quarterbacks in the NFL, ranking with Baltimore's John Unitas and Washington's Sonny Jurgensen. An unheralded 17th-round draft choice out of the University of Alabama, where he had spent the end of his career on the bench due to a bad back, Starr joined the Packers in 1956 as a long-shot rookie. He played sporadically his first three years, serving as backup to Babe Parilli and later Lamar McHan. Shortly after Lombardi arrived as head coach in 1959, he watched Starr throw a poor pass that was intercepted during a scrimmage.

"Starr!" the coach yelled. "You could see that the ball was going to be intercepted when you threw it. One more like that and you're gone!"

The son of a regular army master sergeant, Starr grew up on air force bases and army posts, and he calls everyone "Sir." To this day, he remains quiet and unfailingly polite. He spent most of his first couple of years in Green Bay staring at his shoes. He rarely looked anyone in the eye, and his voice portrayed more quiver than confidence. When Lombardi became head coach of the Packers in 1959, he thought Starr was too nice and too self-effacing to ever develop into the kind of commanding field leader that Charlie Conerly had been for Lombardi in New York.

"The opinion around (Green Bay) and in the league was that Starr would never make it." Lombardi said in his book, *Run To Daylight.* "They said he couldn't throw well enough and wasn't tough enough, that he had no confidence in himself and that no one had confidence in him."

Slightly built at 6-1, 190 pounds, he didn't have great arm strength and his background as a college quarterback at Alabama didn't inspire the confidence of his Packer teammates. His leadership qualities were still dormant; most of the time, his teammates didn't even know he was around.

Starr was labeled "Mr. Milquetoast" by some, and he seemed to epitomize baseball wise guy Leo Durocher's adage that "Nice guys finish last." He didn't smoke, rarely drank or swore, and asked his teammates to pick up after themselves in the locker room to make the trainer's job easier. Yet while some writers tried to make Starr seem unnaturally nice, he refuted their claims.

"I'm not that 'nice guy' stuff," he said at the time, "nice on the football field or at home. Ask the players. Ask my wife."

Starr loved to tell teammates the story of how he barged home one afternoon, spanked one of his children for tracking mud across the carpet and then yelled at his wife, Cherry, for not mailing some letters that day.

"I've got a jillion things to do," he shouted. "A jillion things. And I've got to go to a banquet over in Appleton tonight."

"What kind of banquet?" asked Cherry.

Starr hesitated. "I'm receiving a nice-guy award."

"You're putting me on."

It wasn't until a game in 1961 against the Chicago Bears that

Starr shook his nice-guy image. Chicago middle linebacker Bill George, who had earned a reputation as a ferocious blitzer, broke through the line and delivered a vicious forearm that bloodied Starr's nose and mouth. Standing over the fallen quarterback, George growled, "That'll take care of you, Starr, you sissy."

Starr jumped up, and through cracked lips, said, "Screw you, Bill George, we're coming after you."

That game proved to be one of the defining points of Starr's career, since his steely response inspired his teammates. They looked at him and saw what Kramer called "a gentle manliness . . . an iron in him." With careful nurturing from Lombardi, Starr grew in confidence and eventually became the leader of Green Bay's offense. Though he was criticized by some as being a push-button quarterback who followed Lombardi's orders like an automaton—writer Elinor Kaine likened him to a robot, "competent but uninspired"—Starr reveled in his role of being an extension of his coach on the field. It meant, he said, that he had absorbed Lombardi's teachings and applied them successfully.

Some NFL observers downgraded Starr's impact on the Packers' early championship years because of the overwhelming success of the running game. In reality, Starr was a heady quarterback who took full advantage of all the parts of the Packers' precision machine. He didn't pass often because Lombardi didn't need him to, because Green Bay's attack was geared to the ground game. He is the only Hall of Fame quarterback not to have thrown 300 passes in a season at least once, but when the running game slowed, Starr stepped to the fore and passed the Packers to an NFL title in 1966 and victory in Super Bowl I, where he was named Most Valuable Player.

"In recent years, the burden has fallen more and more on Bart," Kramer said at the time. "Before it was Jimmy Taylor and Paul Hornung. Now Jimmy and Paul are gone and the burden is on Bart. He carries the whole thing."

Starr was the quarterback as master technician, refining his play through meticulous, year-round study of game films. He gradually emerged as the quintessential example of the quarterback as coach on the field. Starr's intelligent play-calling, deft ball-handling techniques, and textbook mechanics made him a complete quarterback, and he pried defenses apart with precision short- and medium-range passes from sideline to sideline and over the middle. Over the course of the 1964-65 seasons, he threw 294 consecutive passes without an interception, a mark that stood as an NFL record for the next two decades. He was unparalleled when it came to completing clutch third-down passes, and his performance in pressure situations made him the best big game quarterback of the sixties.

"The true test of a quarterback," Starr said, "is how you perform when you *have* to win."

His performance in clutch situations speaks volumes about the soft-spoken Starr. In six NFL championship games, he threw eleven touchdowns and just one interception, and his post-season rating is the highest in NFL history.

While he never developed the daring, throw-deep style of Unitas, to whom he was often compared, Starr shrugged off his critics in much the same style he shrugged off onrushing defenders.

"The Packer system is conservative," he said. "We play ball-control football. We use a lot of running plays and short passes. We try to make as few mistakes as possible. It would be great to throw the long pass and hear the crowd roar, but what good is a big roar from the crowd if it's for an interception?"

Starr learned to speed-read defenses, and of the 65 or 70 plays the Packer offense ran in a given game, Lombardi only sent in approximately ten or so. Starr became adept at the art of calling audibles, changing plays at the line of scrimmage after diagnosing the defensive alignment. He engaged in a cat-and-mouse game of mental gymnastics with defensive signal-callers, and kept them off-guard by calling audibles almost half of the time.

Because Lombardi demanded his players be tough-minded and play through pain, Starr often hid his injuries from the coaching staff. He played with a cool disregard for danger, staring down a furious rush and holding the ball until the final second as he scanned the field for an open receiver. His unwillingness to risk a turnover allowed him to post a startlingly low career interception rate, but it also exposed him to damaging hits.

In 1961, he played with a torn stomach muscle so painful he could hardly stand straight enough to pass. When one of his teammates advised him to tell Lombardi of his injury, Starr replied grimly, "Coach has enough problems without worrying about me. I can play with it."

In 1965, the Baltimore Colts knocked Starr out of the Western Conference playoff game with bruised ribs and a sore back. One week later, with his ribs corseted and taped, Starr walked on to a snow-swept field in Green Bay and threw an early touchdown pass to set the tone for a 23–12 win over Cleveland in the NFL title game.

From 1960-67, Starr's record as a starter was an outstanding 82-24-4, and he quieted his critics by carrying the bulk of the offense as the Packers graduated from a running team to a passing team. He led the NFL four times in percentage of passes completed, and was the league's passing champion three times. Said one NFL coach, "I wish there was a way to ban Bart Starr from the game he plays against us. For his team, he is the perfect quarterback."

Starr's appearance in the starting lineup against the Giants midway through the '67 season marked the beginning of Green Bay's turnaround. Though he started slowly in the first half, he brought the Packers back from a 14–10 deficit at the break by coolly dissecting the Giants' defense and sending his backs into the vulnerable areas. By game's end, the Packers had rushed for 249 yards, their highest total since 1962, and destroyed the Giants, 48–21.

Green Bay won three of its next four games, as Starr led an attack that scored 31 points against St. Louis, 55 against Cleveland and averaged more than 27 points per game. By late November, all the parts of the Packer machine were meshing smoothly. With their offense and defense in championship form and their special teams sparked by Williams, a kick-return specialist who was nicknamed

"The Roadrunner" for his game-breaking speed, the Packers clinched the Central Division title in Week Eleven with a 17–13 win in Chicago. One week later, Green Bay ran its record to 9-2-1 with a 30–27 victory over the Vikings, then closed its season with a pair of narrow losses to the Rams and Steelers.

Just as the Packers struggled to find their offensive consistency throughout much of the 1967 campaign, the Dallas Cowboys searched for the solution to their defensive problems. Landry's unit had earned fame the previous season as the best young defense in the NFL. The Cowboys' front four was the stingiest in the league, allowing the fewest yards on the ground and a total of just six rushing touchdowns in 14 games, and their pass rush produced an NFL high of 60 sacks.

Dallas was not as impressive, however, in 1967. While they again led the league against the run, they allowed almost twice as many touchdowns (11) on the ground, and their sack total fell to 45. Dallas' defensive problems were symptomatic of their overall struggles in 1967. Even though they were in the NFL's weakest division, the Cowboys barely survived close encounters with Capitol rivals Philadelphia, Washington, and New Orleans.

At the season's mid-point, Dallas was just 5-2 following a 21–14 loss to the Eagles. But with its back to the wall, Doomsday returned to form, holding its next two opponents to a total of 17 points in a pair of Cowboy victories.

Fronting the Dallas foursome was right tackle Bob Lilly, a 6 ft. 5 in., 260-pound blend of strength, quickness, and intellect that was unrivaled in his era. With his red hair and freckles, Lilly may have looked like a grown up Huck Finn, but his playing style was pure Paul Bunyan. In 1964, Lilly broke the first block applied to him every time. In a 1967 game against the New Orleans Saints, he was double-teamed 27 times, and he broke through the wall of blockers 24 times. In 14 years with the Cowboys, Lilly missed just one game.

"He was a massive man and seemed indestructible," George Allen, the late coach of the Rams and Redskins, once said. "He made plays all over the field."

Despite the number of great players in Dallas franchise history, Lilly is known as "Mr. Cowboy." A two-time member of the All-Southwest Conference team during his career at Texas Christian University, Lilly was the Cowboys' first draft choice in 1961. A year later, he was the first Dallas player ever to be named to the Pro Bowl. In 1964, Lilly was the team's first all-pro player, and in '66, he was the focal point of a team that delivered the first divisional championship in team history. He was also the anchor of a defense that led the Cowboys to their first world championship in 1971, and the club's first Hall of Famer in 1980. Small wonder then, that Lilly also established himself as first in the hearts of Cowboy fans.

Landry said that a player like Lilly comes along once in a coach's lifetime. "There is not one man that can contain Bob Lilly," Landry said. A panel of NFL coaches, players, historians, and sportswriters named Lilly the greatest defensive tackle in history, ranking him ahead of other Hall of Famers like Merlin Olsen, Joe Greene, and Alan Page. Minnesota guard Ed White, who played opposite Olsen and Greene and was a teammate of Page, said Lilly was "number one, without question." Allen once called Lilly a combination of Deacon Jones and Gino Marchetti.

"Lilly was almost as good a pass rusher as either," Allen said, "but a better run defender than both." He called Lilly the smartest, coolest defensive lineman he coached against in a career that spanned two decades. "We tried everything against him," Allen said, "but we couldn't confuse him or contain him."

Lilly's position coach, Ernie Stautner, was a Hall of Fame tackle in his own right, but even he admitted he wasn't in Lilly's class. "He could do things I couldn't do," Stautner admitted. "He was the best defensive tackle I ever saw."

Deployed in the four-point lineman's stance common to Landry's flex defenses, Lilly defeated blocking schemes even though he was double-teamed and sometimes triple-teamed. Stautner recalled grading films and watching in awe as Lilly avoided the offensive lineman's blocks by grabbing the guard by the shoulder pads and throwing him out of the way. "He throws guys into the dirt like they weren't even there," Stautner said.

Lilly's immense strength earned him a reputation at TCU, where, finding a Volkswagen in his parking place in front of the university library, he lifted the front end of the car onto the sidewalk, then walked around and lifted the back end over the curb as well.

Wearing the plum-colored uniform of TCU, he was called the "Purple Cloud" because he seemed to be everywhere on the field. As he matured in Dallas, however, Lilly was no longer a mere cloud. Wearing number 74 and dressed in Cowboy blue-and-silver, he had grown into a swift-moving, southwestern storm front that scattered NFL offenses and scuttled their best-laid blocking schemes.

Lilly's forte was crowding the line of scrimmage and then blowing into the backfield by anticipating the snap count. Cowboy center Mike Connelly, frustrated at his inability to block Lilly during scrimmages, said once that Lilly "slithers *around* blockers."

Though he was a great instinctive player, Lilly didn't rely on his natural abilities alone. He kept notes on every offensive lineman he faced, and referred to them to see when an opponent was disguising his intentions. Lilly studied opposing blockers before each play, looking at their knuckles to see what the play was going to do. If the guard's knuckles were white from the pressure of him leaning on them, Lilly knew the guard was getting ready to drive into him, which meant a running play. If the guard was light on his knuckles, Lilly knew he was leaning his weight back to get into position to pass-block.

Lilly's first move on every play was to grab the offensive blocker by the shoulder pads, and get a feel for his first move. Whichever direction the opponent began to move—inside or outside—Lilly shoved him in that direction.

An outstanding photographer, Lilly found himself on the other end of the lens more often than not. He once did a hair tonic commercial in which he argued against "greasy kid stuff." Looking into the camera, Lilly issued a mock growl and said, "I just had my damn hair done. Wanna make something of it?"

In reality mild-mannered and even-tempered, Lilly had the perfect personality to play Landry's patient read-and-react defense. Though he was held on virtually every play, Lilly kept his cool most of the time. One opposing guard who had spent the afternoon holding and tripping Lilly, shook his head afterward and said, "He never says a word, just plays his game."

Lilly seemed to keep football in perspective, and in late 1967 a tragic event undoubtedly put more of his focus on his personal life. He and his family lost a child near the end of the '67 season. Lilly and his wife Kitsy were the parents of three children—Bob Jr., Katherine, and Christienne, ages four to two—when they welcomed a fourth baby, Carmen Elizabeth, into their home in late fall. Tragedy entered their lives when Kitsy discovered that their new baby daughter, just seven weeks old, had passed away from a mysterious illness.

Few were eager to challenge Lilly, and he succeeded in helping lead Dallas to a division title. The "Doomsday" defense denied New Orleans an upset in the rain-drenched Cotton Bowl when middle linebacker Lee Roy Jordan recovered a Saints' fumble at the Dallas six to preserve a 14–10 win.

In a Thanksgiving Day game against St. Louis, "Doomsday" held Cardinals' back Johnny Roland, the NFL's second-leading rusher, to just 27 yards on 15 attempts, and put unrelenting pressure on quarterbacks Jim Hart and Charley Johnson in a 46–21 victory.

The offense regrouped as well. Backup quarterback Craig Morton provided a 24–21 win over Pittsburgh by rolling right late in the game and finding tight end Pettis Norman for a touchdown pass. Halfback Dan Reeves scored four TDs in a 37–7 win over Atlanta, and receiver Lance Rentzel hauled in 13 passes for 223 yards against Washington.

With the regular season behind them, the Cowboys could finally set their sights on the prize they had come so agonizingly close to obtaining the previous New Year's Day. After losing to Green Bay in the 1966 league title game, Dallas coaches and players dedicated themselves to keeping an "Appointment with Destiny," picking up on the title of their team's 1967 highlight film.

With the regular season behind them, Dallas was just one win away from a second summit meeting with Green Bay.

The NFL playoffs were about to begin.

Chapter Eight

The NFL Playoffs

A HALF-DOZEN SPORTSWRITERS SURROUNDED VINCE LOMBARDI as the Green Bay head coach held court in the tower suite of the Hotel Pfister in Milwaukee.

Friday, December 22, 1967, marked the eve of the Western Conference championship game between the Packers and the Los Angeles Rams in Milwaukee's County Stadium. In the fading twilight outside, Christmas shoppers puffed clouds of steam as they hustled through the 20-degree cold and into warm, brightly decorated stores.

In less than 20 hours, the Packers would be opening the National Football League playoffs against a Rams' team that had beaten them two Sundays earlier in Los Angeles on a blocked punt late in the game. The Rams had celebrated their victory with locker room remarks that they had broken the Packer "mystique," and the oddsmakers agreed, installing head coach George Allen's team as the favorite.

As Lombardi discussed the game with the assembled writers, Red Smith of *The New York Times* listened as he expounded on a theme that Smith felt was the core of the coach's existence—commitment to excellence and to victory.

"As St. Paul wrote in one of the Epistles, 'Know ye not that they which run in a race run all, but one receiveth the prize? So run, that ye may obtain.'"

Lombardi's listeners exchanged sidewise glances, but they waited until they were in the corridor outside to comment.

"How about that? St. Vincent de Paul!"

"The Gospel according to Lombardi."

Smith headed back to his room to check chapter and verse in the Gideon Bible. "The man had it right," he said later.

Though he coached with a religious zeal, Lombardi didn't make it a practice to quote scripture in the locker room. But he began the week groping for a way to fire up his team, and he knew that to beat the Rams, the Packers had to run the ball effectively against a defensive line known as the "Fearsome Foursome."

In a team meeting the Tuesday before the game, Lombardi said that while many people who enter a race just think about finishing, the Packers thought only about winning. Paraphrasing St. Paul, he told his players to "run to win. Everything you do this week, run to win."

He repeated the phrase at practice, reminding his players so often that middle linebacker Ray Nitschke said the words were burned into his brain. "I kept saying to myself, 'I'm running to win, I'm running to win,'" Nitschke said.

Out in L.A., Allen was also scheming to win. A defensive mastermind, he had stopped Lombardi's drive to a title in 1963, when as defensive coordinator of the Chicago Bears, his unit held Lombardi's offense to a total of 10 points in two games.

Allen would try to thwart Lombardi again with a Ram defense that featured all-pros in Merlin Olsen, Deacon Jones, linebacker Maxie Baughan, and free safety Eddie Meador. They constituted the focal point of a team that captured the Coastal Division with an 11-1-2 record. Quarterback Roman Gabriel, halfback Dick Bass, and ends Jack Snow and Bernie Casey led the most prolific offense in the NFL, but it was the battering Rams' defense, with its glamorous nickname, that garnered the publicity and brought the Hollywood crowd to the Los Angeles Coliseum.

As a unit, the Rams offered the strongest defensive challenge Lombardi ever faced as Packers' head coach. Baughan was its signal-caller and leader, and Meador was a resourceful gambler in the secondary whom Allen felt "made plays you didn't think he could make."

As good as Baughan and Meador were, they were overshadowed by the tremendous play of the twin pillars on the left side of their line, Olsen and Jones. Drafted in the first round out of Utah State University in 1962, Olsen joined Jones, end Lamar Lundy, and former Giant Rosey Grier on a front that became the best in the game.

At 6-5, 270 pounds, Olsen was a prototype for modern defensive tackles. A member of Phi Beta Kappa in college, he combined brains with brawn. A gentle giant, Olsen refused to believe a player had to "hate" his opponent. "If you are motivated by pride and the desire to win," he said, "you will want to dominate your opponent, but that is a lot better thing than hatred on which to tie your success."

His temperament allowed him to make the transition from playing with the "Fearsome Foursome" to playing the title role of *Father Murphy* on the NBC television series. He also was an NFL analyst for NBC, appeared as a regular on the TV show *Little House on the Prairie,* and was a commercial spokesman for FTD florists.

But his nice-guy image belied the intensity he brought to pro football. Olsen studied the game, applied a thinking man's approach to his position, and went to the Pro Bowl 14 times in his 15-year career. Marion Campbell, a former player and coach in the NFL, called him "one of the smartest players I've ever been around," and Torgy Torgeson, a player and coach in the NFL since the fifties, said Olsen had "some of the best techniques of any lineman ever."

Olsen's techniques meshed perfectly with Jones, who entered the league as an obscure 14th-round pick. A product of South Carolina State College, Jones arrived on the West Coast in 1961 and quickly found out there were 10 pages of Joneses in the L.A.

phone book and some 30 David Joneses. He devised a publicity scheme to set him apart from the pack because, as he said, "no one would ever a remember a player with the name of David Jones."

He took the nickname "Deacon," which he had earned in college after leading the team in prayers. When an opposing player asked what Jones prays for, one of the Deacon's teammates answered, "That he doesn't kill anybody." It wasn't long before NFL quarterbacks were praying for the same thing.

"When Jones is chasing me, I have a one-word audible," said Fran Tarkenton, a Hall of Fame quarterback with the Minnesota Vikings and New York Giants. "The word is 'Help!'"

Jones became a starter at end when Gene Brito was hospitalized with a muscle disease known as myasthenia gravis in 1962. Jones proved himself a pioneer, popularizing the head slap, where a defensive lineman strikes the blocker with a blow to the helmet, and the term "sack," used to describe trapping the quarterback.

In an era when pro football was becoming a practicing religion, this Deacon from the Deep South spent autumn Sundays delivering fire and brimstone sermons to opposing ball carriers. "If I'm blocked," he said once, "I'll claw my way in. If I'm knocked down, I'll crawl. If I get through to that man with the ball, I'll hit him high and try to make him fumble."

Dressed in Ram navy-blue and white, with his long arms covered by pads and tape, the sight of number 75 lined up at left end became one of the staples of the sixties. Allen said at the time that quarterbacks started off each play with one eye on Jones. "He was a pass defense all by himself," Allen remarked at the time.

Jones mixed a flamboyant personality with a fiery playing style. Game films show him exploding off the line, head-slapping the tackle with his left hand, and pulling the quarterback down with a swipe of his right arm. He ranged the field making tackles, and once ran stride for stride with speedy Redskins' receiver Bobby Mitchell for ten yards before hauling him to the turf. When a coach asked him why he waited to make the tackle, Deacon answered, "I wanted to find out if I was as fast as Mitchell. And I was."

Banners in the L.A. Coliseum proclaimed him the "Secretary of Defense" and in his 14 years in the NFL, he was named all-pro six times and played in eight Pro Bowls. He was the NFL's Defensive Player of the Year in 1967 and '68.

Jones and Olsen played side-by-side for ten seasons, and together they perfected moves that made the "Fearsome Foursome" one of the great defensive lines in history. Their most common maneuver was a stunt, or loop, in which Jones stepped to his right just before the snap of the ball, and Olsen slid to his left to loop behind Jones. The move allowed the two linemen to exchange rush lanes, with Jones barging inside and Olsen roaming outside.

"Deac and I had it all together," Olsen said. "He knew what to expect from me and I knew just what he'd do."

"We have our own signals," Jones explained at the time. "Maybe one is going to rush inside, so the other rushes outside. Maybe two are going to fire in, so the other two lay back. We let each other know what we're going to do."

The "Foursome" underwent changes in personnel in 1967, Roger Brown replacing the retiring Grier at left tackle. Physically, the Ram front was huge. Lundy was 6-7, 260; Brown 6-5, 300 pounds, and together with Jones and Olsen, the Foursome averaged 6-6, 275 pounds per man.

The Ram defense peaked late in the season, holding four of five opponents to seven points or less. Needing a win over rival Baltimore in the season finale to clinch the division, the Rams shut down Colt quarterback John Unitas in a 34–10 win.

L.A.'s game plan for Green Bay focused on Bart Starr. Allen felt the Packers' quarterback was "technically perfect . . . the master of all the short passes from sideline to sideline and across the middle." The L.A. coach thought Starr executed plays with precision and the touch of a fine surgeon. "He cut defenses apart," Allen said. The Rams planned to mix their defenses and show Starr different coverages. "Make him guess or gamble a little bit," Allen noted.

Responsibility for running the Rams' complex defense fell to Baughan, one of the top field strategists in the league. It was common to see Baughan carrying a thick orange notebook which held hundreds of play diagrams and scouting reports. He studied film of opposing offenses, searching for clues as to which of the Rams' 150 defensive plays would work best. "He had a lot of leadership in him," Allen said at the time, "and he fired up his side."

Baughan's style was almost as fiery as his red hair. The big linebacker became embroiled in a "signal-jamming" controversy during a regular season game against San Francisco. Just before 49ers' quarterback John Brodie would yell "Go!" at the line of scrimmage, Baughan would shout "Show!" To 49ers' linemen, the words sounded similar, particularly when mingled with the sounds of the crowd, and caused San Francisco players to jump offsides in more than one third-down situation.

While Allen concentrated on Starr, Lombardi focused on the Rams' defense. "Their front four presented a serious problem," he said then, "because of their size and quickness and experience."

To counter the quick charge of the "Fearsome Foursome," he put in a series of quick-hitting running plays, and altered his blocking schemes to double-team Jones, who had enjoyed success against Green Bay all-pro tackle Forrest Gregg in previous games. On one occasion, Jones sacked Starr four times, and the Packers' quarterback said Deacon was in on him so quick, "I thought he was one of my own backs."

Gregg was a textbook blocker, a master of technique. Though he was big at 6-4, 250, he never tried to overpower his opponents. Relying on finesse, Gregg would slide with his defender, maneuver him, shield him away from the pocket. He played the tackle position like a technician, and his hard work, skill, and consistency led Lombardi to call him, "the finest player I have ever coached." High praise, considering Lombardi coached more than a dozen Hall of Fame players in his career.

During his 15-year career, Gregg earned all-pro honors at both tackle and guard, and he played in a then-record 188 straight games. Gregg studied his position, watching reels of film of all-pro tackles like Baltimore's Jim Parker and New York's Rosey Brown. Eagles' pass-rushing specialist Joe Robb called Gregg the greatest tackle he ever faced. "He'd be four yards deep," Robb said, "still blocking on me before I could set up."

Allen considered Green Bay's offensive line the finest ever, and called Gregg its anchor. "He had quick hands and feet and superior intelligence," Allen said. "He did his little dance and turned people around."

As great as Gregg was, even he acknowledged the problems Jones presented. "You just can't fire out at him," Gregg said. "You fire out hard and he's gone, slipped around you. You have to be controlled, keep your balance, and try to move with him."

As Gregg prepared for Jones, right guard Jerry Kramer got ready to face Olsen. Best known for pulling and leading the Green Bay sweeps, Kramer was also a tremendous drive-blocker. As the Packers rose to power in the sixties, Kramer and Fuzzy Thurston became the most publicized pair of guards in NFL history. Countless photos showed them escorting Jim Taylor and Paul Hornung to the outside on the sweep. An articulate and introspective man, Kramer brought offensive linemen out of obscurity, thanks in large part to his best-selling book, *Instant Replay*.

Having played side by side for more than a decade, Kramer and Gregg knew each other's moves almost instinctively. When defenses shifted at the line of scrimmage, Kramer would say, "Forrest," and Gregg would answer, "Yeah," and they would both carry out their assignments. "I'd know exactly what he was going to do," Kramer said, "and he'd know what I was going to do."

Asked about Olsen by a Milwaukee sportswriter, Kramer described the Rams' tackle as "very big, very strong, has great speed, great agility, is a very smart ballplayer, gives at least 110 percent on every play." And, deadpanned Kramer, those were Olsen's "weak points."

The matchups on the right side of the Packers' offensive line were critical. Gregg versus Jones, and Kramer versus Olsen, offered confrontations between four all-pro players. While the left side of the Rams' defense is the finest in history, the Kramer-Gregg pairing is possibly the greatest guard-tackle tandem ever on the right side of an offensive line.

Game day in Milwaukee was greeted by typical Packer weather. Saturday, December 23 offered a combination of snowy, steel-gray skies and temperatures in the high teens. The mood among Packer backers was as somber as the weather. The Rams entered the game riding an eight-game win streak; the Packers had lost their last two games of the season, including a heartbreaker in L.A.

"The faithful hereabouts weren't so faithful," noted then *Green Bay Press-Gazette* sports editor Art Daley. "They felt the Packers would lose to the Rams."

Lombardi, too, sensed the prevailing attitude of impending defeat among Green Bay's usually boisterous fans. "For some reason," he told Daley, "they got off the Green Bay bandwagon."

In the locker room before the game, Lombardi pulled on a beige overcoat, covered his graying hair with a tan fedora, and delivered a speech that made his players see red.

"This," he said, "is the game I wish I could play myself. If I could, I'd be sure how it could be played. There are 50,000 people out there, waiting for you to come out of this dressing room. They're all your family and friends... They came here to see you, and any time you let a team sit in California and say how they've broken your magic and what they're going to do to you, they're challenging you, and if they get away with it, it will be something you'll have to live with the rest of your lives.

"This," he said, "is the most important game of your life."

The speech galvanized Green Bay's veterans. Ray Nitschke sat in front of his locker growling, and split end Boyd Dowler ran to the bathroom and threw up. Lombardi had so aroused his team that Willie Davis felt they were "running heavy" as they left the locker room and took to the thick, winter-brown turf inside County Stadium. "You could hear (our) feet pounding," said Davis, who admitted to being so fired up it took him two series to settle down.

Defense dominated the early going, and it wasn't until the five-minute mark that the Packers put together the game's first sustained drive. Moving from his own 13 to the 43, Starr hit Carroll Dale for a nine-yard gain, but Dale fumbled, and Chuck Lamson recovered for the Rams at the L.A. 48.

Gabriel took quick advantage of the turnover. He handed off to fullback Les Josephson for a five-yard gain, and a facemasking penalty added 15 yards. Bass ran for three yards, and Gabriel, stretching his 6-4 frame to its fullest, tossed a 29-yard pass to Casey down the left sideline for a 7–0 lead.

The Rams' defense forced three Packer turnovers early on, and Lombardi, his face reddened by the cold, raged on the sidelines. "What the hell's wrong with you anyway?" he shouted at tight end Marv Fleming, whose failure to turn around on a short pass resulted in an interception. Deacon Jones, who called Lombardi "The Little Tyrant," heard the Green Bay boss bellowing, and couldn't help but smile. Things were going L.A.'s way.

Gabriel mounted another drive into Green Bay territory, and with the ball resting on the Packers' 24-yard line, kicker Bruce Gossett attempted a field goal that would give the Rams a 10-point lead. Even Lombardi recognized that a score here would put the Packers in a deep hole. But Green Bay linebacker Dave Robinson blocked Gossett's kick, forcing a shift in the game's momentum.

In the second quarter, Tom Brown returned a punt 39 yards to the Rams' 47, and two plays later, halfback Travis Williams sped past Olsen and Jones on a long trap play and raced 46 yards for the tying touchdown. Known as "67" in the Packers' terminology, the play was designed for left guard Gale Gillingham to pull and help Gregg double-team Jones to the outside. Kramer drove Olsen inside, and Williams shot through the opening. It was textbook blocking, and as Lombardi noted later, "We worked it just like the diagrams say."

Williams, who idolized Chicago Bears' star back Gale Sayers, was a sturdy back blessed with sprinter's speed. He was 215 pounds and ran the 100-yard dash in 9.3 seconds. He set an NFL record in his 1967 rookie season by returning four kickoffs for touchdowns, including one for 104 yards against the Rams in L.A. "The Roadrunner's" guiding principle was simple: "Go full speed," he said once, "and see what happens."

Willie Wood's 44-yard return of Gossett's short field goal attempt gave Green Bay another scoring opportunity. Kramer reminded his mates to "run to win," and Williams burst 15 yards up the middle. Starr followed with a 17-yard TD pass to Dale, and the Packers led 14–7 with 47 seconds left in the half.

While the pregame publicity focused on the "Fearsome Foursome," it was the Packer defense that was controlling the game. Right tackle Henry Jordan slipped past guard Tom Mack to sack Gabriel five times. An exceptional run-pass blocker, Mack made 11 Pro Bowl appearances in a 13-year career that lasted until 1978. Football historian Beau Riffenburgh once called him "the perfect guard," but Mack struggled to contain the veteran Jordan, whose variety of moves was the most extensive in the league. "There's no tackle in this league," Colts' Hall of Fame offensive tackle Jim Parker said once, "with Henry's moves."

Jordan's inspired play was symbolic of the entire Packer defense. Nitschke was enjoying himself so much he didn't want to leave the field. When the Rams moved close to a first down on one occasion, Nitschke yelled at the referee, "Give 'em the first down. We're not ready to stop."

Allen said later that when Nitschke got wound up, he could "take apart an offense all by himself." Watching from the press box,

Red Smith called Nitschke "a living flame." Nitschke played with Lombardi's "run to win" theme on his mind. When he chased down a back, he was running to win. When he blitzed Gabriel, he was running to win. Thirty years later, he said he still thinks of the phrase often.

The Packers' ground attack put the game away in the third quarter. Playing with a charge as spirited and unified as Patton's Third Army, Green Bay engineered an 80-yard march capped by Chuck Mercein's six-yard score off a veer play. Running to win, Mercein cut behind Gillingham's block, skipped through Meador's arms and dove into the end zone for a 21–7 lead.

A graduate of Yale, Mercein was drafted by the New York Giants in 1965. Though he led the team in rushing in 1966, a personality conflict with head coach Allie Sherman led to Mercein being released before the start of the '67 season. "There was a strange disharmony between myself and the coach because I came from Yale," Mercein recalled. "He always had a funny feeling about my going to Yale rather than to a bigger school."

The truth was, Mercein was recruited by some 50 schools, including most of the Big Ten programs, but chose Yale because of its academic reputation. Discouraged at being put on waivers, Mercein clung to a notion he believes in to this day. "It's funny how when looking back over things, if you hang in there, go through rough spots, keep trying and don't give up, good things happen."

He was close to signing with the Washington Redskins when Lombardi lost Jim Grabowski and Elijah Pitts to injuries in mid-season. Lombardi contacted his old boss, Giants' owner Wellington Mara, to ask about Mercein.

"I was all packed and ready to go to Washington when Lombardi contacted me on Sunday night," Mercein said. "He asked me, 'Have you signed with Washington yet?' I said, 'No,' and he said, 'Well, if you get on the next plane and come out here, you'll be part of the next world championship team. We're going to go to the Super Bowl and you're going to help us get there.'

"I was thrilled. I said, 'Coach, I'll be there.' I hung up the phone, turned to my family and said, 'Unpack the car.' I arrived in Green Bay the next day and Lombardi was terrific to me from the very start, as were the players, Bart Starr and Forrest Gregg. They said, 'We really need you,' and Lombardi said, 'Just do what you're capable of doing and you'll help us win.' I felt immediately at home."

Starr's play-calling and the slippery field kept the "Fearsome Foursome" off-balance. The Packers neutralized Jones with double-team blocking by Gregg and 250-pound tight end Marv Fleming. Engaging in a strategic mental war with Baughan, Starr varied his calls, sending his backs first to one side and then the other, pulling the guards for power sweeps and quick-hitters, and completing a variety of passes. "It was a typical Starr game," writer Milton Shapiro said. "Nothing spectacular, no bombs, just beautiful football."

Starr threw for 222 yards, and moved the ball to the Rams' two with a long completion to Dale. Still running to win, Williams' TD closed the scoring at 28–7.

"Everybody's been saying we were dead," Lombardi remarked after the game, "that we'd won in a patsy division, that we weren't the Packers we once were. We had something to prove."

While the Packers celebrated their win over the Rams, the Dallas Cowboys were preparing to host the Cleveland Browns in the Cotton Bowl the following afternoon in the Eastern Conference championship. The key for the Dallas defense, which led the NFL in rushing yards allowed, was to contain Cleveland halfback Leroy Kelly, the NFL's rushing leader with 1,205 yards.

A future Hall of Famer, Kelly was in his fourth year as a pro and second as a starter. Jim Brown's surprising retirement following the 1965 season gave Kelly the opportunity to join Ernie Green in the starting backfield. The Philadelphia native responded, leading the Browns to a 9-5 record and the Century Division crown.

At 6 feet, 205 pounds, Kelly didn't physically resemble the 6 ft.

1 in., 235-pound Brown, but their styles were similar. Like Brown, he rose slowly after being tackled. But again like Brown, Kelly would explode into the line on the next snap of the ball. He had the fastest first step in football, and slid around tacklers with a series of fakes and sidesteps, changing direction more sharply and at a higher speed than any NFL back. His flat-footed style of running allowed him to thrive in the off-track conditions that prevailed in Cleveland's Municipal Stadium late in the season.

Kelly was the perfect back for head coach Blanton Collier's offense. A former assistant to Paul Brown, whom he replaced as Cleveland head coach in 1953, Collier was a cerebral coach. The former school teacher was distinguished-looking in his fedora and black-frame glasses. He avoided the pep talks and sideline prancing that other coaches practiced, relying instead on a mature approach reflected by the Browns' style of play.

Collier's refined offense required players to think on the move, as evidenced by their top play, the strong-side sweep. Kelly keyed an offense that included quarterback Frank Ryan, receivers Gary Collins and Paul Warfield, and a line headed by perennial all-pros Dick Schafrath at tackle and Gene Hickerson at guard. As good as Cleveland's offense was, its defense was suspect, and there were questions as to how the Browns could cope with the Cowboys' offense.

Sunday, December 24 found downtown Dallas drenched in warm, cloudless sunshine, and a Christmas Eve crowd of 70,786 crammed into the Cotton Bowl for the Eastern Conference championship. Cowboy fans, many of them wearing white Stetson hats and waving blue-and-silver banners, stood at the sight of starting halfback Dan Reeves leaving the field in the first quarter with an injury. But rookie Craig Baynham entered the game and opened the scoring when he beat linebacker Dale Lindsey in the right corner of the end zone and snared a three-yard touchdown pass from quarterback Don Meredith.

Dazzling in their white-and-silver uniforms, Dallas made it 14–0 later in the quarter when fullback Don Perkins crashed into the end zone from four yards out. Dallas upped the score to 21–0 in the second quarter when split end Bob Hayes sped past the Browns' secondary for an 86-yard scoring pass from Meredith.

Wearing the dark brown jerseys and burnt-orange helmets that made up one of the classic uniforms in the NFL, Cleveland finally got on the scoreboard late in the half when Ryan hit tight end Milt Morin on a 13-yard TD. Dallas decided the issue in the third quarter, as Baynham and Perkins scored on one-yard touchdown runs, and cornerback Cornell Green returned an interception 60 yards for a score. Meredith, who had been maligned in Dallas for years, departed to a standing ovation at the start of the final quarter. As he left, he shook the hand of each offensive lineman.

One play that typified Dallas' determination this day came when outside linebacker Chuck Howley saved a touchdown by running the quicker Kelly down from behind after a 46-yard run. The play brought the disbelieving Cotton Bowl crowd to its feet.

Baynham blasted to his third TD on a one-yard plunge in the final quarter. Dallas head coach Tom Landry called the Cowboys' 52–14 victory the most impressive in team history. "It was our best game," he said, "because so much was at stake and we did everything well."

Left behind in the locker room celebration was a long season of injuries and inconsistencies. Having claimed their first-ever postseason victory, the Cowboys were heading to Green Bay for the NFL championship game.

It was a rematch the Cowboys, and NFL fans, had waited a year for.

Chapter Nine

Game Day in Green Bay

D ALLAS KICKOFF RETURN MAN SIMS STOKES stood shivering on the goal line at the south end of Lambeau Field, awaiting placekicker Don Chandler's game-opening kickoff. Patches of snow covered the brownish-green field, and the chipped ice sparkled like frozen diamonds in the dazzling sunshine.

It also lent what Green Bay fullback Chuck Mercein remembers today as a rough, abrasive feel to the playing surface.

"It was like stucco," Mercein said. "It made Astroturf feel like a pillow."

Green Bay head coach Vince Lombardi had the "electric blanket" installed beneath Lambeau Field's bluegrass sod prior to the 1967 season, and General Electric issued a press release at the time stating that "September-like" playing conditions would prevail through the season. "Instead of a frozen field," the release read, "the Wisconsin contests will be played on a green, soft, frost-free turf."

But the plastic-coated cables buried six inches beneath the field's surface didn't do much good when the air temperature dropped below 20 degrees. So instead of the "soft, frost-free turf" that G.E. had promised, players were forced to deal with a field that Dallas defensive tackle Bob Lilly remembered being "like a scrub board in the center of it, where we had worked out, and total ice at the end of it."

Defensive end George Andrie had talked Lilly into taking the field for pregame drills, facetiously called "warm-ups" this day, without his waist-length, blue woolen team jacket.

"He said, 'Bob, we're going to have to be leaders out there today,'" recalled Lilly. "He said, 'You and I have to go out there for warm-ups without our warm-up jackets on.'

"I said, 'Oh,' and I'm thinking to myself, 'I've never been in weather like this.' But I let him talk me into it, and as soon we walked out of the locker room door I knew I was a fool. And good ol' George probably thought he was a fool too, because we literally had icicles hanging out of our noses.

"As soon as we got back in from warm-ups, I stripped down, put on two pairs of long-handles (thermal underwear), and wrapped Saran Wrap around my shoes.

"We didn't wear gloves, because our defensive line coach, Ernie Stautner, said we couldn't. But Green Bay came out wearing gloves and turtlenecks, and I'm thinking, 'Man, we must not know what they know.' And we sure as hell didn't, because we had frostbite all over.

"I played in a lot of games where it was zero degrees or a little above, and it never bothered me. We'd have heaters at the game and you'd come off the field and be kind of warm. And we had heaters that day too, but we never got warm. *Never.* We just froze to death. I think we thought more about the weather that day than about the game."

The Packers were suffering too. "It was like playing inside a meat locker," said Mercein, looking back. "I'll never forget the feel of the football. I've never felt leather that cold."

Sitting on its tee at the Green Bay 40-yard line was "The Duke," a Wilson football that received its nickname in the thirties after New York Giants' co-owner Wellington Mara, who was called "Duke" by boyhood friends. Wilson officially named their NFL ball "The Duke" in 1941, and inscribed the words on the side of the ball, where it remained as a trademark until being retired in 1969.

As Chandler strode towards the ball, one writer, taking note of the minus-34 degrees wind-chill factor, turned to Bob Woessner of the *Press-Gazette* and said, "Three to one it breaks when he kicks it." A full-throated roar rose from the sellout crowd of 50,861 as Chandler's kick cut through the frozen sunshine.

The 48th title game in NFL history was underway, ending the fans' year-long wait from the previous New Year's Day, when the Packers defeated the Cowboys, 34–27, in a classic championship.

Stokes settled under the ball at his five-yard line, slipped at the gold-painted seven-yard hash mark, and veered right, gaining 25 yards before Green Bay's Bob Hyland knocked him to the ice-glazed turf at the 33-yard line.

Outside the stadium, Titletown was teeming with excitement. Fans who didn't have tickets to the sold-out game gathered in restaurants like Kroll's Cafe or downtown taverns to watch the game on television with friends. Restaurant tabletops were covered with "Know Your Packer" placemats, and various eateries carried menus offering the "Linebacker Special," a steak-and-eggs breakfast, and an appetizer known as a "Quick Opener." Storefront windows carried not only holiday decorations but large cardboard cutouts of Packer helmets bordered by the words, "Titletown, U.S.A." Flatlow's Infants' and Children's Wear was selling one-piece terry cloth pajamas colored Packers green-and-gold and carrying the team logo on the front. For older children, Prange's department store offered an official Packer shop that carried a green-and-gold cardigan sweater outfit that included cufflinks and tie clasps with the team logo.

Everything from delivery trucks to doormats bore Packer colors, including the park benches and fire hydrants. Bilotti's Forum, an upper class restaurant located near Lambeau Field, backlit its green planters with soft yellow lights. The walls of Holzer's Drug Store, on the corner of Pine and Washington in downtown Green Bay, were covered with Packer memorabilia, including a fragment of the goal post that was torn down following the '61 title win.

Written on the post was the final score, "37–0."

Unlike the previous week, when a sense of foreboding surrounded the playoff game against the Rams, Packer fans seemed convinced that a win over the Cowboys was forthcoming. The reason for this confidence centered on Lombardi, who was considered virtually unbeatable in big games. Sportswriter Jerry Izenberg of the Newark (N.J.) *Star-Ledger* labeled him "Invincible Vince," and it was the opinion of most Packer fans that Lombardi was in top form during the injury-ridden '67 campaign.

"The 1967 season was Lombardi's best coaching job," remarked Art Daley, who was sports editor of the *Press-Gazette* at the time. "They were a dominant team in '66, but in '67, they had a fight on their hands."

Writing for the Sunday morning game-day edition of the *Press-Gazette*, Daley tapped out a story that focused on the mood of Green Bay's suddenly fickle fans:

"The big game . . . and the eyes of Texas . . . are upon us.

"And nobody in Packerville seems to be alarmed over the possibility that the Packers could actually lose."

Daley proved prophetic when he wrote later in the story that "certain intangibles" would prevail in the game, things beyond the strategy of the two teams. One of those intangibles, he wrote, would be the weather.

Born in St. Paul, Minnesota, Daley had been a Packers' beat reporter since 1941, so he was used to the harshness of midwestern winters. But waking up at 7:30 A.M. on December 31, 1967, Daley's first thought was, "God, it's cold. It must be 20 below."

Too cold, it turned out, for the Packers' cheerleaders, "The Golden Girls." Moments before kickoff, they had lined up on the field holding individual placards spelling "Happy New Year." To scattered applause, they quickly hurried off the field and into the warmth of their dressing room, where they stayed for the rest of the afternoon.

As the Dallas offense and Green Bay defense took the field for the first time, referee Norm Schachter noticed that umpire Joe Connell had a problem. As umpire, it was Connell's job to blow his whistle to start the game, but when he tried, all he got was a soft *tweet* rather than the normal high-pitched shrill. The wooden ball in his whistle was frozen, but making matters worse for Connell was that when he took the metal whistle out of his mouth, some of his lower lip came with it. He had forgotten to use a rubber mouthpiece, and blood flowed down his chin. Standing on the Dallas sideline, defensive tackle Bob Lilly saw Connell's lip, and noticed that the blood had frozen on the umpire's chin.

Schachter looked at Connell's lip, which was soon treated with petroleum jelly, and told his officiating crew not to use their whistles any more that day—another first. Not only was this the coldest game in pro football history, it was also the only game ever to be played without benefit of an official's whistle. Schachter and his crew spent the rest of the afternoon calling out to the players, "Stay away!" and "Keep off him!"

Led by quarterback Don Meredith, the Cowboy offense immediately revealed its game plan. A year earlier, Dallas head coach Tom Landry had confused Green Bay with his multiple offense and its myriad of formations. Attacking the Packer flanks with off-tackle plays, reverses, and quick sideline passes, the Cowboys piled up 23 first downs and 27 points, two points less than Phil Bengston's unit had allowed in their four previous title games combined.

The Cowboys were confident they could move the ball on the Packers again. There was a feeling in the Dallas organization that the maturing Cowboys were a better team than the aging, and in some cases, aching, Packers. One writer described Dallas as "a younger, faster version of the Packers," and Cowboys' defensive coordinator Dick Nolan said there wasn't any doubt the Cowboys had the superior team. "Tom knew it," Nolan said. "I think everybody did."

"Green Bay was really beat-up when we played them," Lilly recalled, "and we were relatively healthy going into that game. We really felt that due to their injuries and all, that we had the better team."

Dallas fullback Don Perkins said the Cowboys believed they could "beat the stuffing out of the Packers," and Dallas owner Clint Murchison confidently told a reporter before the game, "It's too cold for the Green Bay passing game, and we'll win with our running."

Condensed clouds of steam crystallized in the air as the Cowboy offense and Packer defense faced each other on the first play from scrimmage. Starting at center for Dallas was Mike Connelly, a 32-year-old backup who was starting for injured Dave Manders. A preseason knee injury had sidelined Manders for the season, and the Pro Bowl center was balancing himself on crutches and trying to stay warm inside his five layers of clothing. Manders had put on backup defensive end Larry Stephens' size-15 boots so he could layer his socks, and covered his face with a full ski mask. Standing on the sidelines, Manders saw the steam from the exhaling of the fans and thought it looked like some kind of eerie fog.

Connelly had been picked up by the Cowboys in 1960 after being cut by the Los Angeles Rams. A graduate of Utah State, Connelly was an ex-Marine. He started for the Cowboys through 1964. He suffered a knee injury in 1965 and lost his starting job to Manders, but Connelly worked hard to excel on special teams. Listed at 235 pounds, he was actually much lighter, but he fooled the coaches by hiding weights in his boxer shorts before weigh-ins. Still, his greyhound build—he was 6-3—and speed made him effective at cutting down middle linebackers.

As Connelly settled into his stance and gripped the frozen ball, his eyes focused on Green Bay middle linebacker Ray Nitschke. The offensive game plan worked up by Landry and assistants Ermal Allen and Jim Myers called for the Cowboys to neutralize Nitschke and prevent him from pursuing ball carriers. Offensive tackle Ralph Neely recalled Myers, the Cowboys' offensive line coach, putting particular emphasis on stopping Nitschke.

"Any time we played the Packers, our number-one priority was blocking Ray Nitschke," Neely remembered. "We knew if we were going to be successful, we had to block Nitschke."

Fans in Green Bay listening to the game on WTMJ Radio heard broadcaster Ted Moore call the opening play from scrimmage:

"Don Meredith has the team set out of the I-formation. (Dan) Reeves goes to the left side and they're in a slot formation already. Meredith goes back to throw a pass on the first play from scrimmage . . . fires . . . It is complete to Bob Hayes across the 40-yard line to about the 44 . . . and Willie Wood knocks him out of bounds."

Having backpedaled three steps, Meredith hit Hayes on the left sideline for a ten-yard gain and a first down. For Hayes, the reception was an ice-breaker in more ways than one. Bracketed by the Packers' defense in the '66 title game, Hayes, whose flashing smile and flying feet made him a fan favorite, finished that game with one catch for one yard. Seeking to get Hayes involved from the outset, the Cowboys lined him up in the left slot and isolated him on Green Bay linebacker Lee Roy Caffey. Hayes eluded the slower Caffey, and caught the ball just before sliding out of bounds.

Responsibility for reading the complex Cowboy offense rested on Nitschke. While most NFL teams employed six different formations and approximately 40 plays, Neely remembered Dallas using as many as 18 different formations, out of which Meredith could call any one of 20 plays, a total of 360 plays in all.

Nitschke knew Cowboy coaches had put in long hours trying as he said, "to think of ways to outmaneuver us," and he also knew the success of the Packer defense would come down to a guessing game between him and Meredith. "He'd be trying to fool me," Nitschke said. "By calling defensive audibles at the line of scrimmage, I'd be trying to stop him from doing it."

Nitschke was a thorough student of the game. Bengston said at the time that if someone wanted a lightning review of the plays and formations the Cowboys would use against the Packers, they should ask Meredith, but "if he's unavailable, ask Nitschke."

As he watched films of the Cowboys, Nitschke looked for keys to Meredith's play-calling. He took notes on when the Dallas quarterback was most likely to go to his tight end, and whether he threw to Reeves on first or second down.

Even though the Cowboys would mix things up and try to throw him off, Nitschke realized Meredith would follow certain patterns that had worked before. Since every quarterback had players and plays he favored in given situations, Nitschke studied Dallas films and played the percentages. Even though Meredith wouldn't always do what the Packers expected, Nitschke felt if the Cowboys followed their pattern even 55 percent of the time, Green Bay would be in position to stop them more than half the time.

As the Cowboys shifted from their I-formation (*See Diagram 5*) into a slot set, Nitschke pointed to the moving backs, his raspy voice cutting through the cold air as he called out the play. Nitschke was so adept at recognizing formations some opposing players thought he did it to mock them. In a 1970 game against Pittsburgh, Steelers' running back Preston Pearson watched as Nitschke shouted to his teammates where the next play was going. If Nitschke yelled that it was an end sweep, it was a certainty that quarterback Terry Bradshaw had called that play in the huddle. If Nitschke yelled to look out for a post play, the Packers were sure that's what Bradshaw would do. "It made us sick," Pearson said, "to see Nitschke standing back there, not bothering to conceal his contempt."

Nitschke read opposing offenses so well that even when enemy quarterbacks changed plays at the line of scrimmage by calling out audibles, Nitschke thought along with them. Minnesota Vikings' all-pro center Mick Tingelhoff remembered quarterback Joe Kapp changing a play at the line of scrimmage, and then hearing Nitschke tell defensive tackle Ron Kostelnik where the play was going. Kostelnik shifted his position and stopped the runner for no gain. "They know our offense as well as we know it," Tingelhoff said.

The guessing game between Nitschke and Meredith continued

as Dallas moved to a first down on its 43. Halfback Dan Reeves, who was wearing a neck roll to protect an injury sustained in the playoff against the Browns, followed Neely for a four-yard gain.

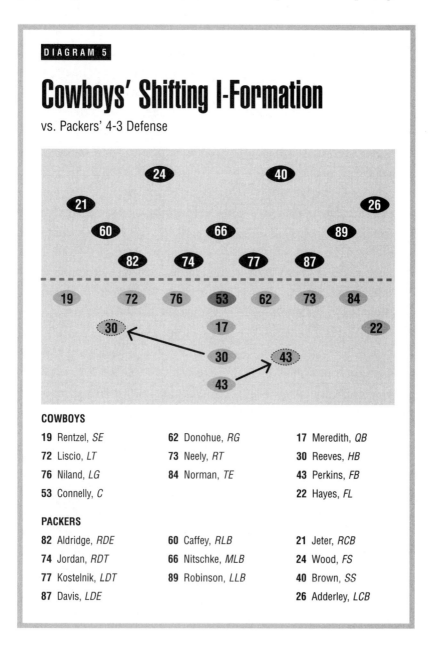

DIAGRAM 5

Cowboys' Shifting I-Formation

vs. Packers' 4-3 Defense

COWBOYS

19 Rentzel, *SE*	**62** Donohue, *RG*	**17** Meredith, *QB*
72 Liscio, *LT*	**73** Neely, *RT*	**30** Reeves, *HB*
76 Niland, *LG*	**84** Norman, *TE*	**43** Perkins, *FB*
53 Connelly, *C*		**22** Hayes, *FL*

PACKERS

82 Aldridge, *RDE*	**60** Caffey, *RLB*	**21** Jeter, *RCB*
74 Jordan, *RDT*	**66** Nitschke, *MLB*	**24** Wood, *FS*
77 Kostelnik, *LDT*	**89** Robinson, *LLB*	**40** Brown, *SS*
87 Davis, *LDE*		**26** Adderley, *LCB*

Continuing to attack the Packer flanks, Meredith threw incomplete to flanker Lance Rentzel on the right sideline. On third down, Reeves ran right again, but was stopped for no gain by Herb Adderley, who stepped up from his left cornerback position to make the stop.

In the pressbox, CBS-TV color analyst Frank Gifford told his viewing audience the Dallas offense was trying running plays to "get a feel of the game, a feel of the field, and a sense of what the weather will do to their game plan."

Turning the game back over to play-by-play announcer Jack Buck, who was scheduled to broadcast the first half while Ray Scott did the second, Gifford reached for a Styrofoam cup that a pressbox attendant had filled with hot coffee and left on a ledge in front of him. Picking up the cup, Gifford realized he'd need an ice pick to drink it. The coffee had frozen solid, and as he turned it over like a Popsicle, Gifford joked to his listeners, "I think I'll have another bite of my coffee."

Among the media struggling with the cold down on the field was photographer Vernon Biever and his 15-year-old son, John. Considered by many the first team photographer in NFL history, Vernon got his start with the Packers in the late forties.

"I was an army photographer in Germany and France for two years," he recalled, "and then I worked for the *Milwaukee Sentinel.* I went to the Packers in the late forties and said, 'How about giving me a field pass and I'll give you memories of the game.' The first game I did was the Packers and the Bears in Green Bay."

The biggest problems facing Vernon and John were the hard ground and the inadvisability of handling the metal cameras barehanded. "You had to wear gloves because the cameras were metal," Vernon said, "and photographers hate working with gloves on because it's tough to focus and difficult to load and unload the cameras. You had to go near the heaters to keep your hands warm. And it was difficult kneeling because the ground was so hard."

Having met the initial charge of the Dallas offense and limited it to 14 yards, the Packer defense felt relief on the Green Bay sideline. Despite the Cowboys' success against them a year earlier, Green Bay made few changes in their defensive game plan for the rematch. They were concerned with Hayes as a long-ball threat, and with Reeves and Perkins, whom they considered quick, powerful runners. But the Packers' primary concern focused on the Cowboys' shifting formations. In Dallas the previous January, Nitschke had been lured out of position by the pre-snap movement of the backs, and Green Bay had been victimized by Dallas draw plays.

Their plan was to present a stable defensive picture by refusing to be faked into what their coaches called "unnatural alignments." With their reverse screen passes, flanker screens, and end reverses, the Cowboy offense had the most complex attack in the league, and by utilizing men-in-motion plays and Meredith on rollouts, Landry looked to force the defense to meet him on his own terms.

Believing that shaking up their defense would be a sign of weakness that would undermine the confidence of their players, Packer coaches decided to run their usual plays.

Forced to punt, Danny Villanueva spiraled a kick that Green Bay return man Willie Wood caught at the 16 and returned two yards before slipping to the turf. Lambeau Field was alive with cheers and noise-makers as the Green Bay offense trotted onto the field for the first time.

True to form, the Packers opened with a running play. Throughout the Lombardi era, the Packers had been criticized by some fans for "wasting" the first play of every game with a line plunge by a running back. Green Bay coaches believed that the same people who booed their play selection were the same ones who liked to see the first play from scrimmage go 20 yards to assure everyone it was going to be a good day.

But the coaches felt most Green Bay fans were more sophisticated, having been educated to basic football during the sixties. They could watch the game closely to see how strong the Packers looked, where they were wearing down the opposition, how much time they were using to control the ball, and how they maintained their field position. Most Packer fans knew how to watch line play. Those who only watched the backs and receivers were the ones booing.

Driving past Lambeau Field the night before the game, Packer center Ken Bowman had noticed Lombardi's car sitting alone in the parking lot. A solitary light was on in the coach's office, and Bowman could see the reflection of a projector. Lombardi was studying films, still searching for an advantage some 12 hours before kickoff.

The coach's planning paid immediate dividends. Having studied the Dallas defense on film, Lombardi installed a new play to take advantage of middle linebacker Lee Roy Jordan's strong pursuit. Known as "41-Special," the play called for left guard Gale Gillingham to pull right and influence Jordan into thinking the play was going in that direction. Bob Hyland, starting at center, was expected to block Lilly, while fullback Chuck Mercein sealed off Jordan and led halfback Donny Anderson into the hole.

The play worked just as Lombardi diagrammed it. Churning across the slick turf, Anderson followed his blocking for five yards, then unexpectedly fumbled the ball. Mercein covered it for the Packers, preventing an early turnover.

On second-and-five, Anderson ran right, this time behind guard Jerry Kramer and tackle Forrest Gregg, and gained four yards. Carrying a third time, Anderson hit the middle for another four yards and a first down. Packer fans recognized the early trend. On three consecutive running plays, Starr probed the left flank, right flank, and middle of the Dallas "Doomsday" defense, and Anderson averaged better than four yards per carry.

Drafted in 1965 out of Texas Tech, where he led the team in rushing, receiving, punting, and scoring, Anderson was a product of the fierce signing war with the American Football League that marked pro football in the mid-sixties. The Packers outbid the AFL's Houston Oilers for the right to sign Anderson, and the price tag was a hefty $600,000, a staggering sum at that time. Anderson's versatile skills had led Green Bay fans to think of him as the "next Paul Hornung," but he never reached those heights. By the time Anderson became a starter, Lombardi was on the verge of retiring, and so were many of the team's veterans.

Like Hornung, Anderson was a big, blond, handsome type who liked the night life. Teammates called him the "Golden Palomino," and though he never emerged into the superstar player Hornung had been, Anderson made valuable contributions to the Packers' success in 1967. As a player, this historic game was his finest hour.

Lombardi's strategy to attack Landry's flex defense and its alternating offset linemen was to run at the "bubble," or the lineman who was off the ball. The Cowboys believed that by placing an end and tackle a yard off the ball in a staggered formation, they fouled blocking assignments by making the offense "go get" the offset lineman. When that happened, Cowboy linebackers were free to fire through the gaps.

Green Bay's well-schooled offensive line foiled Landry's flex schemes by exploding off the ball and pushing the sliding Dallas defenders further back into the bubble area. Bowman, who alternated at center with Hyland, felt the Cowboys were reading the offense and not being aggressive on this initial series.

If the Cowboys were cautious, it was because they believed that to beat the Packers, they had to play an almost perfect brand of football.

"It wasn't hard to prepare for them," Lilly reflected. "The thing was, we knew they weren't going to make an error. They didn't get penalties. They didn't hold a lot, and they didn't let the quarterback get hit most of the time. You didn't really get to Starr that often. And they were as excellent at run-blocking as they were at pass protection.

"Lombardi really had them well-trained, and we just knew we couldn't make a lot of mistakes or they were going to beat us. That's how they beat most teams. They just didn't make any errors."

With the Cowboys' defense conscious of the run, Starr switched to a pass play. The Packers' quarterback retreated into the pocket, but the left side of his line gave way, and Lilly and end George Andrie flowed through the opening to sack him for a nine-yard loss. Facing a second-and-19 from his own 22, Starr's pass to tight end Marv Fleming over the middle was broken up by left safety Mike Gaechter, but a pass interference call against the Cowboys gave Green Bay an automatic first down at their own 31.

Starr followed with a pass to Anderson in the left flat that gained 17 yards, and Anderson put the Packers into Cowboy territory for the first time with a three-yard pickup on "41 Special." Mercein drove for two more yards, and another Cowboy penalty— a holding call against left end Willie Townes on Starr's incomplete pass to Anderson—moved the ball to the Dallas 42.

Starr, who Detroit Lions' tackle Alex Karras once said had "all kinds of guts on third down," converted a third-and-nine play with a pass over the middle for 17 yards to flanker Carroll Dale. With the ball at the Dallas 24, Starr threw incomplete to split end Boyd Dowler, then found Dale on the left sideline for 15 yards and a first-and-goal at the nine.

As the Packers marched down the field on their opening drive, writers in the front row of the press box were struggling to follow the action. The condensation from their breath quickly iced the windows, and they were forced to lean forward and try to scrape the ice away with any sharp-edged object they could find. Watching from his seat in the last row of the press box was the *Press-Gazette's* Daley, the Packers' hometown paper—which had assigned 14 staff members to cover the historic game. As a longtime Packers' beat reporter, Daley should have been sitting in the front row, but most of the front-row seats that day went to writers from the metropolitan morning papers. Watching his colleagues below chipping away at the ice, however, Daley felt happy with the seating arrangement.

"Everyone was cold in the press box," he said. "But some of the morning paper guys down in the front row looked like they were freezing to death. I was a little warmer back in the third row."

Running "41 Special" again, Anderson earned a yard through the middle. Standing behind center on second down from the seven, Starr studied the Cowboys' man-for-man coverage in the secondary. With the 6-5 Dowler owning a seven-inch height advantage on Cowboy right cornerback Mike Johnson, Starr changed the call at the line of scrimmage. Instead of another line plunge, he changed to a quick inside pass to Dowler.

WTMJ listeners heard Moore make the following call:

"And it's second down and goal-to-go for the Packers on the Cowboys' eight-yard line. Green Bay back in the huddle, and now they break out. Dale goes to the right side, flanked out about 10, 12 yards. Dowler's split about five on the left side.

"Starr . . . begins the count, takes the ball, pumps one up the middle and the pass is complete to Dowler in the end zone for a touchdown! He was wide open, and the Green Bay Packers draw first blood . . ."

At the snap, Dowler ran straight at Johnson, driving him back, then cut in front of him, shielding the smaller man off the ball. Starr dropped back five steps, beating a Cowboy blitz, then spiraled a pass over the outstretched left arm of Lilly. Dowler, an ex-hurdler from the University of Colorado, leapt slightly to cradle Starr's pass in the middle of the end zone. Chandler provided the extra point, and the Packers led, 7-0.

"Their cornerback lined up outside of me and stayed there, and he had no help inside," remembered Dowler. "It was a quick post from the weak-side tight end position, and Bart read the blitz and threw a quick pass."

Marching his team 82 yards in 16 plays, Starr had provided a textbook example of how to pick apart a defense. He balanced his play selection perfectly, calling eight runs and eight passes. Probing every angle of the "Doomsday" defense, Starr settled on the Cowboys' right side, where Johnson, in just his second season, had difficulty matching the experience of Dowler, a nine-year veteran, and Dale, who was in his eighth season.

Starr had thrown to Johnson's side twice, completing both

passes to Dale, then switched Dowler to that side. The big flanker tested Johnson first to the outside, then curled inside for the touchdown pass.

One of the ten cameramen capturing Dowler's TD for NFL Films was Art Spieller, who was stationed just inside an opening in the metal scoreboard above the south end zone. Over breakfast at The Northland Hotel that morning, Spieller and the rest of the NFL Films crew had discussed how they would handle the extreme cold. One thing they decided was to take the oil out of the cameras so it wouldn't freeze up.

Spieller had covered himself from head to toe with many layers of clothing, then topped it off with a ski mask. A heater was placed inside the scoreboard to help keep him warm, but as he positioned himself behind the opening, all Spieller could think of was how cold he was.

"My feeling was, 'Am I going to live through this thing?'" said Spieller, shortly before his retirement from NFL Films in early 1997. "I felt my life was going to come to an end in Green Bay and I was going to freeze to death in that scoreboard and no one would know I was there."

Near the end of the first quarter, WTMJ listeners heard a commercial promotion for an ice capades show ironically called "Holiday on Ice." With New Year's Eve temperatures in Green Bay at minus-16 degrees, the "Holiday on Ice" promo seemed highly appropriate for the occasion.

Following the commercial, Moore told his audience, "We'll be all right here if our can of 'de-icer' holds out."

It was that kind of a day in Titletown. But with their beloved Packers carrying a 7–0 lead into the second quarter, Green Bay fans were warmed by the thought of another NFL title.

Chapter Ten

Wind Chill and the Will to Win

A S THE FIRST QUARTER CAME TO AN END, CBS Director Tony Verna adjusted his headset in the network's control room and told his associate producer to run commercial "Five."

Since they needed to get 18 one-minute commercials into their three-hour broadcast, CBS had set a prearranged pattern for their use. Commercial One was set to run before the opening kickoff, and Two, Three, and Four were planned for the first quarter. Commercial Five came at the end of the first quarter, and as Verna cut away from the action on the field, he eyed the monitors in front of him, scanning the field as he might if he were among the more than 50,000 fans at Lambeau Field.

Throughout the afternoon, CBS cameras panned the crowd, and their close-up shots of fans bundled in bright hunting gear and ski clothing provided a nationwide viewing audience with stark images of the arctic conditions in Green Bay. "There were some dandy outfits," CBS color analyst Frank Gifford said, and most of them involved stocking caps with small slits for the eyes, nose, and mouth. Some wrapped their faces in woolen scarves, while others covered their heads with blankets.

Choreographing CBS's coverage, Verna was one of two directors and five producers on a staff headed by executive producer

Bill Fitts. Seated behind a telecommunications panel of four alternating white-and-black phones and 12 viewing screens of varying sizes, Verna monitored the game through shots taken by one of CBS's five cameramen on the field. His job was to make split-second choices of which view of the game he wanted on the air. Verna compared it to "playing blindfold chess." Regardless of which team won the game on the field, it was Verna's responsibility to make sure CBS was the biggest winner in the eyes of the 30 million viewers.

With his dark hair and sideburns, Verna in 1967 could easily have passed for a post-graduate student, but he had 14 years of experience in TV sports coverage. Football, more than anything else, was in his blood. He studied game films and carried a 36-page "play book" that served as a guide for the positioning and minute-by-minute moves of men and their equipment. Verna had an intimate knowledge of the game, and it was said by one observer that he drilled his technicians and production people "with the single-minded drive of an electronic Vince Lombardi."

"Tony, at that time, was far ahead of everybody else that was directing," recalled Tom Brookshier, who was a sideline commentator for CBS that day. "He was really trying to do the special isolated stuff. I remember the year before, we had done the first isolated replay, and he said, 'Hey, Tom. I've got something I'm going to try. I'm just going to put a camera on a lineman.'

"Well, we were doing a Dallas game, and I said, 'Put it on (Cowboys' guard) John Niland.' Niland pulled out and fell down over somebody else, it was the darndest thing. And we laughed so much. We said, 'Well, here's what this great guard did on this play.'

"We had instant replays, but this was the first time we had ever seen an isolated replay. In those days, Tony was the guy who thought ahead most of the time."

During his career, Verna had seen TV sports coverage evolve from a single commentator and one cameraman positioned high above the 50-yard line to batteries of cameras accompanied by expert analysis from a play-by-play broadcaster and his color commentator. TV coverage in the sixties expanded to include zoom lenses and sideline microphones, and the sights and sounds of modern pro football became so vivid to viewers that *Time* magazine said bulldozing backs sometimes seemed to blast over the goal-line and land on the living-room rug.

Verna's co-director was Bob Dailey, who was in charge of the pregame, halftime, and postgame segments. During World War II, Dailey had been one of the U.S. Army photographers allowed into the infamous German concentration camp, Auschwitz.

"He would never talk about that," remembered Brookshier. "He was a real gentleman, a great personality. He'd smoke with a long cigarette holder, and he'd turn the collar up on his trenchcoat. He was real interesting."

The CBS production crew for its national telecast of the '67 championship included Verna and Dailey; producer Bill Creasy; an associate producer in charge of commercials; and a "tape AD," or associate director, who handled highlights for the halftime and postgame shows and helped Creasy log the plays.

"We really loaded up for that game," remembered Brookshier. "The year before, the Packers intercepted Dandy (Don Meredith) in the end zone on the last play of the game, so this (rematch) was the ultimate playoff game. It was more important than the Super Bowl."

The technical people on hand were involved with the video aspect of the broadcast, and it was their duty to prevent the jerseys from being green on Camera Two and purple on Camera One, a common occurrence when daytime light changes.

Working with broadcasters Gifford, Jack Buck, and Ray Scott in the broadcast booth were a cameraman, a stage manager with cue cards, a statistician, and spotters. On the Friday before the game, the CBS crew held a production meeting to review the two teams.

The idea was to put together what Fitts called "a frequency report" similar to each coach's scouting report.

The cameramen also held a meeting, discussing what to do on running and passing plays, kickoffs, and punts. Patterns of coverage were set, and the cameramen were told that if something occurred they hadn't anticipated, they were to use a "color" shot of the sidelines or the crowd.

CBS covered the game with a six-camera unit, putting five cameras on the field and the sixth in the broadcast booth. Three of the five cameras were placed on the 50-yard line to handle the play-by-play. Camera One carried a wide-cover shot of the outside flanker and provided viewers with the basic formation as the teams broke from their huddles. Once the flankers had established their positions, Verna would cut to Camera Two, which was focused just inside the flankers and provided pictures of the offensive and defensive lines. Since Camera Two could pick up the pass rushes, blitzes, and basic coverages, its cameraman was instructed to follow the play.

Camera Three provided what Fitts called "impact shots"— medium close-ups of players getting off the ground after being tackled. Cameras Four and Five got the isolated shots. Located on the 50-yard line, Camera Four focused on line play, isolating the pull of the guards on a sweep play or a defensive lineman shedding a block to get to the ball carrier. Camera Five was situated in the end zone, and its cameraman isolated receivers on passing plays.

To heighten the drama and intensity of the game for its television audience, CBS put field microphones on both sidelines. Each microphone was covered with a sponge designed to enhance the sounds of blocking and tackling while filtering out wind noise. For a couple of minutes in the first half, these sounds were muffled by the cold hands of Green Bay halfback Donny Anderson. Following the Packers' first quarter touchdown, Anderson was sitting on the bench trying to warm up when he saw the field microphone dangling in front of him. Thinking it was some new kind of heating equipment, Anderson reached up and wrapped his hands around the mike.

Serving as CBS sideline reporters were Brookshier and former New York Giants' kicker Pat Summerall. Though the network arranged for them to do interviews on the field 30 minutes before kickoff, Lombardi exploded when he saw them on his sideline. "This is my office!" he shouted. "Get the hell outta here!"

Trailing 7–0, the Dallas offense tried to emerge from its deep freeze at the start of the second quarter. Facing a second-and-ten on his own 32, Cowboys' quarterback Don Meredith wobbled an incomplete pass to flanker Lance Rentzel. On third-and-ten, Meredith's pass to halfback Dan Reeves was almost intercepted. Danny Villanueva followed with a punt to the Packers' 32-yard line.

Returning to the field, the Green Bay offense revealed a new backfield. Replacing Anderson and fullback Chuck Mercein were Ben Wilson, a former Los Angeles Rams' fullback, and rookie halfback Travis Williams.

Starr opened the series by sending Wilson off the left side for a 13-yard pickup. With a first down at the Green Bay 45, Starr gave the ball to Williams, who veered left behind tackle Bob Skoronski for a seven-yard gain into Cowboy territory. At the same time, a large cloud of white smoke was suddenly visible on the Packers' sideline. The hot air blowers inside one of the canvas dugouts had run out of gas, and the bench was engulfed in white smoke and diesel fumes that smelled like the back end of a bus. Packer players inside the tent jumped up and ran, and among those emerging from the cloud and muttering about "damn diesel fumes" was backup offensive tackle Steve Wright.

At 6-6, 250 pounds, Wright had the physical makeup to be an outstanding player, but his relaxed attitude and his penchant for finding trouble followed him through a career that saw him play for six different NFL teams. Wright's casual style angered the strict Lombardi, and during their three years together on the Packers, the wise-cracking Wright and his win-at-all-costs coach were often at odds.

Before one game, while most of the players put their pads on and prepared to gather together for Lombardi's pregame speech, Wright headed into the bathroom. After some time, Wright emerged, pants down around his ankles, just as Lombardi was hitting the high point of his talk.

Turning around, Lombardi saw the grinning Wright, standing half-naked in the middle of the locker room.

"What are we running here?" Lombardi screamed. "A damn nursery? Can't you do anything right, Wright?"

Now, in the most memorable game of his life, Wright was in trouble again. As Skoronski came off the field to adjust his helmet, Wright was milling around with the other players, trying to decide whether it was safe to go back into the tent once the smoke cleared. With Skoronski out of the game, Packer coaches began screaming for Wright. "But I don't have my helmet!" Wright said. "I can't find it. It's lost!"

Wright had left his helmet in the tent, which was still spitting smoke and fumes. With the coaches screaming, "Wright! Hey, Wright! Get in the game!" Wright began tearing around inside the smog-filled tent looking for his helmet. "I can't find the damn thing!" he shouted. Finally, defensive tackle Lionel Aldridge handed Wright his helmet to wear. Running onto the field, Wright slammed Aldridge's helmet on, then realized it was too big. The helmet wobbled over Wright's head as he ran, and the chin strap hung halfway down his neck.

When Starr called for another off-tackle slant left, Wright groaned. "I'm freezing cold," he thought, "my system is like molasses, and I can't move." Breaking from the huddle, Wright looked across the line at George Andrie, the Cowboys' 6–6, 250-pound defensive end. The two men had a lot in common besides their near-identical physical size. Both had been branded "Bullwinkle" by their teammates; Andrie because the cartoon moose was his favorite thing to watch during road games, and Wright because he was always pulling the wrong way on the Packers' sweep and running into his own men, prompting center Ken Bowman to repeat Bullwinkle's line, "Go, go, go, but watch where you're going."

Wright had faced Andrie once before, in an exhibition game in Dallas. Andrie bull-rushed Wright in that game, knocking him over easily. In a team meeting, Lombardi ran the film back and forth five times, and the sight of Wright in his stance, then on his back, in his stance, on his back, made nearly everyone laugh. Everyone except Lombardi. "What do you have," Lombardi asked Wright, "a rubber band on you?"

Wright always took the coach's criticism with a bemused smile, and the sight of his big tackle grinning back at him infuriated Lombardi. "Damn it, Wright," he yelled, "wipe that silly smirk off your face!"

As Wright bent at the waist to get into his stance opposite Andrie, the front of his oversized helmet slid down to the bridge of his nose. Unable to see anything but the frozen ground, Wright stared warily at it. "It's like concrete," he thought. "Hitting it would be like diving into an empty swimming pool."

The ball was snapped, Wright hit the ground and immediately tore the skin off both elbows. While his large helmet bobbled around on his head, Wright somehow managed to block Andrie enough to allow Williams a two-yard gain. Later, as Wright came off the field, he looked out of the corner of his eye. Lombardi was staring at him and his huge helmet, and Wright knew what his coach was thinking. "Lombardi," Wright said, "is looking at me like, 'You're a football player?'"

Williams' short gain brought up a third-and-one at the Dallas 43. Throughout his career, Starr had made many big plays on third-and-short situations inside enemy territory. In the early years of the

Lombardi era, third-and-one automatically meant an off-tackle run by bruising fullback Jim Taylor. The Packers had so much success with the play that defenses began stacking the line to stop it. When they did, Starr would fake the handoff to Taylor, drawing the defensive secondary up close to the line, then drop back five yards and throw deep to a sprinting end for a big gain.

The play worked with such regularity that it became known around the NFL as the "Bart Starr Special." Split end Boyd Dowler, who was on the receiving end of many of those Starr touchdown passes, recalls it being called something else in the Packers' playbook.

"'Pass 36, X Post,'" Dowler recalled. "We ran that thing year after year and got away with it. I remember lining up near the opposing team's sideline on third-and-short, and their players would be yelling to the defense, 'Look out for the play-action! Look out for the play action!' And the cornerbacks would look over and say, 'Yeah, yeah.' And then the ball would be snapped and we would run right by them and catch a pass for a touchdown. It worked every time, and I never could understand why the defensive backs thought they could stop a third-and-one run anyway."

Schooled in the nuances of defensive football by head coach Tom Landry and assistant Ernie Stautner, the Cowboys were one of the most intelligent teams in the NFL. Like everyone else watching the game, the Cowboys must have figured that Starr would take one of his calculated risks. Even the writers in the press box figured out what was coming next. *Green Bay Press-Gazette* sportswriter Bob Woessner noted, "Third-and-one . . . watch Starr hit Dale for a TD."

Whether it was because the arctic cold was enough to freeze a man's mind as well as his body, or whether the Cowboys didn't believe Starr would risk a pass into a wind that was slamming into his face at 15 miles per hour, the Dallas defense was unprepared for what followed.

Calling "Pass 36, X Post" in the huddle, Starr faked a handoff to Wilson, who headed left, causing all-pro free safety Mel Renfro to read a running play and take a step towards the line. Wilson blocked blitzing linebacker Dave Edwards, and Starr lofted a high spiral downfield to the streaking Dowler (*See Diagram 6*).

Ted Moore made the call on WTMJ radio:

"Ball is at the Cowboys' 43-yard line. Twelve minutes and 42 seconds remaining here in the first half of play. It's third down and a yard to go for the Green Bay Packers. They're out in front of the Cowboys by a score of seven-to-nothing.

"(Ken) Bowman leads the team up to the line of scrimmage, gets over the ball at center. Starr . . . begins the count, takes the ball, fakes a hand-off, back to throw, fires a long one . . . It is complete to Boyd Dowler and he'll go . . . into the end zone for a touchdown! Bart Starr faded back and pumped a long one to Boyd Dowler, who got behind Mel Renfro, took the pass in stride at the 15-yard line and raced the rest of the way for a touchdown!"

"We had run a couple of plays in a row to that side," Dowler said, "and in the third-and-short situation, the safety bit on the play fake and I ran by him. Bart threw a very easy ball to handle. He wasn't known for having a real strong arm but he was very accurate. He always threw to the right guy. That's why he completed something like 60 percent of the passes he threw in his career.

"At first I thought his pass was too far, but the wind held the ball up and it stuck to my hands. The ball was hard and slick and cold, and my hands were cold, too. So I had to rely on the basic fundamentals of catching a football, which was to get my hands up together and make the catch."

Caught on a friendly Canadian current, the ball hung in the air for an extra split-second, almost as if waiting for Dowler to run under it. CBS cameras isolated Dowler as he hauled it in off the end of his fingertips at the Dallas 15, and outran Renfro to the end zone. Renfro dove and grabbed Dowler's ankle at the two-yard line, and the big end rolled on his right shoulder as he fell across the goal line. As Don Chandler kicked the extra point to make it 14-0, Woessner wrote, "When will the other team learn to stop that play?"

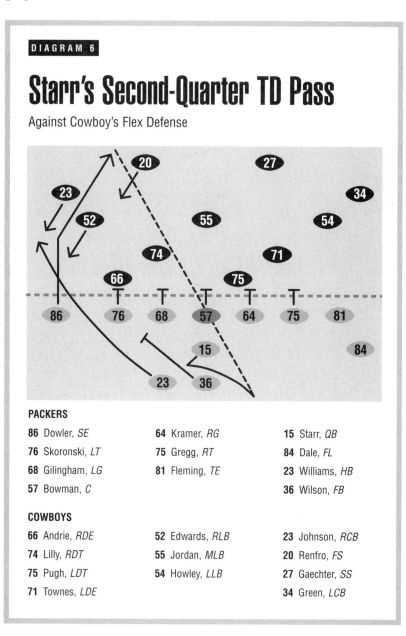

DIAGRAM 6

Starr's Second-Quarter TD Pass

Against Cowboy's Flex Defense

PACKERS

86 Dowler, *SE*	**64** Kramer, *RG*	**15** Starr, *QB*
76 Skoronski, *LT*	**75** Gregg, *RT*	**84** Dale, *FL*
68 Gilingham, *LG*	**81** Fleming, *TE*	**23** Williams, *HB*
57 Bowman, *C*		**36** Wilson, *FB*

COWBOYS

66 Andrie, *RDE*	**52** Edwards, *RLB*	**23** Johnson, *RCB*
74 Lilly, *RDT*	**55** Jordan, *MLB*	**20** Renfro, *FS*
75 Pugh, *LDT*	**54** Howley, *LLB*	**27** Gaechter, *SS*
71 Townes, *LDE*		**34** Green, *LCB*

Dowler's second touchdown of the game was indicative of the kind of big-play performer he was throughout his career in Green Bay. Having been a single-wing quarterback at the University of Colorado, Dowler assumed he'd try out for the position when the Packers made him the 25th pick in the 1959 draft. Since single-wing quarterbacks sometimes were required to catch passes as well as throw them, Dowler had experience as a receiver. After taking over Green Bay, Lombardi held a meeting for his quarterbacks in June of 1959. Dowler was sitting there taking notes—"I guess I thought I was a quarterback," he said with a short laugh—when Lombardi pointed a finger at him and said, "Dowler, you're a flanker."

"So," Dowler said, "I promptly became a flanker. We went out to the field and I think I dropped every other pass they threw to me. I was in shock for a day. I didn't know how long I'd be around after that. But at Colorado, I had spent my winters running indoor track and my summers running outdoor track, and I think that helped me a lot. Not being a receiver at college I didn't have any bad habits to break. I think it only took me a couple of weeks to adjust to the NFL."

Dowler earned NFL Rookie of the Year honors after catching 32 passes and averaging more than 17 yards per reception. With his big body and enjoyment of contact, Dowler was a solid blocker, something an end had to be in Lombardi's system of sweeps and slants.

"We always tried to run the ball first," Dowler said. "But we weren't three-yards-and-a-cloud-of-dust like people said we were. We'd throw the ball 20, 25 times a game, and we'd throw to a lot of people—backs, wide receivers, tight ends. We spread it around a lot, we didn't just throw to one receiver. If you were thrown to six times a game, that was pretty good. But if the ball was thrown to you, you'd better catch it."

On his first touchdown pass to Dowler, Starr had exploited the coverage of a single man, right cornerback Mike Johnson. On Dowler's second TD, Starr exploited the entire right side of the Dallas defense. Running three straight plays to the Cowboys' right, Starr set Renfro up to move closer to the line of scrimmage on third-and-one. Though most NFL quarterbacks tried to avoid throwing in Renfro's direction, Starr went after the future Hall of Fame safety. When Renfro closed in, Starr sent Dowler deep and hit him in stride for the score.

Throughout the 1967 season, Dallas defensive backs had been able to mask their mistakes with speed and quickness. The Cowboys gave up 21 touchdown passes during the season and allowed opposing quarterbacks to complete almost 54 percent of their passes.

Because of the field conditions in Green Bay, the Dallas secondary couldn't use its speed to outrun coverage mistakes. Green Bay's receivers were drilled to run precise patterns, and the Packers' no-frills passing attack was not dependent on good weather conditions. Unlike the Cowboys, whose offense and defense was built on quickness, the Packers relied on executing a handful of basic plays to perfection.

Starr had burned the Cowboys for 304 yards and four touchdowns in the 1966 championship game in Dallas, and he knew how to exploit their defense.

"Bart was really good at calling plays," reflected Lilly. "Boyd Dowler would tell him when he had a man beaten (in pass coverage) and Bart knew exactly what to do.

"They'd nickel-and-dime you with three yards here, five yards there, and then he'd throw a 40-yard pass. He didn't throw long often, but when he did, he usually connected."

Down 14-0, the Cowboys looked like a beaten team. Dallas players herded themselves into sideline dugouts, leaving Landry standing alone like a late-day commuter at a vacant bus stop. The Cowboys' coach would look around, and the sight of the near-empty sideline struck him as being strange, if not downright eerie.

"Everybody would be back at the heaters trying to stay warm," Landry said later. "I was all by myself, just like I was up at the North Pole."

As the second quarter wore on, the cold became even more intense. The sharp wind slapped at the players' clothing like a razor blade on a barber's strap. The slightest contact with the field's chipped-ice surface felt like a major collision. Playing in Green Bay had never been a picnic for opposing teams; Detroit Lions' defensive tackle Alex Karras said once that the Packers "get you up there in that freezing frontier town, beat the crap out of you, and then make you take a cold shower."

But it was the cold air, not a cold shower, that was uppermost in the minds of the Cowboys. They cut arm and head holes in large plastic garbage bags and wore them under their white nylon jerseys. Some Dallas players were genuinely concerned for their survival. They had difficulty breathing because the air was so brittle, it burned their lungs.

"That was the only game in my career in which I can honestly say I was wishing it would just hurry up and be over," Dallas allpro right tackle Ralph Neely said. "You always want to play your best, but all I wanted to do that day was get inside and get warm. I took my foot and put it in front of one of those big ol' kerosene heaters and even though I smelled leather, I never felt anything. My shoe was burning, but I couldn't feel anything. You couldn't run around fast enough to get warm. You couldn't do it. You couldn't run or cut or anything. You just tried to get in each other's way.

"I had a doctor tell me a few years ago that my lungs were probably burned that day from the cold air. You tried to block the cold out and not think about it during the game because there wasn't anything we could do about it."

Meredith's face froze, and he had trouble calling plays in the huddle. His fingers were so frozen he could hardly bend them.

"My hands grew colder with each drive," he said later. "When your hands are as cold as mine were, you can't wing the ball, and you have to wing it, you have to spiral it in a wind like that."

Unable to get a feel for the icy leather, Meredith lobbed soft passes that wobbled in the wind. "We're in trouble," Rentzel thought.

Watching the Cowboys' offense from the sideline, Lilly shared Rentzel's concern. "The field was slick," Lilly recalled, "so you could not play like you normally do. The plays that we were running didn't work, because every time we tried to do something, we slipped and fell down. So that takes a lot away from you, and it did to the Packers too.

"But the cold was something we never really overcame mentally. And I think that was the one advantage Green Bay really had, because they were more used to cold weather and we weren't. We were used to playing in really nice weather in Dallas."

In an attempt to warm his hands between plays, Meredith cut slits in the side of his jersey to keep his hands next to his body. Split end Bob Hayes ran pass patterns with his hands down the front of his metallic silver uniform pants. It didn't take long for the Green Bay defenders to pick up a key on the Cowboys' play-calling; they watched Hayes when he came out of the huddle. If Hayes kept his hands under his uniform belt, the Packers knew he was not the intended receiver. If his hands were out of his pants, Green Bay shifted its defense accordingly.

Bringing the ball back to their own 40 on the ensuing kickoff, the Cowboys failed to gain a yard on their first two plays. On third down, left cornerback Herb Adderley leapt to intercept Meredith's pass at the Dallas 47 and returned it 15 yards. Jogging onto the field to the roar of the crowd, Green Bay right guard Jerry Kramer found himself thinking that if the Packers scored again, they would demoralize Dallas.

Those same thoughts undoubtedly shivered into the minds of the Cowboys. Pushed to the precipice of defeat, the Dallas defense responded. Wilson was stopped for no gain on first down, and Edwards batted Starr's pass to the turf. One play later, Andrie sacked Starr for a 10-yard loss, taking the Packers out of field goal range.

The defensive stand stirred the Cowboys. Following an exchange of punts, the Packers got the ball back on their 31 with 4:20 left in the first half. An illegal procedure penalty on first down moved Green Bay back five yards, and CBS's Jack Buck excited Cowboys' fans with his next call:

"Starr fades . . . he's being rushed . . . and hit by Willie Townes, the ball is loose . . . Andrie has it, he's in for a Dallas touchdown!"

Looking to pass on second down, Starr was caught in a pincer move by Andrie and left end Willie Townes. Starr looked to scramble, but Townes knocked the ball free. Andrie reached down, scooped the ball up at the seven and raced for the end zone. Green Bay right tackle Forrest Gregg tackled Andrie from behind just after he scored.

"The receivers couldn't make their cuts on the icy field and I couldn't find anyone to throw to," Starr said. "I should have pulled the ball to my chest when it was obvious I was going to be tackled, instead of letting it hang out there."

Two minutes later, Dallas got another gift when Green Bay's all-pro safety Willie Wood, back to return Villanueva's punt, dropped the ball at his 17 and Phil Clark covered it for the Cowboys. The Dallas offense, still stalled by the deep freeze and the Packers' defense, settled for a field goal. With the scoreboard at the south end of the field showing 32 seconds left in the half, Villanueva kicked a 21-yard field goal that cut the Packers' lead to 14–10.

As the wind-chill factor fell to 40 degrees below zero, it was announced that the halftime show featuring the Wisconsin State University of La Crosse marching band was canceled. Several of the band members had collapsed in the cold while practicing that morning. The remaining musicians made a futile attempt to play before throwing in the towel.

"The first band member to put a metal mouthpiece to his mouth was the trombone player, and he pulled his lip off," recalled Brookshier, who stood on the sidelines with retired Packer Paul Hornung during the first half. "So they canceled the halftime band show, and they said, 'Brookshier, hurry up and get Hornung, he's right there, and interview him.'

"Paul had been standing outside in that horrible weather, and when he got inside at halftime, his voice went into a different tone. It sounded like he was talking with an echo, and he was looking at me like, 'What's happening to my voice?' And I was looking at him like, 'You sound like Daffy Duck.'"

Up in the WTMJ booth, Moore turned the microphone over to Chuck Johnson, sports editor of the *Milwaukee Journal,* for his opinion of the first half.

Johnson: *"On a cold day like this, everybody likes to say this is Green Bay's weather, but it can work both ways. On that last punt, Willie Wood fumbled the ball because he's got cold hands out there. . . . So on two fumbles, they've gotten ten points."*

Walking off the field, Lombardi's thoughts mirrored Johnson's comments. "We gave them ten points," he muttered. "We gave them momentum." Turnovers by Starr and Wood, two of Green Bay's perennial all-pros, turned a two-touchdown lead into a four-point margin, and turned the Cowboys around. They went into their locker room fired up. Players who complained about the weather before the game were hollering, "Screw the cold! Let's go get 'em!" Landry was all business as he and line coach Jim Myers changed blocking assignments to adapt to the field conditions.

"We can move the ball on the ground," Landry told his team, "if we keep hitting the way we did in the second quarter. There's no reason why we can't win it!"

In the Green Bay locker room, receivers coach Bob Schnelker recommended a change in strategy. He told Starr to take shorter drops to foil the Dallas rush, and throw quick passes to his backs.

Offensive line coach Ray Wietecha was more animated.

"Don't let up out there," he said. "There's a lot of money riding. Get tough, dammit, get tough!"

For Green Bay, a game that once had the look of a rout had grown into a grim battle for survival.

Vernon Biever

Despite the coldest New Year's Eve in Green Bay history, Packer fans filled historic Lambeau Field for the game that came to be known as the Ice Bowl.

Vernon Biever

Vince Lombardi's "Run to Daylight" theories
revolutionized NFL offenses in the 1960s.

Vernon Biever

An outstanding strategist who became the father of modern defenses, Tom Landry was Lombardi's coaching equal.

Vernon Biever

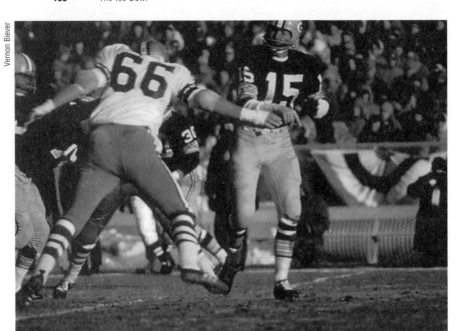

Despite unrelenting pressure from Dallas defenders like George Andrie (66), Green Bay quarterback Bart Starr gave the Packers an early 14–0 lead with two touchdown passes.

Vernon Biever

Green Bay wide receiver Boyd Dowler makes a catch in front of Dallas cornerback Mike Johnson. Dowler led all receivers in the Ice Bowl with four catches for 77 yards, and scored the Packers' first two touchdowns.

Vernon Biever

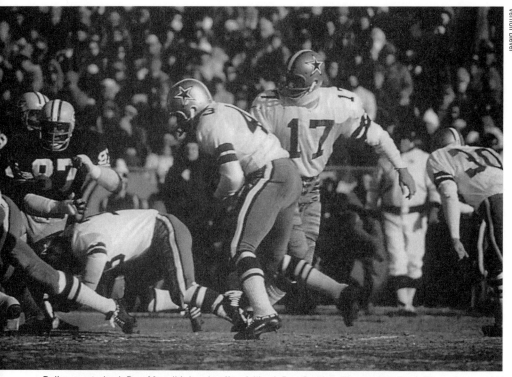

Dallas quarterback Don Meredith hands off to fullback Don Perkins. The combination of the sub-zero cold and the Green Bay defense kept the Cowboys' high-powered offense in check for much of the afternoon.

Vernon Biever

From left, Dallas defensive starters Jethro Pugh, Cornell Green, and Mike Gaechter huddle in a heater-warmed tent installed on the sidelines to battle the minus-50 degree wind chill.

Vernon Biever

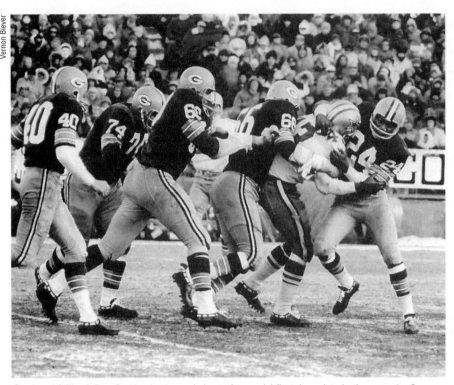

Cowboys' fullback Don Perkins is stopped short of a crucial first down late in the game by Green Bay free safety Willie Wood (24) and a host of Packer defenders.

Dallas receiver Lance Rentzel hauls in a 50-yard TD reception off an option pass from Dan Reeves on the first play of the fourth quarter. The score gave the Cowboys their first lead of the game at 17–14.

Vernon Biever

Vernon Biever

Green Bay halfback Donny Anderson takes Bart Starr's pass and negotiates the icy field for a six-yard gain to start the Packers' dramatic game-winning drive. Closing in for Dallas are left corner-back Cornell Green (34) and left linebacker Chuck Howley (54).

Vernon Biever

Green Bay fullback Chuck Mercein, who joined the Packers in midseason, skates over the ice to pick up a clutch first down on the final drive.

AP / Wide World Photos

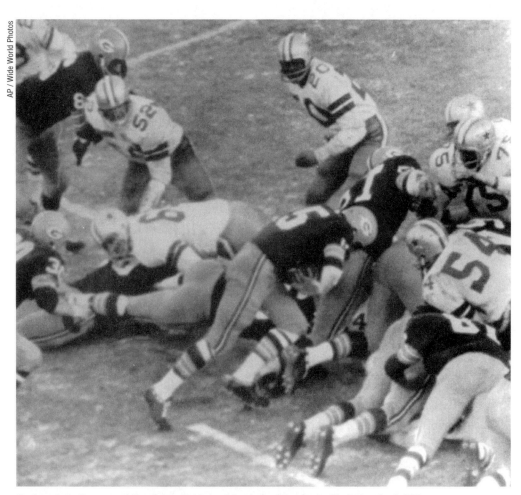

Packers Jerry Kramer and Ken Bowman stopped Cowboys defensive tackle Jethro Pugh (75) with a double-team block, and Bart Starr plunged through the opening to clinch the game for Green Bay in the final seconds of the fourth quarter.

Chapter Eleven

"Doomsday" Dominates

CURRENTS OF COLD AIR CONTINUED TO WHIP through Lambeau Field as Dallas placekicker Danny Villanueva prepared to kick off to start the second half.

Even Packer fans who had long made a ritual of preparing for cold-weather contests were having trouble coping with the glacial winds. Knowing ticket-holders had avoided bathing the day of the game so as not to strip their skin of its protective oils, which would have made them more susceptible to windburn.

The biggest problem facing the fans was keeping their feet warm. Many wore wool socks—"woollies" to the natives—which protected the skin from moisture, and some of Green Bay's mill workers went to the game wearing their steel-toed work shoes. Others chose Canadian-made rubber boots whose felt inserts and comfort ratings to 40 below zero made them the choice of ice fishermen. Still, there were complaints among fans in the second half that they couldn't feel anything from the knees down.

WTMJ broadcaster Ted Moore recalled his seat being "dead on the 50-yard line," and as cold as it was in the broadcast booth, he felt fortunate to be inside. "It was a heckuva lot better in the booth than it was for the people outside," he said, although visibility was a problem. "We were broadcasting that game out of an eight-inch circle because there was a half-inch of frost on the windows."

Moore arrived in Milwaukee in 1958 to be program announcer at WTMJ, which had been the voice of the Packers since the thirties. When the play-by-play spot opened up in 1960, Moore took over, not realizing that his job was subject to the approval of Green Bay's head coach. The game that secured Moore's future was the Packers–Chicago Cardinals exhibition on Labor Day. After listening to the taped rebroadcast, Lombardi sent word to WTMJ that Moore was "okay."

"Lombardi scared the hell out of me," Moore said. "I did a studio show with him, and he could be affable, but he didn't really trust anyone in the media, except for maybe a few New York writers. He intimidated people, and you could not get close to the man."

From 1960–68, Moore was WTMJ's lone announcer on Packer broadcasts. For home games he invited *Milwaukee Journal* sports editor Chuck Johnson into the booth for a halftime interview, and road games sometimes saw him team with a broadcast partner. But it wasn't until 1969 that Moore had a full-time color analyst by his side.

"There was not a lot of hype back in those days," Moore said. "Early in the week I would do a TV show with Lombardi, and we'd do a pregame show for the radio and that was it. I worked with a spotter to my left and a statistician to my right, so basically we had three people in the front row of the broadcast booth."

Moore's broadcasting manner was clipped and concise, similar to that of Ray Scott, who at the start of the second half of the 1967 championship game replaced Jack Buck as the play-by-play announcer for CBS-TV. It is Moore's call, not Scott's, however, that accompanies the NFL Films clip of the Ice Bowl's fabled ending.

As the second half started, Villanueva squibbed a kick to the Packers' up men. Linebacker Lee Roy Caffey handed the loose ball on his 37-yard line and returned it seven yards.

Feeling his team had lost their concentration late in the first half and had begun thinking "more about the cold and the conditions than about our own execution," Green Bay quarterback Bart Starr returned to the ground attack that had worked earlier.

Just as he had started the Packers' first scoring drive by using halfback Donny Anderson on quick-hitting running plays, Starr sent Anderson off the right side for a three-yard pickup before defensive tackle Bob Lilly hauled him down. Though it was just one play, the Packers' lack of execution caused concern among their offensive linemen. Green Bay had been successful against the Cowboys' flex defense earlier by exploding off the ball and driving the Dallas defenders back into the "bubble" left by the offset, or flexed, defensive tackle. The ground was hard, but there were spots on the field that hadn't iced over completely, and the Packers found that by putting most of their weight on their toes, they could dig their cleats into the ground and gain a foothold to push off from.

With this bit of knowledge, the Packers had spent the first quarter-and-a-half moving the Cowboys on running plays and checking them on passing plays.

By the second half however, field conditions had dramatically worsened. Green Bay center Ken Bowman said the icy field "messed up our plan." In order to drive block, the Packers needed traction. With the Packers unable to surge off the ball, the Cowboys' offset linemen had an extra split-second to see the blocking scheme develop, and they stopped Green Bay's ground game before it could get started.

By his own recollection, left guard Gale Gillingham had "a pretty good first half against Lilly." On the first play from scrimmage in the third quarter however, Lilly moved past Gillingham so quick the Packer lineman couldn't believe it. "I was skating around just trying to make contact with him," Gillingham said. Bowman and Gillingham couldn't figure out what was wrong. Why did Lilly and the other Dallas linemen have such superior footing when the Packers were waltzing around so unsteadily they could barely stand up?

Gillingham glanced at the Cowboys' shoes, and noticed some

of the Dallas defenders had changed into a soccer-style shoe which provided superior traction. A few others had removed the rubber tips from their cleats in hope that the exposed metal posts would cut through the ice and give them traction.

Cowboy quickness showed again on the second play, when Starr dropped to pass and was sacked by left tackle Jethro Pugh for a four-yard loss. It was the second sack of the game for Pugh, a third-year player and 11th-round draft pick out of tiny Elizabeth City State Teachers College in North Carolina.

Nicknamed "Buzz" by his teammates, short for "buzzard," Pugh was a prime example of the excellent scouting system employed by the Cowboys' director of player personnel, Gil Brandt. Under Brandt, the Cowboys placed such an emphasis on scouting they were able to find what he called "sleepers," unheralded draft choices like Pugh, at obscure colleges across the country. The Cowboys' championship game roster was dotted with sleepers—Pugh, tight end Pettis Norman from Johnson C. Smith, tackle Jim Boeke from Heidelberg—and the success of Pugh led Brandt to comment in 1967, "I'm sure that somebody stops at Elizabeth City State Teachers College every year now."

The 6 ft. 6 in., 275-pound Pugh anchored the left side of the Dallas defense from 1967–78, but defensive line coach Ernie Stautner had initial concerns about him. In his 1965 rookie camp, Pugh was slow to commit himself to a play because he was afraid to make a mistake. Cowboy coaches kept telling Pugh he would improve with experience, but Jethro wasn't sure how much difference experience could make. "You either beat a guy or you didn't," he would reply. Pugh worried so much he developed an ulcer, but eventually he came to understand what Stautner meant when he talked about the value of experience. "I've learned a lot," he said at the time, "about what my blocker is trying to do to me."

Pugh knew what Green Bay right guard Jerry Kramer would try to do; the two had first squared off the previous summer in an exhibition game in Dallas on August 28. Knowing Pugh had been a substitute in 1966, the veteran Kramer didn't expect too much from him in 1967. But Pugh, who had great quickness off the ball, surprised Kramer with his speed and gave him problems on the Packers' first two or three passing plays. Kramer recovered, and used his experience and drive blocking to get into Pugh at the snap and not let him use his quickness.

Kramer followed the same technique in the first half of the '67 title game. Putting most of his weight on his toes and digging his cleats into the ground, he handled Pugh pretty well in the first half, popping him more than he would under normal weather conditions, and preventing Pugh from getting his hands on him.

But Pugh's sack of Starr, the Cowboys' fifth of the day, was a clear signal the second half would be much more difficult for the Green Bay linemen.

Taking over after a Packer punt, Don Meredith and the Dallas offense came to life for the first time that day. Though the Cowboys had 10 points on the scoreboard, the icy field left their speed-oriented offense impotent for much of the first half. Keying the Cowboys' resurgence was halfback Dan Reeves.

The current head coach of the Atlanta Falcons, Reeves as a running back suffered from flat feet, wasn't very fast, and violated the ball carriers' code with his straight, up-and-down style of running. A former farm boy, he was called "Frog" by his teammates after joining the Cowboys as a free agent in 1965. Reeves was a split-T quarterback at South Carolina, where he specialized in the rollout play. Because South Carolina was just an average team during Reeves' career there, he rarely had a chance to break the kind of big play that gains headlines. Since they weren't involved in championship games, Reeves also didn't have the opportunity to show scouts what a clutch performer he was.

With pro teams focusing on college quarterbacks like Craig Morton and Jerry Rhome, both of whom were drafted in 1965 by the Cowboys, Reeves went to the Dallas training camp in Thousand Oaks and tried out for several positions. He earned a spot at halfback largely because Mel Renfro endured an injury trying to make the switch from the secondary to the offensive backfield. Though he showed just average speed, Reeves had great field vision, was football smart, and owned a nose for the goal line.

After spending much of the '65 season on special teams, Reeves led the team in rushing in 1966 and was second on the club in receiving, behind split end Bob Hayes. By 1967, Reeves was a fixture at halfback, teaming with fullback Don Perkins in a backfield that was both deep and versatile. Reeves was also effective as a receiver both short and deep. "Dan Reeves probably has an ingredient that you just can't measure in football players," Brandt said then. "He has the desire to win, and he has the ability to make the big plays just like (Paul) Hornung."

Like Hornung, Reeves was a triple threat. He retained enough of his college quarterbacking skills to be effective on the Cowboys' version of the halfback option, a play Dallas would spring on Green Bay to great effectiveness in the Ice Bowl.

Displaying the big-play capabilities Brandt had spoken of, Reeves started the Cowboys' first drive of the third quarter with a seven-yard reception from quarterback Don Meredith. Perkins picked up eight yards through the Packers' line, and Meredith followed with a 14-yard pass to tight end Frank Clarke for another first down.

With the ball at the Dallas 40, Reeves followed the blocking of right guard Paul Donohue and tackle Ralph Neely for eight, then ran right again and picked up 20 more yards before being hauled down from behind by outside linebacker Lee Roy Caffey. On first down at the Green Bay 32, Reeves got the call a third straight time, and he responded by sweeping left behind guard John Niland and tackle Tony Liscio for three more yards. Meredith then connected with flanker Lance Rentzel for a first down at the Packers' 18.

Confidence was contagious in the Cowboys' huddle. They had opened the second half running and passing freely on the proud Packer defense, and their success led to four straight first downs and field position deep in Green Bay territory. Rentzel however, paid the price for his catch. Colliding with the concrete-like surface for the first time in the game, he felt at first as if he couldn't get up. "I'd never felt anything like it," Rentzel said. Though he rose and remained in the game, his back hurt him the rest of the day.

Dallas was driving, but on a play that proved to be a foreshadowing of things to come, Caffey slowed the Cowboys' march by breaking into the backfield on a pitchout and knocking Reeves to the ice for a four-yard loss. Meredith followed with an incomplete pass to Rentzel, who was still having trouble breathing in the icy air. Facing third-and-14, Meredith dropped back to pass, but with his receivers having trouble running their intricate patterns on the slick surface, he broke from the pocket. Running to his left, Meredith negotiated nine frozen yards before Caffey slammed him from behind and stripped the ball loose. Green Bay left cornerback Herb Adderley fell on the fumble at the Packers' 13, and middle linebacker Ray Nitschke ensured the turnover when he dropped and covered Adderley in his padded arms.

Though Reeves gained 50 yards running and receiving in the third quarter and the Cowboys made repeated stabs into Green Bay territory, Caffey continually stepped up to make the key defensive play. A fourth-year linebacker out of Texas A&M, the 6 ft. 3 in., 250-pound Caffey was the least known of Green Bay's outstanding linebacking trio, which Dallas head coach Tom Landry recognized at the time as "the best in football."

As a threesome, Nitschke, Robinson, and Caffey appeared to be stamped out of a cookie cutter. Each was 6 ft. 3 in. and approximately 250 pounds, and all three earned all-pro honors in the midsixties. Though their backgrounds differed, their lifestyles were strikingly similar. Each had three children, and each was married for more than 20 years. Fittingly, they each eventually retired in a city close to their roots. A native of Illinois, Nitschke retired following a 15-year career with Green Bay. Robinson, an easterner who was born in New Jersey, retired with the Washington Redskins following his 12th season; and Caffey, a southwesterner from Thorndale, Texas left the NFL in his 10th season following a short stint with the San Diego Chargers.

Of the three, Caffey was the most frequent target of head coach Vince Lombardi's criticisms. Though Lombardi looked on all his players much as a stern but loving father looks upon his offspring, there were several players whom the coach referred to as his "gifted children." The gifted ones, like Caffey, were those expected to excel because of their God-given abilities. When they failed to perform at the level Lombardi felt they should, they felt his wrath on the practice field.

Caffey had a casual attitude towards football practice, and at times loafed through linebacker drills, infuriating Lombardi. "Caffey, that stinks! You have the size, the strength, the speed, the mobility, everything in the world necessary to be a great football player, except one thing. You're too damn lazy!"

In quieter moments, he would pull his linebacker aside and tell him, "Lee Roy, if you cheat on the practice field, you'll cheat in the game. If you cheat in the game, you'll cheat the rest of your life. I'll not have it."

Looking to rebuild his aging linebacking corps in 1964, Lombardi was initially excited to obtain Caffey in a trade with Philadelphia. The Eagles selected Caffey out of Texas A&M, which he had originally attended on a basketball scholarship, picking him up on the seventh round of the '63 draft. Caffey played fullback and linebacker with the Aggies, but on draft day weighed just 208 pounds. When the Eagles told him to report to camp at 240, Caffey went on a diet of egg-filled milk shakes and began a strict weightlifting program.

Caffey was with the Eagles for one season before being sent to Green Bay in a highly-publicized trade involving Packers' all-pro center Jim Ringo. But Caffey's poor practice attitude concerned Lombardi, who told him in 1964, "You don't have this ball club made by a long shot! You might not be here five minutes, you big turkey!" Lombardi, the master motivator, tried several methods in search of a way to inspire Caffey to play better. Sideline footage shows him threatening Caffey with job security. "I'll tell you, Lee Roy, you're not going to get your job back unless we get a better performance."

Contract negotiations during the off-season found the two men across the table from one another, and Lombardi would tell Caffey, "You may wonder why I yell at you a lot. Every team has to have a whipping boy, and I use you as my whipping boy."

"I don't care how you use me," Caffey responded, "just as long as you pay me."

Despite his constant criticism, Lombardi made Caffey one of the highest paid linebackers in the NFL. Though he started at right out-side linebacker, Caffey could also fill in at middle linebacker, which he did when Nitschke was hurt in 1965. Caffey's first start at his new position was one of the turning points of his career. In a game against division rival Detroit, Caffey struggled early as the Lions jumped to a 21-3 halftime lead. During the break, he was so upset with the belief his play was costing the Packers, he had tears run-ning down his cheeks as he sat in front of his locker. But one by one, Packer players began dropping by.

"Now Lee Roy," Nitschke said, "here's what you did wrong." As Nitschke gave him a crash course in middle linebacking, Starr patted Caffey on the back. "Don't worry," Starr said. "We're going to win."

Buoyed by the confidence of his teammates, Caffey played an inspired second half, and his blitzes helped shut out the Lions as Starr threw three touchdown passes and ran for a fourth in a 31-21 win. At that point, Caffey realized what made the Packers special.

"It was all the guys, working together," he said. "We never got down on one of our teammates when he wasn't playing well."

As the third quarter of the '67 championship entered its final minutes, the Cowboys were threatening again. Taking over on the Green Bay 44 following a short punt from the Packers' Don Chandler, Dallas began another drive. Again it was Reeves who was the Cowboys' catalyst. On first down, he swept left for 11 yards before Caffey combined with cornerback Bob Jeter to bring him down. Meredith found Reeves for a three-yard gain, and Reeves ran right for two more.

As the Cowboys huddled on third-and-five at the Green Bay 30, Packers' defensive coordinator Phil Bengston sent in a daring call. In his nine years as Lombardi's chief defensive lieutenant, Bengston had used various signals to communicate his call from the sidelines to Nitschke on the field.

In earlier years, Bengston had waggled his fingers for a blitz, and Nitschke in turn called the play in the defensive huddle. When opponents started to pick up on Bengston's call from their sideline, he changed it to more subtle signals, such as straightening his tie, adjusting the brim of his fedora, or tossing a blade of grass in the air as if he were testing wind direction. Bengston changed his blitz signals frequently to keep teams from decoding his silent messages. At times the Packer coach delivered two signals, and depending on whether Bengston slipped his hand in his pants pocket or not, Nitschke knew the second signal preempted the first.

Bengston's decision in this key third-down situation against the Cowboys was to send Caffey on a weak-side linebacker blitz. It was the perfect call. Since Dallas scouting reports noted that the Packers blitzed their linebackers on third downs less than 5 percent of the time, they weren't expecting such a play. Also, Bengston knew the Cowboys had been victimized by several weak-side blitzes during the year. Meredith was injured in the fourth game of the season after suffering a clothesline tackle by the Washington Redskins weak-side linebacker, Chris Hanburger.

With the Cowboys unprepared to pick up the blitz, Caffey shot into the Dallas backfield and hit Meredith high, dropping him for a nine-yard loss. It was Caffey's fifth tackle of the quarter and his seventh of the game, and it was a crucial play that pushed Dallas further out of field-goal range. Villaneuva's subsequent 47-yard attempt fell four yards short.

Big plays by the Packer defense prevented the Cowboys from scoring in the third quarter, but Dallas defenders delivered far more bruising punishment to Green Bay's offense. Starr was sacked three more times in the third quarter as Jethro Pugh, George Andrie, and Dave Edwards took turns knocking him to the hard ground. The word around the NFL on stopping Lombardi's offense was to gang-tackle them and break down their precision. "Doomsday" did that in the third quarter, yielding just one first down and a total of eight yards.

As the cold intensified, so did the hitting. Neely remembered seeing Reeves' lip split open following a hard tackle, but because it was so cold, there wasn't any trace of blood. Neely spent the afternoon dueling Green Bay all-pro Willie Davis, whom he still regards as the best defensive end he faced in his career.

"I played against a lot of great defensive ends," Neely said. "Willie Davis, Deacon Jones, Bubba Smith, Jim Marshall. Jones was probably faster than Willie, but for intelligence and all-around ability, Willie was a more complete player.

"Willie was a delight to play against because there was no mouthing. If anything, he'd get up as we walked by each other and say, 'Good block.' It was always business. He'd try to knock the hell out of you, make no mistake about that. But there was no trash.

"I was always a Packers fan. Except for when we played them, I always rooted for the Packers. You could get a bunch of players together in a room during a Pro Bowl game, and within five minutes, the Cowboys and Packers would migrate together. We'd all be sitting together, drinking beer or whatever. There was a tremendous amount of mutual respect for each other. When Herb Adderley and Forrest Gregg came over to play for us near the end of their careers, they were happy to be with the Cowboys."

The intensity of the game, however, strained relations between players. After his missed tackle allowed Don Perkins to gain five yards during the second half, Nitschke kicked at the ground in a fit of frustration and anger. Some Cowboy players, however, thought Nitschke's kick was aimed at Perkins. Reeves in particular, became incensed, calling Nitschke "an animal."

But Nitschke wasn't angry with Perkins. He was mad at himself for not making the play when he had the opportunity. The previous January, Perkins had become the first and only back to ever rush for 100 yards in a playoff game against Phil Bengston's defense, when he gained 108 yards on 17 carries.

At 5-10, 200 pounds, Perkins wasn't fast on long runs, but he had great acceleration in short bursts. He could cover ten yards faster than anyone in football, and he was strong and tough; he once played an entire quarter with a broken arm. From 1963 until his retirement following the 1968 season, Perkins was one of the NFL's best backs, running for 6,217 yards and averaging 4.1 yards per carry. Many of his yards came despite playing behind a weak offensive line in the Cowboys' formative years. He played in five Pro Bowl games, and gave the fledgling Cowboys credibility. A gentleman who exhibited virtually no ego, Perkins retired from the game following the '68 season to spend more time with his family.

Since Perkins was primarily his responsibility, Nitschke made up his mind prior to the title game in Green Bay that Perkins wasn't going to get anywhere near 100 yards again. On this play, Nitschke diagnosed the play and hit Perkins at the line of scrimmage, but the Cowboy back wouldn't go down. Nitschke tried to get his arms around him, but Perkins bounced off and picked up five yards.

"I kicked the ground because I was disgusted with myself," Nitschke said. "I didn't have anything against Perkins."

Defense dominated the third quarter, but the Dallas offense reversed the trend on the first play of the fourth quarter. Rentzel noticed that Reeves' success on the left-side sweep was causing right cornerback

Bob Jeter and free safety Willie Wood to step up to stop the run. Rentzel passed the information along to Meredith during a timeout between quarters, and suggested a play to the Dallas quarterback, who was facing second-and-five at midfield.

"This is what we've been waiting for," Rentzel said in a burst of frosty air. "They're playing the run. Let's throw the option."

Meredith nodded, bent into the huddle, and through frozen lips, called "Fire Pitch." Designed by Landry, "Fire Pitch" was a half-back option pass from Reeves to Rentzel, and as was often the case, it worked to playbook perfection *(See Diagram 7)*.

Over the course of the 1966 and '67 seasons, Reeves had thrown 13 option passes, completing seven of those for two touchdowns. A quarterback at South Carolina, Reeves usually took Meredith's handoff and swept to his right, where he had the option of throwing or running.

Realizing teams would be ready for the option right, Landry gave the play a new look by sending Reeves rolling to his left. Because the play would force Reeves, who was right-handed, into the unnatural position of having to stop, turn his body, and throw, Landry figured defenses would never expect such a maneuver.

The play had resulted in a big gain against the Philadelphia Eagles earlier in the season, and it caught the Packers by surprise. Reeves took Meredith's handoff and swept left, just as he had several times before during the game. Wood, an all-pro veteran, saw Rentzel take a wide position at the line, which indicated a pass play. When Wood and Jeter saw Reeves running to his left, they immediately thought "sweep," and rushed to stop him. Rentzel simulated a run block on Wood to fool Jeter, then headed downfield past the startled cornerback.

"Oh my Lord," Jeter thought. "What have I done?" In the Packers' coaching booth, defensive backfield coach Jerry Burns gasped. One of Green Bay's main coaching points for the secondary was "You cannot play defensive halfback or safety without knowing where your help is at all times." Wood and Jeter had violated their own principle on this play by not communicating, and it cost them.

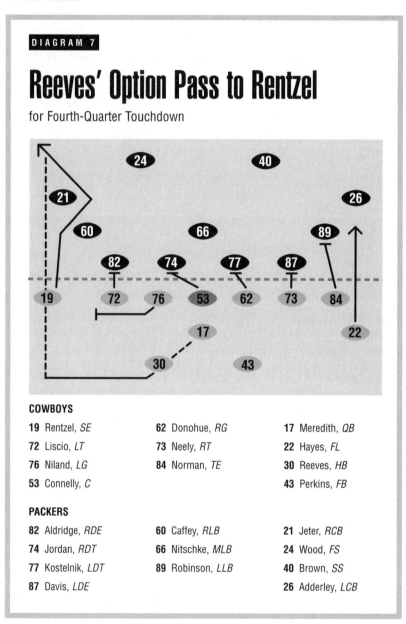

DIAGRAM 7

Reeves' Option Pass to Rentzel

for Fourth-Quarter Touchdown

COWBOYS

19 Rentzel, *SE*	**62** Donohue, *RG*	**17** Meredith, *QB*
72 Liscio, *LT*	**73** Neely, *RT*	**22** Hayes, *FL*
76 Niland, *LG*	**84** Norman, *TE*	**30** Reeves, *HB*
53 Connelly, *C*		**43** Perkins, *FB*

PACKERS

82 Aldridge, *RDE*	**60** Caffey, *RLB*	**21** Jeter, *RCB*
74 Jordan, *RDT*	**66** Nitschke, *MLB*	**24** Wood, *FS*
77 Kostelnik, *LDT*	**89** Robinson, *LLB*	**40** Brown, *SS*
87 Davis, *LDE*		**26** Adderley, *LCB*

"I was slow mentally on that play," Jeter said later. "We knew all about Reeves' option pass (but) I didn't react. Wood moved up to meet the run. It was my job to drop back and protect against any pass. I saw Reeves cock his arm. I tried to get back, but when the ball was in the air, I knew it was gone."

Seeing Reeves' pass arcing through the late afternoon sunshine, Rentzel suddenly experienced an inner warmth. "It was going to be a touchdown," he said later. "I really knew it, and it was the most marvelous feeling in the world."

The feeling was fleeting. Rentzel looked back over his shoulder for the pass, and realized it was short. "I have to slow down," he thought. "No, I have to stop! I'm going to slip on the ice!"

Feeling his feet sliding out from under him, Rentzel watched as the ball changed directions in the wind. He kept his balance by standing still, and hauled in the frozen ball. Praying for solid traction as he ran, he outraced strong safety Tom Brown to the corner of the end zone. "When I crossed that goal line," Rentzel said, "I was suddenly very warm."

Moore's call on WTMJ was accompanied by the stunned silence of the Lambeau crowd:

"Cowboys out of the huddle, up to the line of scrimmage. Second down and five at the 50-yard line. There's a pitchout to Reeves, he'll throw the option pass, way downfield. . . . It is complete to Lance Rentzel! He's at the ten, the five, and into the end zone for the touchdown!

"A pitchout from Don Meredith to Dan Reeves, who went to his left and threw the option pass to Lance Rentzel, a 50-yard touchdown pass . . . and the Dallas Cowboys have taken a 16–14 lead over the Green Bay Packers very early in the fourth period. . . ."

The touchdown carried a note of irony, since the halfback option was Lombardi's pet play, and had been since he and Landry were coaching colleagues in New York nine years before. And the two backs who had made it famous were both in attendance—Frank Gifford in the press box and Paul Hornung as a guest on the Green Bay sideline.

Given the lead for the first time at 17–14 following Danny Villaneuva's extra point, the great Dallas defense went out to win it. They allowed the battered Packer offense one minor drive, but it stalled on the Cowboys' 33, and Chandler's 40-yard field goal to tie the game fell short.

Meredith led the Cowboys back onto the field with 9:44 remaining, and the feeling in their huddle was to keep the ball as long as they could and run the clock down. But the frozen field and the fired-up Green Bay defense prevented it. Dallas did manage two first downs, but with his backs and receivers slipping on the ice, Meredith threw incomplete on second and third down and the Cowboys were forced to punt. Villanueva's kick was handled by Wood on his own 23, and he returned it nine yards to the 32.

There was 4:50 showing on the scoreboard clock as the Packer offense took the field for the last time. Separating them from a date with destiny was 68 yards of ice-slick turf and a defense known as "Doomsday."

Chapter Twelve

The Drive

HERE WAS SOMETHING SOMBER IN THE GRAYING SKIES over Green Bay as the Packers huddled on their own 32-yard line late in the fourth quarter. The brilliant sunshine that marked the early afternoon hours of this New Year's Eve day was fading fast. The sun, which seemed to have spent itself in a futile effort to provide temperatures warmer than 13 below zero, had grown pale. Surrendering to the bitter cold, it began a rapid descent behind the scoreboard at Lambeau Field, leaving the field covered by shadows.

Buffeted by a slashing wind and battered by the Dallas defense, the Packers had managed just two first downs since the second quarter. They had lost a two-touchdown lead, and now trailed 17–14. Equal parts ice and frozen dirt stained their yellow-gold pants and forest green jerseys, and the reflection of the stadium lights flared on their bright yellow helmets. Green Bay head coach Vince Lombardi shoved his gloved hands deep into the pockets of his beige camel-hair overcoat. His face was bright red from the cold, and the gap-toothed grin that had flashed when the Packers led in the early going was replaced by a hard, thin line.

Across the field, the Dallas sideline was warmed by what receiver Lance Rentzel called "a fantastic feeling" that accompanied a victory they could finally anticipate, a victory that seemed too good to be true.

"I thought we were going to win the game," Dallas offensive tackle Ralph Neely remembered. "We were having some success at that point."

To some observers, the gloaming descending on Green Bay was symbolic. The men that Lombardi had pushed and pulled and wrung every emotion from for nine years were aging. They were men of declining skill, and many were contemplating retirement. For frost-bitten Packer fans, this was the twilight of their gods.

Green Bay right guard Jerry Kramer had spent a long afternoon hand-fighting Dallas defensive tackle Jethro Pugh to a standoff. Kramer was one of the best drive-blockers of his era, and he had moved Pugh on running plays. But the immensely strong Cowboy tackle had beaten Kramer on occasion when he slipped past him for a sack. As Kramer bent his battle-scarred helmet into the huddle, the Packers' all-pro felt the razor-sharp gusts of wind, and experienced a sudden, sinking feeling. Maybe, he felt, the time had come for the Packers to lose. Kramer, however, refused to resign himself to defeat. If we do lose, he thought, we'll go down swinging.

Setting the tone for Green Bay's drive to destiny was quarterback Bart Starr. Though some have criticized him as Lombardi's robot, Starr was his own man as a field general. He was in total command when it came to calling plays, and he exerted authority over both his personnel and his coach. When Lombardi would stick his head into a Packers' practice huddle and say, "All right now. I want you to run a 36," Starr would respond, "Wait just a minute. I'm running this huddle." On such occasions, Lombardi quietly stepped back.

Bill Curry, who played center for both the Packers and the Baltimore Colts during the sixties, said that while legendary quarterback John Unitas carried himself in a charismatic way, he lacked Starr's presence of leadership. "Starr," Curry said, "was the *master* of the huddle."

With his body already wracked by the rigors of a long season of injuries, Starr had endured additional punishment at the hands of the Dallas defenders, who broke down his blocking and sacked him eight times for losses totaling 76 yards. He had been knocked to the stone-cold surface on several other occasions just as he released the ball, and the repeated groundings left the southern gentleman battered soft like a bruised Georgia peach.

Yet just as he had throughout his career, Starr reacted to the tough, pressure-filled situation with pure steel. With conditions steadily worsening, he knew, as all the Packers did, that this would be their last opportunity to mount a sustained drive. Starr looked at the faces in the huddle, and thought everyone wore a look that said somehow, some way, they were going to win the game. "It was," he said, "the greatest feeling in the world."

In a voice raw and hoarse from shouting signals in the biting wind, Starr said firmly, "Let's get it done."

As the sun set behind the scoreboard, huge shadows were cast across the field. The temperature was now minus-19 degrees, with a wind-chill factor estimated at 46 below zero.

Several of the players were suffering frostbite in their fingers and toes; Green Bay middle linebacker Ray Nitschke's feet were so numb they felt detached from his body. Six of his toes were blistered from frostbite, and his feet were swelling inside his shoes.

Despite the brutal weather conditions and the lateness of the hour, fullback Chuck Mercein felt a surge of confidence in the huddle.

"Starr had a very commanding presence," Mercein said, "but in a very quiet way. He was a tremendous leader, and tremendously respected, and so whatever he would say, it was enough. He wasn't a big talker in the huddle; he didn't say a lot of things. But at the beginning of that drive, according to my recollection, he did say, 'Let's get it done,' something just as simple as that, nothing rah-rah. But I do remember very well the feeling in the huddle, which was calm, poised, and confident. There wasn't any nervousness; I didn't feel any panic. I just felt a tremendous solidarity and determination."

Halfback Donny Anderson shared that determination, and he attributed the feeling to his head coach. "Nine years of Vince Lombardi was in that huddle with us," he said.

Though he was far removed from the huddle, WTMJ announcer Ted Moore felt that same confidence.

"After doing Green Bay games for eight years," Moore recalled, "I felt that as long as that guy in the camel-hair coat was on the sidelines, the Packers could pull the game out."

Bolstered by Lombardi's fire and Starr's cool command, the Packer offense looked at the frozen landscape that was Lambeau Field, and with the confidence of champions, set out to conquer it.

"That was the point," Starr said later, "where our mental conditioning took over."

First-and-ten at the Green Bay 32; 4:50 remaining: Starr began the drive with a play-action pass to Anderson. Before the Packer offense took the field, Anderson had talked to Starr on the sidelines and told him he could get open because the Dallas linebackers were dropping back to help double cover the wide receivers. Starr processed the information, and after faking to both backs, took a short drop in the pocket.

In the WTMJ booth, Moore began the play-by-play radio call of what he remembers as the most historic drive he's ever covered:

"Starr . . . begins the count, takes the snap. Play-action pass, he's back to throw, gets the pass away, it's complete to Donny Anderson . . . Anderson's across the 35 to the 38-yard line . . ."

Game films show Anderson roll behind Starr following the faked handoff, then drift into the flat. Sensing pressure up the middle from Dallas defensive tackle Bob Lilly, Starr kept the Cowboy linebackers off guard by not looking in Anderson's direction until the last second. He took a short step to his right to evade Lilly, then passed to Anderson, who gained six yards before being stopped by cornerback Cornell Green and outside linebacker Chuck Howley.

Second-and-four at the Green Bay 38; 4:27 remaining: With the Dallas defenders back on their heels, Starr turned and handed off to

Mercein, who picked up a textbook block by Anderson on Howley and ran right for seven yards before being wrestled out of bounds by Lee Roy Jordan.

Moore: *"Starr . . . hands off to Chuck Mercein . . . sweep to the right side, he's out of bounds near the 45-yard line. Lee Roy Jordan knocks him out of bounds and the Packers have a first down . . ."*

As Dallas middle linebacker, it was Jordan's job to match wits with Starr. Considered by many the inspirational leader of the "Doomsday" defense, Jordan, like Starr, was a graduate of the University of Alabama, where he earned All-America status and was called by Crimson Tide head coach Paul "Bear" Bryant "the finest athlete I ever coached." Like Starr, Jordan was a student of the game. During the final five years of his career, he made it a point to have his contract with the Cowboys include a home projector so he could watch game films after hours.

Drafted by the Cowboys in 1963, Jordan originally played out-side linebacker his rookie year before being sidelined for the final six games by a kidney injury. His physical toughness and intelligent play impressed Cowboy coaches, who moved him to middle linebacker in 1964. At 6 ft. 2 in., 215 pounds, Jordan was small for the position, particularly when compared to the other great middle men of his era—Ray Nitschke, Dick Butkus, Tommy Nobis—all of whom were in the 6-3, 250-pound range. But his fierce play earned him the nickname "Killer," and he used his massive hands to tear the ball loose from opposing runners. Cowboy line coach Ernie Stautner said at the time that if Jordan weighed as much as Butkus, "they'd have to outlaw him from football."

Jordan brought an intensity to big downs that few of his defensive peers could match. He was the vocal leader on the field, rallying his teammates individually and demanding they raise their intensity to match the moment. As the Green Bay drive began to gain the momentum of a slow-moving glacier, Jordan exhorted the Cowboys to make a big defensive play.

First-and-ten at the Green Bay 45; 3:57 remaining: Having tested the

Dallas flank with both the short pass and the outside running game, Starr hit Boyd Dowler over the middle with a medium-range pass. The big flanker had been double-teamed following his two touchdown receptions earlier in the day, but he shook free and made the catch at the Dallas 45.

Moore: *"The Packers are going to have to keep this drive going. . . . Starr takes a quick snap from center, back to throw, spots his man, fires, and the pass is complete to Boyd Dowler at the 42-yard line and Dowler is belted to the ground . . ."*

Fighting for extra yardage, Dowler was grabbed from behind by Green, forearmed in the helmet by linebacker Dave Edwards and then spun to the ground, where his head banged violently off the glazed turf. Amazingly, he held onto the ball, but the double blow left Dowler stunned, and he headed to the sidelines, replaced by 35-year-old Max McGee, whose seven catches and two touchdowns had made him the hero of Super Bowl I.

First-and-ten at the Dallas 42; 3:30 remaining: With the ball inside Dallas territory, Starr decided to switch tactics again. Having hurt the Cowboys with a pass over the middle, he sent Anderson wide on an option sweep to the right. But Dallas left end Willie Townes anticipated the play and ran untouched between the Packers' pulling guards, Kramer and Gale Gillingham. Townes grabbed Anderson deep in the backfield and, with a massive bear-hug, dropped him for a nine-yard loss.

Moore: *"Green Bay at the line of scrimmage . . . Starr begins the count, gives off to Anderson and Anderson is nailed . . ."*

Townes' big play was his second of the game. His second quarter hit on Starr resulted in a fumble recovery and touchdown by defensive end George Andrie. Townes' speed was a continuing source of surprise to the Packers. Listed at 6 ft. 5 in., 260, Townes played heavier than that. His teammates called him "Baby Cakes" because of his on-going weight problem, and he ate his team meals at the camp's "Fat Man Table."

Yet he remained exceptionally fast for his size, and his speed was even more deceiving because he had the long strides of a hurdler, which he had been at the University of Tulsa. A second-round pick by the Cowboys in the 1966 draft, Townes was hit with several $500 fines for being overweight. Tired of turning his money back over to the team, Townes bought what he called "heavy scales" and weighed himself at home. He later told team officials the fines were unfair because the sea level was different in Dallas. "It makes you five pounds heavier," he said.

Townes' play on Anderson brought a sense of satisfaction to coach Ernie Stautner. The Cowboys required each of their rookies to take personality tests, and Townes' answers revealed a man whose relaxed attitude masked a sense of insecurity common to first-year players. But Stautner worked to make Townes more aggressive, and he made several spectacular plays during the 1967 season.

Second-and-19 at the Green Bay 49; 2:52 remaining: Returning to a play that worked earlier in the drive, Starr looked left and passed right to Anderson. Having concealed himself behind Kramer and tackle Forrest Gregg in the Green Bay blocking scheme, Anderson was again left open in the right flat. Catching the ball at midfield, Anderson sidestepped Howley, who slipped to the ice, and gained 11 more yards to the Dallas 39 before being tripped up from behind by a diving ankle tackle from Pugh.

Moore: *"Starr takes the snap, he's back to throw. . . . He's got the time, flips out to the right side to Donny Anderson! Gets by one man and is down to the 39 of the Dallas Cowboys . . ."*

Across the frozen tundra of Lambeau Field drove a Green Bay offense determined to make up for miscues that had provided Dallas with 10 points. Dowler said later that although the Cowboys' offense only made one big play all day, that being the Reeves' option pass for a touchdown, they still had 17 points on the board. Starr said the offense felt responsible for the tough situation it was in. His fumble gave Dallas one touchdown, and Willie Wood's fumble gave them a field goal. Said Starr, "I know that definitely crossed my mind."

It crossed Nitschke's mind as well. Standing on frost-bitten feet on the Packers' sideline, he shook his frozen right fist into the air and in his gravel-like voice shouted to the offense, "Don't let me down! Don't let me down!"

Third-and-eight at the Dallas 39; 2:00 remaining: With his wide receivers having difficulty running their patterns on the ice, Starr continued to focus on his backs. Since Dowler was out of the game, the Cowboys had rotated their double-coverage to end Carroll Dale. Realizing the Cowboys were still playing him loose, Anderson relayed the information to Starr.

"Bart," he said, "if you'll dump the ball off to me, I can pick up eight or ten yards every play."

Taking seven steps straight back in the pocket, Starr threw to Anderson on the right side. Catching the pass at the 37, Anderson skated over the slick ice and again eluded Howley, who slipped and fell at the 35. Known to his teammates as "Hogmeat," Howley was one of the top outside linebackers of his era, and a key member of the Doomsday defense. A six-time Pro Bowl player, he was regarded as an outstanding open-field tackler, but he was victimized twice on this drive by the slippery conditions.

Moore: *"We have two minutes remaining in this football game. The Green Bay Packers are down by three points . . . Starr takes the ball, backpedals, looks downfield, flips a short pass . . . complete to Anderson! He's at the 35, moves to the 30 and the Packers have a first down!"*

Safety Mel Renfro hit Anderson at the 32, but the halfback, who at 225 pounds had a 35-pound weight advantage over the Cowboys' all-pro, fell forward for an additional two yards.

First-and-ten at the Dallas 30; 1:35 remaining: Though Mercein rarely said anything to Starr in the huddle, he did approach him following Anderson's two receptions. "I'm open in the left flat," Mercein told Starr, "if you need me."

Starr again made good use of the information given him by a teammate. With his breath forming a frozen vapor trail, Starr took a seven-step drop straight back, and seeing the Cowboys converge on Dale, passed to Mercein in the left flat.

Moore: *"This is a crucial drive, everything from here on in is crucial. Starr takes the snap from center, he's back to throw, flips a pass. . . . It's complete to Chuck Mercein! He's at the 25, the 20, up to the 15, and out of bounds at about the 11! Chuck Mercein, the taxi-squad refugee, has again proven he was a good acquisition for the Green Bay Packers . . .*

"And the Packers have finally solved this great Dallas Cowboys rush. . . . They're throwing the short ones out to the side, throwing the screens, the pops up the middle . . ."

Mercein was not the primary receiver on the play, but as Starr said, "if the linebacker doesn't pick Chuck up immediately when he comes out into his pattern, then I hit him. I saw (right linebacker Dave Edwards) freeze, so I hit Mercein quick. He made the rest of it on his own."

The catch was not an easy one. Films showed the pass to be behind Mercein and to his left, forcing him to twist and make a half-turn to his right.

Mercein put up both hands to grab the ball, and his first thought was of the odd feel of the frozen leather. He pulled the ball in at the 31-yard line in front of Edwards. A three-year starter, Edwards was considered the unsung hero of the Dallas defense. Though he wasn't particularly fast, Edwards used his great strength to control the line of scrimmage. He had tremendously strong hands, and ball carriers found it difficult to escape his grasp. Mercein however, eluded Edwards' reach at the Dallas 25, and got to the 15 before he was pushed off-balance by cornerback Mike Johnson. Still striving for extra yardage, Mercein dove forward, extending his body parallel to the ground as he belly-flopped out of bounds at the 11, completing a 19-yard gain.

The irony of this historic drive is that its success came about because of the Cowboys' own attention to detail. Jordan noticed through film study during the previous off-season that opposing quarterbacks completed medium-range passes on the Cowboys because Dallas linebackers weren't dropping back far enough in coverage.

"As a group, our linebackers weren't consistently getting depth on pass coverage," Jordan said. "We were too worried about screen passes."

Under the direction of linebacker coach Jerry Tubbs, the Cowboys worked on getting deeper drops. But Starr was exploiting their drop coverage by throwing short passes in front of them and relying on Anderson and Mercein to gain yards after the catch.

"Those linebackers weren't able to cover the backs," Mercein remembered. "The two outside linebackers were taking straight drops, like a cornerback would drop, and that way they could maintain their balance, and they could see the field. That was basically the way they were playing their defense, and by just swinging out and getting outside of them, once you did that you were open.

"We weren't the primary receivers, but because of the field conditions and because of the lack of mobility of the outside linebackers, we both were more than safety valves. We were open. They were pretty safe passes too, although the pass to me was kind of high and outside. It kind of floated up there. I wouldn't say Bart pulled the string on it, but he really wanted to be safe and make sure he got it there. Sometimes when that happens, you don't throw it as hard as you might want to and the ball sails a little bit. I don't know if the wind got under it, but I had to jump and make an awkward turn to catch it."

First-and-ten at the Dallas 11; 1:11 remaining: Having just connected with Mercein for a 19-yard gain on a swing pass, Starr called his fullback's number again. The play was "Brown right, 65-Give."

A potentially dangerous play, "65-Give" refuted the critic's claims that Starr was an unimaginative quarterback. The play was aimed at Lilly, the Cowboys' best defender. The design of "65-Give" was for Gillingham to pull right from his guard position as if he were leading Green Bay's famed power sweep. The Packers were banking on the fact that Lilly, a quick and intelligent player, would read Gillingham's pull and follow him down the line. Mercein, who was lined up directly behind Starr, would take the handoff and hit the opening left vacant by Lilly.

The danger was that Lilly was left unblocked. Earlier in the game, he had foiled a Packer sweep by pursuing the play down the line. If he didn't read the sweep again and follow Gillingham, Lilly would be in perfect position to drill Mercein in the backfield.

The Packers used the "give" play sparingly, and Starr hadn't called it all afternoon. In the huddle, he asked left tackle Bob Skoronski if he could get a good block on Dallas defensive end George Andrie, who would be responsible for filling the hole.

"Call it," Skoronski said.

Starr still regards this as the best play he ever called under pressure. The Packers had been saving it for the right time. "This," said Starr, "was the time."

Clapping his gloved hands together in a muffled *clump* as the Packers broke from their huddle, Gillingham spun and headed towards the line. A second-year guard out of the University of Minnesota, Gillingham had replaced the aging Fuzzy Thurston as left guard for the Packers during the 1967 season. His first season had been a learning experience for Gillingham, who patterned his play after Thurston and Kramer. The season opener against Detroit resulted in a 17–17 tie and what Gillingham called "the longest game I can remember." Playing against Lions' veteran Jerry Rush, who may have had the best surname of any defensive tackle ever, Gillingham had endured a difficult afternoon.

As good as Rush was, Lilly provided even more of a problem for Gillingham. "He was very big, very agile, and very quick," Gillingham said. While some tackles were considered "dancers" who would grab a guard by the shoulders, pull to one side and move around him, others were strong enough to simply run over their offensive counterparts. Lilly, Gillingham said, was a combination of both types. "And," he added, "(Lilly) adds a few more (moves) of his own."

The play worked just as diagrammed (*See Diagram 8*). Positioned directly behind Starr, Mercein took the handoff and headed straight upfield. Gillingham pulled out and to his right, as did Anderson. Reading sweep, Lilly took two steps in the Green Bay backfield before he realized it was an influence play. Andrie, who was supposed to cover Lilly's vacated area, slipped on the ice and was covered by Skoronski. Mercein ran through the gaping hole to the five, where he was hit low by Renfro. He bounced off both Renfro and his own man, Forrest Gregg, who had pulled out from his right tackle position to provide downfield blocking. Mercein was finally brought down at the three by another low tackle, this time by Johnson.

Moore: *"Starr has the team at the line . . . takes the snap. . . . It's to Mercein! Pops up the middle . . . inside the five, to the two-yard line! Chuck, how about this one?"*

Chuck Johnson: *"I think Bart caught them looking for something else on that last play, when Mercein went over left guard and down to the three-yard line . . ."*

"It was a *great* call," Mercein said, looking back. "Just a great call. We had run the sweep out of the 'Brown' formation, which is the formation where the fullback is lined up directly behind the center and quarterback. In the 'Brown' formation, you can still run the sweep with the guards pulling. What happens is that the fullback replaces the left guard that pulls and blocks the left tackle, which in this case is Bob Lilly.

"Lilly is so fast and so quick and such a good reader that as soon as our left guard, Gale Gillingham, would pull, Lilly would just follow him down the line of scrimmage and try to make the play from behind, disrupting the sweep. I was finding on those particular sweeps that I was almost clipping Lilly. I wasn't blocking him in the hole, I was blocking him down the line of scrimmage. So what this meant was that if you did have the guts to call the 'give' or influence play, he better take that influence and go down the

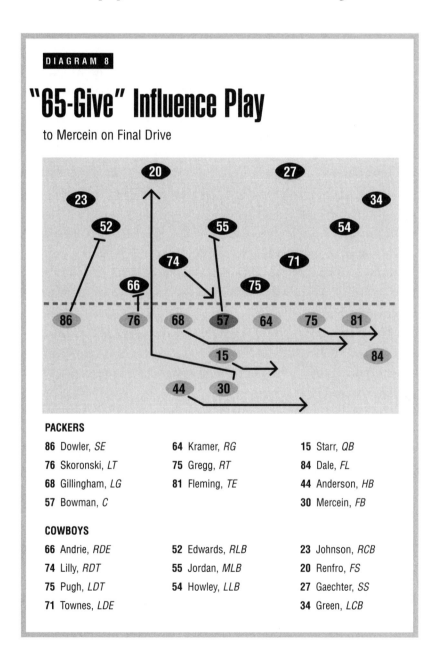

DIAGRAM 8

"65-Give" Influence Play

to Mercein on Final Drive

PACKERS

86 Dowler, *SE*	**64** Kramer, *RG*	**15** Starr, *QB*
76 Skoronski, *LT*	**75** Gregg, *RT*	**84** Dale, *FL*
68 Gillingham, *LG*	**81** Fleming, *TE*	**44** Anderson, *HB*
57 Bowman, *C*		**30** Mercein, *FB*

COWBOYS

66 Andrie, *RDE*	**52** Edwards, *RLB*	**23** Johnson, *RCB*
74 Lilly, *RDT*	**55** Jordan, *MLB*	**20** Renfro, *FS*
75 Pugh, *LDT*	**54** Howley, *LLB*	**27** Gaechter, *SS*
71 Townes, *LDE*		**34** Green, *LCB*

line. Otherwise I'm going to be taking the ball and running into this massive guy and anything can happen.

"But Lilly was true to form, and did take the influence of the guard pulling and followed him down the line of scrimmage. Bart, instead of faking to me and handing to Donny on the sweep, gives me the ball, and I run right through a vacated hole. Another important part of that play was that Skoronski made a great seal block on their defensive end."

Along with being known as an influence play, the "give" play is also called a "sucker" play because the offense is trying to sucker the targeted defender out of position. In Lilly's case, the Packers have always refrained from using the term "sucker" because they felt it demeaned the Cowboys' tackle, whom they respected greatly. Lombardi called Lilly "the heart and soul" of the Dallas defense.

"That play wouldn't have worked against a slower player," Mercein said, and Dowler agreed. "You couldn't run that against a big slow guy," Dowler said, "because he would be standing there in the hole."

The films show Lilly doing what he was supposed to, which was follow the guard. Green Bay's big threat was the halfback sweep, and three times in the first half Lilly had caught Travis Williams from behind on the play.

"George Andrie was supposed to move into the gap and make the play," Lilly said. "George did what he was supposed to do, too. He moved in, but it was slick on that frozen field and he slipped and fell down. And that was it."

Still, the play has irked Lilly for years. "I ran into Bob a few years ago," Mercein said, "and he said to me, 'You know, Chuck, that play was not my responsibility.'"

Second-and-two at the Dallas three; 54 seconds remaining: Following the first of their allotted three timeouts, the Packers ran a goal-line play that Paul Hornung had made famous in the early sixties.

Moore: *"The Packers are at the line of scrimmage . . . the handoff to Donny Anderson, he is very close. He's got the first down but he doesn't have the touchdown . . . he smashed over right tackle. He is inside the two-yard line . . ."*

Anderson veered left on a quick trap and plunged headlong, just as Hornung used to, into the middle of the line. Jordan, Howley, and Renfro converged on Anderson at the one.

First-and-goal at the Dallas one; 30 seconds remaining: Conserving a timeout, the Packers huddled quickly. Gillingham told Starr, "Run over there. Run that '55-Special.' They can't stop that."

The "55-Special" was designed for Anderson, who was lined up to Starr's left, to run behind Kramer and Gregg. When Starr called the play, Kramer thought, "Well, this is it, toad. They're putting it directly on your back. Yours and Forrest's."

Moore: *"The clock is running . . . the Packers are inches away from the winning touchdown . . . Bart Starr hands off to Donny Anderson . . ."*

Anderson took the ball and, unable to get traction on the ice, turned around at the line and tried to back into the end zone by digging his heels into the ground and pushing off. Pugh drove low and fast past Kramer, a move known by the players as "sub-marining." He and Lilly hit Anderson in the legs. Renfro further stacked Anderson up by rushing in from his safety position and hitting him high.

Second-and-goal at the Dallas one; 20 seconds remaining: Starr took his second timeout, then returned to the huddle and called "55-Special" again.

Moore: *"This has got to be sheer tension . . . Starr has the team set at the line. The handoff goes to Donny Anderson . . ."*

Anderson, who was lined up this time behind Starr and to his right, slipped again on the ice as he surged forward to take the handoff. The slip left the Green Bay halfback in a dangerous position—virtually parallel to the ground—and it was all Starr could do to get the ball into Anderson's numb hands. Pugh again submarined past Kramer, and Renfro again came over the top of the line to slow the plunging Anderson.

This play proved critical for three reasons. First, players from both sides swore Anderson scored on this play. Those in the middle of the play say they saw Anderson extend the ball over the goal line, but the officials didn't see it because of the pileup. To this day, Anderson wonders how much different his career would have been had he been remembered as the man who scored the winning touchdown in the Ice Bowl.

The second part of this play is that a fumble occurred when Jordan knocked the ball from Anderson's outstretched hands. On the film, Anderson and Jordan can be seen momentarily wrestling for the ball as they lay at the bottom of the pileup.

The third and final factor is that Anderson's slip at the start of the play convinced Starr he would have to run it himself on the next play. He quickly stepped into the line and, raising his arms, pointed the fingers of his left hand into the palm of his right, the signal for a timeout.

Third-and-goal at the Dallas one; 16 seconds remaining: Twice before, Anderson gained brief glimpses of glory, only to be stopped inches short by both the Dallas defense and the frozen field. With the ball resting on "Doomsday's" doorstep, just 18 inches shy of the gold-painted goal line, Starr knew the Packers were down to just one play. "We had run out of ideas," he said later.

As he headed to the sideline to confer with Lombardi, Starr stopped and looked into the frost-bitten face of Kramer.

"Can you get your footing for a wedge play?"

"Hell, yes!"

Engulfed by noise as he trotted to the sidelines, Starr blocked out the confusion by concentrating on the situation. On the two previous plays, the Packers had run two straight-ahead, short-yardage calls. Anderson gained a yard on first down, and a foot on second down. Packer backs could not accelerate without slipping; Starr said the shadows cast by the scoreboard had left the south end of the field hard as granite. But he also noticed that the activity at the line of scrimmage had broken part of the ice, and he realized he had better footing than either Anderson or Mercein.

Standing on the field, Mercein couldn't help but think that if the turf hadn't been so icy, he would have scored the winning touchdown on the "give" play over Lilly. Yet he also knew how close the Packers had come to disaster on the two previous plays.

"They tried Donny on a couple of dives, he slipped on both and they almost had miscues on both," Mercein recalled. "It was terrifying to see what almost happened. The second play in particular, Donny's almost prone to the ground when Bart gives him the ball. That was an amazing, *amazing* exchange. It was like handing a platter to someone lying on the ground. The ball was handed off maybe a foot off the ground. Donny's feet had slipped out from under him and he was almost parallel to the ground when he got the ball."

As Starr arrived at the sideline, referee Norm Schachter approached Lombardi. "Coach, that was your last timeout. No more. Sixteen seconds left to play and it's third down on the two-foot line."

Lombardi looked at Schachter, then tuned him out. "How that man could concentrate," Schachter said later. Standing nearby, the referee listened as coach and quarterback reviewed their strategy. Schachter was so certain the Packers would play for the tie he began reviewing in his mind overtime procedures: "Get the captains of both teams. Toss the coin. Dallas has to call heads or tails as it is the visiting team. They get that option. After the toss, wait three minutes for television and regrouping by both teams." Schachter had it all figured out, but as he stood on the Packers sideline, he suddenly realized an overtime period wouldn't be needed.

Starr was convinced they could run a "wedge" play. The "wedge" was a short-yardage play in which two linemen double-teamed a defender at the point of attack and cleared a path for the ball carrier. The question of which side to run at—Lilly on the left side or Pugh on the right—had already been decided in the Packers' minds in the days leading up to the game.

"If Lilly was not the best tackle in football, he was close to it," Starr said. "Lilly came in hard and low. Wedge blocking would not work on him. I decided we would have to take our chances running at Pugh."

Green Bay's detailed film study revealed that while Lilly charged in low and hard on goal-line plays, the taller Pugh had a tendency at times to rise up out of his stance, thus presenting a better blocking angle.

As Starr met with Lombardi, several options were discussed. The logical play would have been a field goal to tie the game and send it into sudden-death overtime, but both men quickly discounted that. "We meant to win it in regulation," Starr said.

Lombardi asked about the condition of the field, and Starr said the ground was frozen so hard the Packers could not get a foothold for their cleats. It's hard for the runners to accelerate, he said, and hard for the linemen to block with authority. Everybody, he remarked, is slipping and sliding.

A pass play seemed too risky. Starr's fingers were numb from the cold, and he was having trouble gripping the ball. The passes he had completed on the drive had been difficult ones. "Both Coach Lombardi and I felt we would have to run the ball over the goal line," Starr said. "But which running play should we use?"

Another "dive" play was mentioned, but it required one-on-one blocking, and the Cowboys had penetrated to stop the Packers' previous two dive plays. Green Bay tried a wedge play earlier in the game, and it worked. Lombardi decided to run "31 Wedge," which called for the "three" back, in this case Mercein, to hit the "one" hole, located between Kramer and Bowman. But Starr remembered thinking, "What if Mercein slips, and doesn't reach the hole in time?" Realizing he could get better traction at the line of scrimmage, Starr told his coach he would have a better chance of scoring if he kept the ball instead of giving it to Mercein.

"There's nothing wrong with the plays we've run," he told Lombardi, "it's just that the backs can't get their footing. They can't even stand up and get to the line of scrimmage. The 'wedge' play will work, but the backs can't get there. I'm upright, I can feel my way in for a couple of steps and then just lunge in from there. Why don't I just keep it?"

Lombardi's response was brief.

"Run it," he said, "and let's get the hell out of here."

Schachter said later he heard Starr tell Lombardi, "You know, we won't have time to get a field-goal team in after the play. If we need it."

"You won't need it," Lombardi answered.

Lombardi joked later that he didn't want to settle for overtime because he had compassion for the fans who had suffered in the cold long enough. The fans were indeed suffering; many would be treated for frostbite after the game. But the real reason for his decision was his confidence in his players. "These decisions don't come from the mind," he said later. "They come from the gut."

Across the field, the Cowboys tried to guess what Starr and Lombardi were planning. Dallas head coach Tom Landry looked at the scoreboard, saw there were 16 seconds remaining and no time-outs left for Green Bay. His analytical mind broke down the situation. If the Packers tried to run the ball in and they failed, they wouldn't have any chance to unpile the players and get the field-goal unit in place to try and give Don Chandler a chance to tie the game.

Landry figured the Packers would try a rollout pass, just as he had called in a situation that was strikingly similar at the end of the 1966 championship game in Dallas. Facing a fourth-and-two, Landry ordered a rollout, only to see Green Bay linebacker Dave Robinson slip his block and force quarterback Don Meredith into an off-balance pass that was intercepted in the end zone by Packers' safety Tom Brown.

With Lombardi facing a similar situation, Landry felt sure he knew what the Packers would do. "I thought Starr would roll out, and depending on what he saw, throw to an open receiver or just toss the ball out of bounds to stop the clock and give them time to get Chandler on the field."

For the second time in a decade, Landry was in the role of a defensive mastermind trying to stop a drive of momentous power and significance. In 1958, he had stood on the sidelines at Yankee Stadium and watched Baltimore Colts' quarterback John Unitas direct two classic late-game drives that gave Baltimore a 23–17 overtime win. Nine years later, Starr was repeating what Unitas had done, and the Packers, like the Colts, were one yard away from victory.

A few feet from where Landry stood, Rentzel looked across the field as Starr and Lombardi talked. As an offensive player, Rentzel tried to think along with them.

"What the hell were they going to do on third down with 16 seconds left?" he thought. "Send Anderson on a sweep, with the option to pass or run? A play-action pass, so if it's incomplete, the clock stops, and they can have time to attempt the tying field goal?"

In the press box, the writers were also discussing strategy: Try a field goal? Run Anderson wide? Try Mercein off-tackle? CBS director Tony Verna and producer Bill Creasy were also guessing. Verna had to decide during the timeout where to focus his end-zone camera, Camera Five. He asked sideline reporter Pat Summerall, who was standing in the south end zone, what play he thought Starr would run.

"Rollout pass," Summerall said.

Verna quickly told the end-zone cameraman, "You get Dowler." But the cold had frozen the cables behind the camera during this drive, and the cameraman was unable to turn his focus to Dowler. So Camera Five stayed put behind the Dallas defense, where its position was almost directly behind Pugh.

In the CBS broadcast booth, Gifford wondered if he'd even be able to comment on what was to follow. His body had become almost totally numb from the cold. His fingers were stiff and his throat felt raw every time he tried to speak. But as Starr turned and trotted back to the field, Gifford told his audience:

"Chandler isn't moving. They are going for the win."

Returning to the huddle, Starr called "Brown Right, 31-Wedge." The call surprised Dowler. "I thought Bart might come back with a play-action pass," he remembered. "We had a play-action where I would block and then release and go into the flat. We had that play in the game plan, too."

Mercein however, wasn't surprised by the call. He had gained 34 of the Packers' 67 yards on the drive to that point, and he felt certain he would get the ball one final time. "I knew they were going to run '31-wedge,'" he said, looking back. "I knew it because it was the safest play, and I was hot in a sense, I had a hot hand having a lot of those yards to that point. And I just felt that this would be the call and sure enough, it was. But what Bart didn't say to anybody on the team was that he was going to keep the ball."

"They had their blocking assignments," Starr later explained, "and I didn't want to change anything."

The responsibility of clearing a path for Starr fell to Bowman and Kramer. The two would engage in what the Packers called a "post-drive" block, a high-low double-team in which Bowman would hit Pugh in the chest as he rose out of his stance and Kramer would drive in low, cutting Pugh's legs out from under him. In the huddle, Bowman heard the call and thought, "This is it."

As Lilly stared at the Green Bay huddle, he knew what was coming. The Packers were going to try to run it in. "Hope they run it at me," he thought. He began kicking at the ice with his right foot, trying to get traction on the hard ground. Lilly figured the game would be won by whichever team could get traction on the ice. "If they get a foothold and run the ball," he thought, "we won't be able to stop them."

Pugh, standing next to Lilly, tried to warm his hands by putting them down the front of his metallic silver pants. The coaches hadn't allowed the Dallas linemen to put gloves on, thinking they wouldn't be able to grab and throw Green Bay's blockers. Pugh obeyed his coaches, Townes didn't. "The hell with it," Townes said. "I'm getting gloves and keeping my hands warm."

Pugh's feet were so numb he felt he was standing "in a bucket of ice." He turned to Lilly and said, "We've got to call a timeout to get an ice pick."

He tried kicking at the ice, but couldn't feel his feet; they were frozen from the cold. Reflecting on that day recently, Pugh recalled thinking about his mother during the course of the bitter afternoon. He could hear her say, as if she were there, "What are you doing out in that cold weather, fool?"

Having studied the Packers on film, Pugh was sure he knew what Green Bay would try to do. "Starr doesn't like quarterback sneaks," he thought. "He's going to call the play to Donny Anderson."

The Cowboys earned their "Doomsday" defense nickname in the mid-sixties because of the number of successful goal-line stands they had made. Their attitude toward opposing offenses was summed up at the time by Lilly. "We kind of say, 'Go ahead and run at it if you can make it.'"

Starr began the drive by saying, "Let's get it done," and now, a moment before the Packers broke from the huddle, Mercein heard Starr make a final statement: "We're going in from here."

Mercein was ready. Nine years earlier, the 15-year-old Mercein had sat transfixed in front of a black-and-white TV set as Baltimore Colts' fullback Alan Ameche burst one yard through the gathering darkness and the New York Giants defense to score the game-winning touchdown in overtime in the '58 title game. Ameche emerged as Mercein's boyhood football hero, and there were many similarities between the two men.

Both were natives of Wisconsin, Mercein hailing from Milwaukee and Ameche from Kenosha. Both had been star fullbacks in college, and both were big men physically, each weighing 225 pounds. They looked alike as well, each having brown eyes and black hair. And each had become a key figure in classic games: Ameche in the '58 sudden-death classic, Mercein in the '67 Ice Bowl.

Mercein had followed Ameche's career dating back to Alan's All-America days at the University of Wisconsin, where he won the Heisman Trophy Award as the best collegiate player in the nation. Just as Ameche had put the Colts in position to win the '58 championship by running a trap play up the middle, Mercein had run an influence play up the middle for a key gain. Now, Mercein felt he was going to get a chance to duplicate Ameche's famous one-yard touchdown run.

"I really knew I was going to score," Mercein said. "You play your whole career and practice every day and go through pain, and you just want to be in that position. You think, 'Let me, God, have the chance to perform in a situation like that.' I was just begging, just dying, to get the ball because I feel like I'm going to meet the challenge. I'm convinced I would have scored."

Mercein didn't say anything to anyone at the time, but his left arm was numb. The right arm was tingling from the cold, but his left arm felt heavy and numb, as if he had fallen asleep on it. He had been kicked in the left triceps during a pileup, and though he didn't realize it, a hematoma had developed. In normal weather, the arm would have swelled with blood from the vessels broken by the injury. But because it was so cold, the arm had merely gone numb. It wasn't until he took a hot shower after the game that the hematoma swelled. "My left arm," he remembered, "became as big as a thigh."

Standing on his perch inside the scoreboard, NFL Films production manager Art Spieller focused his camera on the back of the Dallas defense. Like Mercein, Spieller remembered Ameche's run; he had been in the end zone that day as well and got the famous footage of the winning touchdown.

As the Packers approached the line of scrimmage, the temperature was now 20 below zero, and the wind chill a devastating minus-50. Before he signaled the ball in play, Schachter told his officiating crew, "Stay alive. Be awake. Keep on your toes. No more timeouts for Green Bay. Side men watch that damn goal line. If it's in, signal touchdown right away. Don't guess. Give it a good look. We're going to earn our pay on this one play. Heads up."

Schachter took his position along the line of scrimmage on the west sideline, the Packers' sideline, and cursed his luck.

"How in hell do I always wind up in this kind of a situation?" he thought. "What a bitch. Here it comes down to one play, and I'm going to be smack in the middle of it. If Starr doesn't get the touchdown, no Dallas player will get off him. If I stop the clock after the play to haul the Dallas players off him, it just might be enough time for Green Bay to get its field goal team lined up. . . . If I don't kill the clock to pull the Dallas players off Starr, he will never get up in time to possibly get in another play. What a helluva spot for me."

Schachter already had one incident with Lombardi earlier in the fourth quarter. Because of TV obligations, Schachter had to call an additional timeout following an incomplete pass by Starr. If Schachter hadn't ordered a timeout, CBS would been forced to skip a commercial worth $180,000 to the network. When Schachter called for time, Green Bay left tackle and offensive captain Bob Skoronski rushed over to him.

"Who the hell called that timeout, Norm?"

"I did, Bob. I did, Bob," said Schachter, who was so cold he said everything twice.

"What the hell for?"

"The players' pension fund. The players' pension fund."

"Great call, Norm."

Lombardi however, didn't think it was a great call. He began screaming at Schachter. "Norm, you killed our momentum," he shouted. "You shouldn't have stopped the game. We were on the move. Damn it. You killed our drive."

Now, with the game on the line, Schachter looked at Lombardi, with his fur hat and beige coat, standing on the sideline. The referee could imagine the uproar if Starr's play failed and the Cowboys piled on. "What a helluva spot for me," he thought.

Standing in the back of the end zone, photographer Vernon Biever turned to his teenage son, John. "Stay here in case they score a touchdown," Vernon said. "I'll go to the sideline and get the jubilation."

"We had sort of a game plan going," Vernon said, looking back. "We didn't want to be in the same place at the same time."

As young John steadied his metal camera, his father negotiated the difficult footing as he made his way to the Packers' side of the field. "Towards the end of the game the field had a glaze over it," Vernon said. "It was a sheet of ice."

Also standing in the back of the end zone was a knot of newspapermen. Among them was *Green Bay Press-Gazette* sports editor Art Daley. "It was pretty common practice in those days to go down to the sidelines with three, four minutes to go," Daley said. "The field was frozen solid, and everybody was freezing. A friend of mine from the *Los Angeles Times* was wearing just a topcoat."

Win or lose, Daley thought the Packers' final drive was amazing. Daley knew it was in keeping with Lombardi's character that Green Bay would go for the win rather than the tie. "What a way to end it," he thought.

Nitschke thought Lombardi gave Starr one final chance to win the game to show his love and respect for his players. Of the 33 players on the Packers' 1967 roster, 11 of them had been with Lombardi at mud-filled Franklin Field in Philadelphia back in 1960, when the Packers played in their first NFL championship game under Lombardi. Through the years, they had suffered through torturous grass drills on sun-baked ground in July, and celebrated championships on frozen fields in late December. They had played hurt, and they proved that win or lose, they were a brotherhood. Black or white, young or old, they were Lombardi's extended family.

Nobody would have criticized the coach if he had sent the field-goal unit in when the ball was at the goal line, Nitschke said, but to the players, it would have meant something. "It would have meant he didn't have confidence in our ability to take that last step," Nitschke said, "to rise to the limits of our ability when all the chips had been shoved to the center of the table."

Fans at Lambeau Field stood as one and rocked the historic stadium to its frigid core. Many took off their scarves and waved them in the air. Lombardi looked at his team and was heard to say, "If we can't score from the one, we don't deserve to win." Rentzel stared at the field and decided the Packers were going to pass. Silently, he begged them to throw the ball away. "Let them kick the field goal," he thought. "We'll get them in overtime."

A thousand or so plays during the 1967 season had brought Lombardi and Landry to this decisive call, and it was fitting that after all their years together in New York and their years opposite one another in Green Bay and Dallas, the most famous drive in NFL history had come down to one single yard. Lombardi was the leading offensive mind of his era; Landry the dominant defensive thinker. They had spent years parrying one another's coaching philosophies, and they would climax this championship with one final test of strategy.

In the darkening shadows, the Packers' forest-green jerseys appeared black, and the icy vapors of breath from both sides were more distinct. Bob St. John of the Dallas *Morning News* thought the scene on the field did not look real. The players had become gray, ghost-like figures moving at a slow, painful pace.

Before he crouched into his three-point stance opposite Pugh, Kramer kicked at the ice and tried to dig his cleats into the ground. Normally, Kramer would drive forward by pushing off his right, or back, foot, but he felt a small divot in the ground near his left foot. Like a sprinter positioning himself in the starting blocks, Kramer planted his left foot against the divot, and kept his eyes on Pugh's jersey number, 75.

Standing behind Bowman, Starr raised his arms to quiet the crowd. For a split second, a hush seemed to fall over Lambeau Field as 50,861 fans held their collective breath. Starr wiggled his right foot for extra traction.

Moore: *"Here are the Packers . . . Third down, inches to go to pay-dirt . . . 17–14, Cowboys out in front . . . Packers trying for the go-ahead score . . .*

"Starr begins the count, takes the snap . . ."

Going off a quick count to prevent the Cowboys from digging in, Starr took the snap, tucked the ball to his stomach, and immediately dove to his right.

Anticipating the count, Kramer slammed into Pugh so fast the Cowboy tackle had time only to raise his left arm. Pugh later compared his predicament to an Old West gunfight. Somebody pulls the trigger, he said, and it's too late to do anything.

Unable to find any traction, Pugh felt his feet skidding on the ice. Bowman hit him in the ribs, and Kramer drove into him low. The double-team block pushed Pugh back and to his right. Townes fired in from his right to fill the hole, but he was too low to stop Starr (*See Diagram 9*).

Helmet lowered, Starr churned into the opening behind Kramer. As he fell across the goal line, Starr felt someone tugging at his arms, trying to pry the ball loose. It was Howley, who had charged from his left linebacker position and was clawing at the ball.

Still clutching the ball, Starr tumbled into the end zone and NFL history.

In the back of the end zone, John Biever clicked his camera shutter, and the historic moment was frozen, literally, in time.

Moore: *"He's got the quarterback sneak and he's in for the touchdown! . . . And the Green Bay Packers are going to be world champions, NFL champions, for a third straight year!"*

Following Starr into the end zone was Mercein, who had his arms raised in anticipation of a handoff that never came. Most

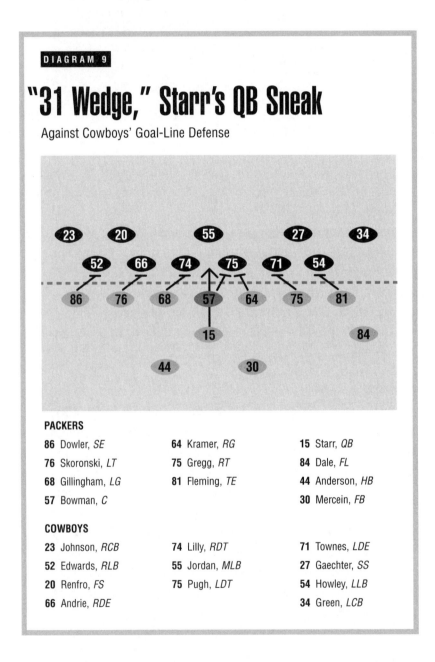

DIAGRAM 9

"31 Wedge," Starr's QB Sneak

Against Cowboys' Goal-Line Defense

PACKERS

86 Dowler, *SE*	**64** Kramer, *RG*	**15** Starr, *QB*
76 Skoronski, *LT*	**75** Gregg, *RT*	**84** Dale, *FL*
68 Gillingham, *LG*	**81** Fleming, *TE*	**44** Anderson, *HB*
57 Bowman, *C*		**30** Mercein, *FB*

COWBOYS

23 Johnson, *RCB*	**74** Lilly, *RDT*	**71** Townes, *LDE*
52 Edwards, *RLB*	**55** Jordan, *MLB*	**27** Gaechter, *SS*
20 Renfro, *FS*	**75** Pugh, *LDT*	**54** Howley, *LLB*
66 Andrie, *RDE*		**34** Green, *LCB*

believe from the photo of Starr's touchdown that Mercein is raising his arms to signal a score, but that's not the case.

"I came over the top of that pile and it looks to everyone like I'm signaling a touchdown," Mercein said. "It's a very famous picture, a terrific picture. But what's really happening there is that I'm trying to indicate to the referees that I'm not assisting him into the end zone, which would have been a penalty. You couldn't push or aid a runner into the end zone, or it would have been a five-yard penalty. He had to go in on his own effort. And I was aware of that. But the thing was, I couldn't stop. I had gotten good traction and had a pretty good takeoff, and there was no stopping. I tried to hold up, but I knew I was going to pile over the top of them. If you're on dry grass, you might be able to halt before you got there. But I came right over the top and I was trying to indicate, 'Hey, I'm not pushing this guy, I'm not assisting him.'"

Moore: *"People are pouring out of the stands . . . They're coming out from all sides, out onto the field. The Packers know they have it won and so does everyone else . . . How about that!"*

The fans in Lambeau erupted as field judge Fritz Graf stood over Starr and signaled a touchdown. Lying next to Pugh in the end zone, Kramer looked back and saw Starr hunched over the goal line. "It was," Kramer said later, "the most beautiful sight in the world."

Pugh was stunned. He couldn't believe it when he saw the officials signaling a touchdown. He was certain he had seen Kramer's right hand come off the ground an instant before the ball, which would have been an offsides penalty that negated the touchdown.

Lombardi, who had been standing stock-still in his fur hat and overcoat, mimicked Graf's signal by taking his gloved hands out of his pocket and momentarily thrusting them over his head.

In the CBS production room, Verna was all smiles. Camera Five, frozen in place, had provided the best angle of Starr's touchdown. Viewers across the country watched the instant replay and dissected the components of the dramatic score. "If it hadn't been for those cables freezing," Summerall said, "we wouldn't have had the shot."

CBS broadcaster Ray Scott told his viewing audience, "You have just witnessed a mind-over-matter masterpiece."

Scott still regards that drive as the greatest in NFL history. "The field was treacherous," he said. "Impossible footing. That last Packers' drive was one of the most spine-tingling drives I've ever seen."

Colts' quarterback John Unitas, who had engineered his own last-minute masterpiece of a drive in the '58 title game, was among the more than 30 million watching on TV. Considered the master of the two-minute march, Unitas said Green Bay's drive "defied the clock and tested Starr's ability under extreme pressure."

In dangerously cold weather and against one of the best defenses of their era, the Packers had driven 68 yards in 12 plays. They conquered the Cowboys and the elements, and in winning their third straight championship, had met the sternest challenge in NFL history, and risen above it. Dowler looked back and said simply, "It was a matter of will over ability."

Chandler's extra point made it 21–17, and following the kick-off, Meredith threw long incompletions to Rentzel and Bob Hayes before the final gun sounded. When it did, Green Bay fans stormed the field and began tearing down the yellow goal posts.

Moore: *"There's the gun! This football game is over, and history has been made . . . The Green Bay Packers have won three straight National Football League championships . . . And the goal posts are coming down here at Lambeau Field . . ."*

The 1967 NFL championship game was over, but the myths and legends surrounding the Ice Bowl were just beginning to crystallize in the cold air.

The Cold Truth

"ALL THE WORLD LOVES A GAMBLER," announced Vince Lombardi, beaming beneath a battery of television lights in the Green Bay locker room. "Except when he loses."

When the Packers arrived from the field, they found their locker room filled with CBS cameramen and wired for sound. Cursing the intrusion, Lombardi ordered the CBS crew to "get the hell out!" Alone for a moment, the players kneeled and quietly recited the Lord's Prayer. Lombardi began to say something to his team, but had to fight back tears of joy. "I can't talk anymore," he said. "I can't say anymore."

Lombardi wasn't the only one crying or on the verge of it. Middle linebacker Ray Nitschke recalled nearly everyone in the locker room being emotional. Guard Fuzzy Thurston, who had played in every Green Bay title game since 1960, wiped the tears from his frozen face. "This was the hardest one of my six," he said. "And the best." The Packers' jubilation wasn't loud and boisterous; *Green Bay Press-Gazette* sportswriter Len Wagner said the only difference between the Green Bay and Dallas locker rooms was "there were more reporters on the Packer side."

Nitschke remembered the Packers' celebration as "a quiet, rewarding, satisfying feeling." Players and coaches were not only numbed by the cold, they were numbed by what they had just accomplished.

Finally able to relax and enjoy the moment, Lombardi made his way to his office, where he stood behind his desk, crossed his arms and grinned his gap-toothed smile at the pool of print and electronic reporters waiting for him to speak. He and his team had achieved their goal, they had won an historic third straight NFL championship. Lombardi's ruddy face, reddened even more by the intense cold, scarcely needed the bright camera lights, it so radiated with the glow of victory.

"We took the gamble," he said, "and it was a gamble. We had the field-goal team ready to go in if we didn't make it. . . . It was very questionable if we would have had enough time."

One reporter suggested to Lombardi that the Dallas defense "could have just sat on Starr for awhile."

"That's right," Lombardi said. "It was a gamble.

"This was it. This was our greatest one. This is what the Green Bay Packers are all about. They don't do it for individual glory. They do it because they love one another."

When someone mentioned the weather, Lombardi smiled. "Cold? What cold? I didn't feel any cold." Asked about his underground heating system, he remarked, "I guarantee this field is the warmest place in Wisconsin today."

He told reporters the victory "took all of our experience, all of our poise." Though Blackie Sherrod of the Dallas *Times-Herald* hailed Lombardi for his "almighty audacity" in going for the win rather than the tie, the coach refused the credit.

At first he laughed off his decision. "I didn't want all those freezing people up in the stands to have to sit through sudden-death overtime," he said grinning. "That just goes to show that I'm not without compassion, although I'm often accused of lacking it."

But as reporters continued to ask about the play, Lombardi pointed them in the direction of the locker room. "The story," he said, "is out there."

Reporters crowded around Starr, who had stripped down to his thermal undershirt as he stood in front of his locker. The Packers' quarterback was smiling but weary; the emotion of the game—and the entire season—had drained him. When asked by a reporter, "What if you hadn't scored on that play?" Starr involuntarily shuddered.

"I don't even want to think about that," he said.

One by one the questions were issued rapid-fire:

"Would the Packers have had time to attempt a game-tying field goal if you had been unable to get in?"

"We had the time. . . . I think we had the time. I hadn't even given (a field goal) a thought."

"Did you consider passing?"

"That close, I felt sure we could get it in on the ground. . . . We just had to get in there."

"When was the last time you called a quarterback sneak?"

Starr smiled. "I can't remember the last time."

Just then a roar went up in the locker room as attention was drawn to a TV monitor that showed that CBS was playing its instant replay of the sneak. There was Starr scoring behind the great blocking of center Ken Bowman and right guard Jerry Kramer. CBS producer Bill Creasy and directors Tony Verna and Bob Dailey were so proud of their camera angle on the play they ran it over and over, treating a nationwide audience as many as 20 times. Millions of football fans who didn't know the names of more than one or two NFL offensive linemen heard the names Kramer and Bowman repeatedly. As he watched the play, all Kramer could think of was, "Thank God for instant replay."

Whether by luck or fate, Kramer had spent the 1967 season recording his thoughts and views on the Packers' season in a tape-recorded diary. Edited by Dick Schaap, Kramer's diary became a runaway best-seller when it hit the book stands in 1968. Fittingly, the book was titled *Instant Replay.*

As Kramer held court with Tom Brookshier, who was wearing an earplug to take instructions from postgame director Dailey, Bowman walked up and said with a smile, "Don't take all the credit,

Kramer. Don't take all the credit. I helped you with that block."

"Shut up, Bow," Kramer said kiddingly. "You've got ten more years to play. You've got plenty of time for glory. Give an old man his day."

Kramer did take time to point out one other thing to his viewing audience. Still rankled by the *Look* magazine article about Lombardi, Kramer told Brookshier, "Many things have been said about Coach, and he is not always understood by those who quote him. The players understand. This is one beautiful man.

"There's a great deal of love for one another on this club. Perhaps we're living in Camelot."

"The interviews we did in the Packers' locker room that day will never be duplicated," recalled Brookshier. "All of them were wahoo and wanted to go on the air. They would come up and say, 'I'm next.' It was much different than having to coax people to talk. It was gung-ho, and you had to be careful with the camera because guys were running around without any clothes on."

Brookshier talked with several Packers, then introduced his next guest.

"Here's Green Bay's madman, Ray Nitschke."

"I was thinking I was being cute," Brookshier recalled with a chuckle. "I looked over and Nitschke, who was a behemoth anyway, was red-faced. He was *furious*. I heard Bob Dailey say in my ear, 'If Nitschke hits Brookshier, let's cut to a commercial.' When Nitschke got on, he said, 'I'm not a madman.' But earlier, I had seen him try to kick (Dallas fullback) Don Perkins and I thought, 'Wow. This guy's wild.'

"When I see him now he says, 'You gave me personality, but I didn't like that when you called me a madman.'"

The words rankled Nitschke, who maintains that he was so angry at himself for missing a tackle that he kicked at the ground, not Perkins. "I'm not a madman," he growled at Brookshier. "I just enjoy football."

Fullback Chuck Mercein, who had been at the stadium since 10:30 that morning, stood in front of his locker unable to believe he had gone from the waiver wire to the NFL title game in two months. Released by the Giants, Mercein didn't even know if he'd be playing football two months earlier.

"It's more than I could ever hope for," he told *Green Bay Press-Gazette* sportswriter Jim Zima. "Thank God I had the confidence in myself and kept on trying and didn't give up.

"I'll never forget that last drive. To see it must have been great but to be in it and feel it was just something else. Thank goodness I was able to contribute. Everybody gave everything they had. We knew what we had to do."

Left tackle Bob Skoronski, the Packers' offensive captain, wiped a smudge of blood off his face as he talked with Tex Maule of *Sports Illustrated*. Skoronski had butted helmets with George Andrie for three hours out in the cold, and the intensity of their private battle left both men marked and weary. Said Skoronski, "This game was our mark of distinction."

While the Packers lingered in their uniforms for another hour, most of the Cowboys dressed quickly. The team's frustration was evident in their mood. Two Dallas coaches, an offensive and defensive assistant, got into a heated exchange with one another in the locker room and had to be separated by the head coach. "What's said in this room," Landry told them, "stays in this room."

Cowboy reporters Blackie Sherrod and Steve Perkins of the Dallas *Times Herald,* and Sam Blair and Bob St. John of the Dallas *Morning News* waited alongside *Green Bay Press-Gazette* sports editor Art Daley outside the Dallas locker room.

Ten minutes went by before Landry emerged. Still dressed in his sideline outfit, the Cowboys' coach ignored the reporters and walked right by them and into another room down the hall. They waited for another five minutes before the door to the locker room was finally opened, but before they could ask any questions of the players, Landry reappeared and ushered the reporters to the center of the room.

As is the case in most losing locker rooms, the questions didn't come easy. Finally, someone asked about the cold.

"Unusual," Landry said quietly. "We were suffering and so were the Packers. You just couldn't do the things you wanted to do on a field like that. It got worse as the game went on."

Asked about Lombardi's daring decision to go for the touchdown, Landry, the decade's defensive genius, seemed stunned by it. "I can't believe that call, the sneak," he said. "It wasn't a good call, but now it's a great call.

"I thought Starr would roll out and, depending on what he saw, throw to an open receiver or just toss the ball out of bounds to stop the clock and give them time to get (placekicker Don) Chandler on the field. If the play they ran had failed, the game would have been over. There's no way they'd have gotten off another play."

Dallas defensive line coach Ermal Allen thought the sneak was a lousy call, and said so.

"I just wish it had failed," he said bitterly. "You think there wouldn't have been a few million words written about that? Then we'd see how smart (Lombardi) felt."

The sting of defeat was evident in the Cowboys' voices. A few blamed the cold. Middle linebacker Lee Roy Jordan said outside linebackers Chuck Howley and Dave Edwards both slipped and fell on key plays during Green Bay's final drive.

"Playing in this weather," Jordan said, "is an injustice."

Defensive tackle Bob Lilly said the ground at the goal line was so hard the game was decided by which team could get traction. "We knew we couldn't stop them if they got the footing," he said.

Daley looked around the room and saw quarterback Don Meredith taking his shirt off as he sat on a table. Answering questions left and right, the battered Texan finally drawled, "All I have to say is, there was trouble on every corner, and it just didn't seem like Christmas out there."

Daley thought Dallas had played well considering they had come out of a warm-weather climate into sub-zero temperatures. But the fact that the Cowboys had now lost consecutive title games to Green Bay in the final minute caused Meredith to say, "I guess we can do everything except win the big one."

Meredith's phrase haunted Landry's Cowboys for the next four seasons. Sportswriters labeled them a team that couldn't win big games, and after upset losses to Cleveland in the 1968 and '69 play-offs and a last-second loss to Baltimore in Super Bowl V following the 1970 season, the Cowboys became known as "Next Year's Champion." It wasn't until 1971, when they defeated Miami in Super Bowl VI, that Landry's team finally quieted their critics.

Frank Gifford made his way to the Dallas dressing room, and he saw Meredith sitting slumped and bare-chested, his head practically between his knees. There was blood on the quarterback's face and a huge bruise under his eye. To Gifford, Meredith looked "like the survivor of a gang-mugging."

Gifford called Creasy and asked, "Why don't we get a camera in here and interview some of the losers, too? Hell, they only lost by a quarterback sneak. And we've got plenty of time to fill."

"Frank, they won't do that. You can't get any of those guys to come on, and we can't ask them. It just isn't done, man."

"So let's be the first. Besides, I think I can get Meredith to talk with me."

Creasy sighed. "If you feel that strongly, go ahead and take a shot."

Gifford approached Meredith, with whom he had become friends, and asked, "Don, why don't you come on and say what you feel about today? It's not like you guys got killed. You got beat on a frozen home field by a lousy quarterback sneak."

Meredith lifted his head. "You really think I should?"

"Yeah," Gifford answered. "I really do."

"Okay."

As Meredith pulled his blood-stained T-shirt back on, one of the CBS cameras was wheeled in from the Green Bay dressing room. A couple of camera lights were set up, and when Creasy gave him the go-ahead, Gifford addressed Meredith.

"Don, you came so close. How does it feel to lose this one?"

"The way I look at it, we really didn't lose it. Dadgummit, we didn't lose anything."

Meredith proceeded to do something that Gifford realized was very "un-Don-like." Choking on his words, Meredith dropped the fun-loving, country-boy façade and poured his emotions out on national TV. He talked about how proud he was of his teammates, how hard they had played that day, how he blamed himself for the loss and how awful he felt for his team.

Gifford later described it as a passionate and spontaneous TV moment. "It was wonderful," he said.

The banner headline in Monday's *Press-Gazette* read "Packer Poise Brings Third Straight," and writers covering the game began their stories with leads that reflected which city they worked in:

Lee Remmel, *Green Bay Press-Gazette:* "'It took all of our experience, all of our poise . . .'

"A proud Vince Lombardi thus summed up one of the greatest moments in the Packers' rich history, a pressure-ridden race against the clock which swept them into the National Football League record book at Arctic Lambeau Field Sunday afternoon. . . ."

Sherrod, Dallas *Times Herald:* "It was the epic Arctic struggle between the Cowboys and the Green Bays, an impossible ballet that somehow retained the best of a jungle trench war. . . ."

Perkins, *Times Herald:* "The Cowboys, visitors to the coldest wasteland on which an NFL title game had ever been played, were beaten more by the 13-below weather than the Packers. . . ."

Blair, Dallas *Morning News:* "No sporting event, with the possible exception of the Winter Olympics, ever had been contested in such brutal conditions. . . ."

Two weeks after the Ice Bowl, the Packers represented the NFL against the champions of the American Football League, the Oakland Raiders, in Super Bowl II. Just as they had the year before, Green Bay gained a satisfying victory for the pro football establishment, beating the rebels, 33–14, in the Miami Orange Bowl. At 6:06 P.M. Eastern Standard Time, Lombardi was hoisted on the shoulders of Kramer and Forrest Gregg, and they carried him off the darkening field and into NFL history.

Because it followed on the heels of the Ice Bowl, Green Bay's victory over Oakland was overshadowed by the championship game that preceded it. To many Packer fans, Lombardi's last stand came not on the spongy turf of the Miami Orange Bowl, but on the now-famous frozen tundra of Lambeau Field.

In the 30 years that have followed, numerous legends and myths about the Ice Bowl game grew, most of them focusing on Starr's quarterback sneak for a touchdown. It's the most famous play in NFL history, and even today, Starr says people still stop and ask him about "that sneak in the Ice Bowl."

The play has intrigued fans for decades for various reasons. First, the sneak was a questionable call at best. Second, Kramer might have been offside on the play. Third, Pugh, who had a great game with several sacks and quarterback pressures, was simply the victim of one of the best double-team blocks in history.

Regarding the play itself, in his 1970 book, *Vince Lombardi on Football,* the Packers' coach told editor George L. Flynn there was "no question about a rollout or a pass or a field goal." There was only one option, he said, and that was to run it in.

But the Packers had failed to score on two previous running plays down close, and they were facing a Dallas defense that earned its "Doomsday" nickname for its rock-solid goal-line stands. More remarkable than Lombardi's decision to run the ball in, however, was Starr's decision to run a quarterback sneak.

Pugh was right when he said the Cowboys knew Starr didn't like to run the ball. Starr himself can recall only one previous occasion when he ran a sneak, and that was in a game several years earlier against the San Francisco 49ers. The weather that day was also cold and icy, and the footing was bad, yet Starr scored that day, too.

Dallas halfback Dan Reeves, who has since gone on to a successful head coaching career in the NFL, still doesn't think the sneak was a smart call. "But," he added, "maybe that's the reason Lombardi won all those championships and I haven't won any."

Still, there's little doubt that if Starr's sneak had failed and the Packers lost, Lombardi would have been second-guessed into the next century—which explains why Landry, who respected Lombardi and was aware of his conventional coaching style, could be seen in the locker room after the game, shaking his head and muttering, "Amazing. An amazing gamble."

Of course, Lombardi and Starr would not have been faced with that difficult call had the officials seen halfback Donny Anderson stretch the ball across the goal line on his run two plays earlier. Every time Anderson sees the NFL Films highlight of the sneak, he wonders what might have been.

"Maybe," he mused, "Donny Anderson would have been a bigger star if he was the one who had scored."

And maybe, if Kramer *was* offside and the officials had called it, Pugh would have shed the label of "The Guy Who Got Blocked on Starr's Sneak."

An outstanding player for 14 seasons in Dallas, Pugh was one of the anchors of the "Doomsday" defense. A quiet man, he played in the shadow of Hall of Fame teammate Bob Lilly. But while the media spotlight rarely focused on him, Pugh's coaches and teammates recognized him for the number of big plays he made during the Cowboys' glory years in the 1970s.

To Pugh's credit, for years he kept to himself his belief that

Kramer was offside on the sneak, simply because he was too classy to make excuses. But he told football writers Dan Daly and Bob O'Donnel in their book, *The Pro Football Chronicle,* that he saw Kramer move before the snap.

"In a goal-line situation like that you key the football," Pugh said. "And I could visualize Kramer's hand moving an instant before the ball did. My first thought (after the play) was, 'We got 'em. He's offsides, and that's cost 'em five yards.' I was shocked when I didn't see a flag. I kept looking around for one.'"

When he saw the game film, Pugh thought, "I was right."

Bowman can't say whether Kramer was offside, but he did say Kramer was quick off the ball. "I remember snapping the ball," Bowman said, "and (Kramer) was gone."

Kramer himself doesn't know whether he moved a second before the snap. In his book *Instant Replay,* Kramer said, "I wouldn't swear that I didn't beat the center's snap by a fraction of a second. I wouldn't swear that I wasn't actually offside."

If Kramer was offside, the officiating crew can't be blamed for missing the call. Slow-motion replays of the film are inconclusive, meaning that if Kramer did anticipate the play, he did it by a fraction of a second, almost impossible for the human eye to detect.

Overlooked in all the mystery of whether or not Kramer was offside is the block Bowman made in helping to move Pugh out of the way. According to the Packer playbook, the design of the post-drive block called for Bowman to hit Pugh high, posting him up as it were, giving Kramer an angle to hit him low and drive him back. Both men did their jobs to playbook perfection, and the credit for this superb performance should have been equally shared. But Kramer's media-friendly personality and his book shifted the public's attention to him.

In the media crush after the game, the 32-year-old Kramer casually swept the 24-year-old Bowman away from the spotlight. Bowman had another decade at least to make another block like that, Kramer intimated.

"Being young and dumb," Bowman said, "I didn't realize a block like that comes along every 50 years."

Pugh's opinion is that Bowman deserves more of the credit. "Kramer had good position," he said, "but Bowman did more of the blocking."

Regardless of who should get the credit, Kramer and Bowman delivered a double-team block that Lilly said was unstoppable. "It was a case of mass against mass," he reflected. "It was two against one. Had it been me instead of Jethro, I would have been the one going backwards."

The controversies and legends that prevail about the Ice Bowl have kept this game fresh in the minds of football fans. Fox sportscaster John Madden said that "anyone who knows anything about football, or follows football will always remember that day."

Green Bay's current Super Bowl quarterback, Brett Favre, said Packer fans are always approaching him and talking about "what it was like to be at the Ice Bowl." Favre has heard so much about the game that even though he wasn't even born yet in 1967, "I feel like I was at the Ice Bowl, too. In Green Bay, that game will always seem like it happened yesterday."

"The sheer elements alone make it memorable," said Remmel, who is now the Packers' Director of Media Relations. "It was the most incredible drive in the history of pro football, and the way it finished . . . Starr scoring with 13 seconds left on a play that was quite a gamble. It was a calculated risk, and it was done in the coldest air-temperature game in the history of the NFL."

Every summer, a Packers' fantasy camp is held in Green Bay in which grown men spend several days with some of the legends of Lombardi. The highlight of the camp comes when each man is allowed to stand at the one-yard line and run a quarterback sneak of his own into the south end zone of Lambeau Field.

Packers' general manager Ron Wolf calls Lambeau Field "hallowed ground," and to fans of the NFL, the history and tradition of

Lambeau means as much to them as Yankee Stadium means to baseball fans and the old Boston Garden and Montreal Forum meant to NBA and NHL fans, respectively.

First-time visitors to Lambeau Field invariably turn their attention to the one-yard line at the south end zone, and whether it is a hot September night or a rainy Sunday afternoon in November, memories of the Ice Bowl remain strong. Time is suspended, and suddenly it is New Year's Eve, 1967 again.

The sun is sinking behind the scoreboard in the south end zone, the field is glistening like a polar ice cap, and the wind-chill factor is 50 degrees below zero. In their stance at the one-yard line are the green-shirted ghosts of the past—Starr, Kramer, Bowman, Mercein, Dowler. Across from them are the "Doomsday" Cowboys—Lilly, Pugh, Jordan, and Renfro—and from these famous, and frozen, faces flow breaths of steam that resemble smoke flowing from a chimney.

On the sidelines stand the legendary coaches—Lombardi in a beige camel-hair coat and black fur hat; Landry, in fur coat and woolen hood. They, along with thousands of frost-bitten and suddenly hushed fans, are poised for one of the NFL's golden moments:

"Starr begins the count . . . takes the snap . . . he keeps it on a quarterback sneak and he's in for the touchdown!"

More than thirty years later, Nitschke still felt the numbing cold that turned Green Bay into a glacier that New Year's Eve afternoon. "I had frostbite in my feet from that game," he recalled. "And I lost 10, 15 pounds from the flu."

More than thirty years later, Starr still felt the emotions of the day. "It was a very emotional game for us," he remembered. "We were mentally drained afterwards, and it took us a long time to get ready for the Super Bowl."

More than thirty years later, Lilly still thought of that day as both the saddest and happiest of his life. "Saddest when we lost," he said, "and happiest when we got on an airplane and took off."

The men who made that afternoon so memorable have gone

their separate ways. Some have passed from the scene. Lombardi, who has become the very embodiment of pro football, passed away from cancer in 1970. His fiery spirit, however, has yet to be buried.

Some of his coaches and players—Phil Bengston, Henry Jordan, Travis Williams, Ray Nitschke—are gone too, taken far too early.

Landry, who coached the Cowboys for their first 29 seasons, died from leukemia in 2000.

Those that remain are involved in a variety of businesses. Starr is a 71-year-old chairman of a health-care realty company in Birmingham, Alabama; Kramer, 67, is a rancher in Idaho; Pugh, 59, owns gift shops in the Dallas-Fort Worth airport; Reeves, 60, is in his seventh year as head coach of the Atlanta Falcons.

Despite their disparate career paths and lifestyles, the 1967 Packers and Cowboys remain forever linked by their Ice Bowl experience. They were the men of winter, drawn together by the warm memories of pro football's coldest day.

"When people find out I played for the Dallas Cowboys," Ralph Neely said over the phone, "the first question they ask me is, 'Did you play in the Ice Bowl?'"

Neely paused, and silence prevailed for several seconds. "That last drive," he said quietly, "was the mark of a champion."

In a voice filled with both disappointment for Landry's Cowboys and admiration for Lombardi's Packers, Neely chuckled softly and said, "Those sons of bitches."

Ice Bowl Starting Lineups   230

Ice Bowl Statistics   231

Ice Bowl Play-by-Play   232

Cowboys Full Team Roster, 1967   238

Packers Full Team Roster, 1967   239

Individual Statistics, 1967 Season Totals   240

Team Statistics, 1967 Season Totals   242

Green Bay Packers 1967 Season   244

Dallas Cowboys 1967 Season   244

All-Time Series, Green Bay vs. Dallas   245

Packers All-Time Season Results, 1960–2004   246

Cowboys All-Time Season Results, 1960–2004   247

Ice Bowl Starting Lineups

Dallas   ## Green Bay

OFFENSE   **DEFENSE**

Bob Hayes .SE   RCB . . . . .Bob Jeter
Tony Liscio . . . . .LT   RDE . . . . .Lionel Aldridge
John Niland . . . . .LG   RDT . . . . .Henry Jordan
Mike Connelly C   MLB . . . . .Ray Nitschke
Leon Donohue . . . . .RG   LDT . . . . .Ron Kostelnik
Ralph Neely . . . . .RT   LDE . . . . .Willie Davis
Pettis Norman . . . . .TE   SS . . . . .Tom Brown
Lance Rentzel . . . . .FL   LCB . . . . .Herb Adderley
Don Meredith . . . . .QB   FS . . . . .Willie Wood
Dan Reeves . . . . .HB   RLB . . . . .Lee Roy Caffey
Don Perkins . . . . .FB   LLB . . . . .Dave Robinson

DEFENSE   **OFFENSE**

Mike Johnson . . . . .RCB   SE . . . . .Boyd Dowler
George Andrie . . . . .RDE   LT . . . . .Bob Skoronski
Bob Lilly .RDT   LG . . . . .Gale Gillingham
Lee Roy Jordan . . . . .MLB   C . . . . .Ken Bowman
Jethro Pugh . . . . .LDT   RG . . . . .Jerry Kramer
Willie Townes . . . . .LDE   RT . . . . .Forrest Gregg
Mike Gaechter . . . . .SS   TE . . . . .Marv Fleming
Cornell Green . . . . .LCB   FL . . . . .Carroll Dale
Mel Renfro . . . . .FS   QB . . . . .Bart Starr
Dave Edwards . . . . .RLB   HB . . . . .Donny Anderson
Chuck Howley . . . . .LLB   FB . . . . .Chuck Mercein

HEAD COACHES

Tom Landry . . . . .Vince Lombardi

OFFENSIVE ASSISTANTS

Ermal Allen . . . . .Tom McCormick
Jim Myers . . . . .Ray Wietecha
Ben Agajanian . . . . .Bob Schnelker

DEFENSIVE ASSISTANTS

Dick Nolan . . . . .Phil Bengston
Ernie Stautner . . . . .Dave Hanner
Jerry Tubbs . . . . .Jerry Burns

Ice Bowl Statistics

SCORING

| GREEN BAY | 7 | 7 | 0 | 7 | — | 21 |
| DALLAS | 0 | 10 | 0 | 7 | — | 17 |

GB   Dowler 8 pass from Starr
(Chandler kick)

GB   Dowler 43 pass from Starr
(Chandler kick)

D   Andrie 7 fumble return
(Villanueva kick)

D   FG Villanueva 21

D   Rentzel 50 pass from Reeves
(Villanueva kick)

GB   Starr 1 run
(Chandler kick)

Attendance: 50,861

TEAM STATISTICS

	DALLAS	GREEN BAY
First Downs	11	18
By Rush	4	5
By Pass	6	10
By Penalty	1	3
Total Yards	192	195
Net Rush Yards	92	80
Net Pass Yards	100	115
Fumbles-Lost	3-1	3-2
Penalties-Yards	7-58	2-10
Punts	8-39	18-29

INDIVIDUAL STATISTICS

RUSHING

DALLAS: Perkins 17-51; Reeves 13-42; Meredith 1-9; Baynham 1-(–2); Clarke 1-(–8)

GREEN BAY: Anderson 18-35; Mercein 6-20; Williams 4-13; Wilson 3-11; Starr 1-1, TD

PASSING

DALLAS: Meredith 10-25-59,1 Int.; Reeves 1-1-50, TD

GREEN BAY: Starr 14-24-191, 2 TDs

RECEIVING

DALLAS: Hayes 3-16; Reeves 3-11; Rentzel 2-61, TD; Clarke 2-24; Baynham 1-(–3)

GREEN BAY: Dowler 4-77, 2 TDs; Anderson 4-44; Dale 3-44; Mercein 2-22; Williams 1-4

OFFICIALS

Referee:	Norm Schachter	Back Judge:	Tom Kelleher
Umpire:	Joe Connell	Field Judge:	Fritz Graf
Head Linesman:	George Murphy	Alternates:	Jim Tunney
			Pat Harder
Line Judge:	Bill Schleibaum		

Ice Bowl Play-by-Play

Date: December 31, 1967

Teams: Dallas Cowboys (9-5) and Green Bay Packers (9-4-1)

At Stake: 1967 National Football League championship

Site: Lambeau Field in Green Bay, Wisconsin

Starting Time: 1:10 p.m. Eastern Standard Time

Network Coverage: CBS Television with broadcasters Ray Scott, Jack Buck, and Frank Gifford, and commentators Tom Brookshier and Pat Summerall

Radio Coverage: CBS affiliate WTMJ with play-by-play by Ted Moore

Weather Conditions: -13 degrees, 15 mph winds and wind-chill factor of -38 degrees

---

FIRST QUARTER

Cowboys win coin toss, elect to receive. Packers to defend south goal.

Chandler kicks off to Stokes on the 5, returns to the 33 (Hyland).

DALLAS

1-10-33 D   Meredith passes to Hayes on left sideline for 10; first down.

1-10-43 D   Reeves runs right side for 4 (Caffey and Jordan).

2-6-47 D   Meredith passes incomplete to Rentzel on right sideline.

3-6-47 D   Reeves runs right side for no gain (Adderley).

4-6-47 D   Villanueva punts to Wood on the 14, returns to the 18.

GREEN BAY

1-10-18 GB   (12:54) Anderson runs left for 5, fumbles; Mercein recovers.

2-5-23 GB   Anderson runs right side for 4 (Jordan).

3-1-27 GB   Anderson runs middle for 4; first down (Renfro and Howley).

1-10-31 GB   Starr loses 9 trying to pass (Andrie and Lilly).

2-19-22 GB   Starr passes over middle to Fleming; Dallas penalized for pass interference; first down.

1-10-31 GB   Starr passes to Anderson on left sideline for 17; first down.

1-10-48 GB   Anderson runs for 3 (Lilly).

2-7-49 D   Mercein runs for 2 (Pugh).

3-5-47 D   Starr passes incomplete to Anderson; Dallas penalized five yards for holding.

1-10-42 D   Anderson run loses 2 (Lilly).

2-12-44 D   Mercein runs middle for 3 (Edwards).

3-9-41 D   Starr passes over middle to Dale for 17; first down (Johnson).

1-10-24 D   Starr passes incomplete to Dowler.

2-10-24 D   Starr pass to Dale on left sideline for 15; first down (Gaechter).

1-Goal-9 D Anderson runs middle for 1 (Jordan, Lilly, Pugh).

2-Goal-8 D Starr passes over middle to Dowler in end zone for touchdown.

Packers 6, Cowboys 0

Chandler kicks extra point.

Packers 7, Cowboys 0 *(Green Bay scoring drive: 82 yards, 14 plays, incl. two penalties)*

Chandler kicks off to Dallas 12; ball out of bounds after being touched by Stephens.

DALLAS

1-10-12 D   (6:02) Perkins runs middle for 5 (Davis and Robinson).

2-5-17 D   Meredith passes to Hayes on right side for 5; first down.

1-10-22 D   Perkins runs left side for 3 (Caffey).

2-7-25 D   Perkins runs left side for 3 (Jordan).

3-4-28 D   Perkins runs right for 5; first down (Wood and Nitschke).

1-10-33 D   Meredith passes incomplete to Reeves on right sideline.

2-10-33 D   Perkins runs for no gain (Kostelnik).

3-10-33 D   Meredith pressured, passes incomplete to Rentzel.

4-10-33 D   Villanueva punts to Wood; fair catch on Green Bay 34.

GREEN BAY

1-10-34 GB (1:57) Mercein runs right for no gain (Jordan).

2-10-34 GB Starr passes over middle incomplete to Dale.

3-10-34 GB Starr passes to Mercein on left for 3 (Pugh).

4-7-37 GB   Anderson punts to Rentzel; fair catch on Dallas 31.

DALLAS

1-10-31 D   (:19) Perkins runs for no gain (Kostelnik and Aldridge).

END OF FIRST QUARTER: Packers 7, Cowboys 0

SECOND QUARTER

DALLAS

2-10-31 D   Meredith passes incomplete for Rentzel.

3-10-31 D   Meredith passes incomplete for Reeves.

4-10-31 D   Villanueva punts to Green Bay 35, ball rolls dead.

GREEN BAY

1-10-35 GB (14:40) Wilson runs left for 13; first down (Renfro).

1-10-48 GB Williams runs left for 7 (Edwards).

2-3-45 D   Williams runs left for 2 (Andrie).

3-1-43 D   Starr passes deep to Dowler for touchdown.

Packers 13, Cowboys 0

Chandler kicks extra point.

Packers 14, Cowboys 0 *(Green Bay scoring drive 65 yards in 4 plays)*

Chandler kicks off to Stephens at 25, returns to Dallas 40.

DALLAS

1-10-40 D   (12:18) Meredith passes long to Hayes incomplete.

2-10-40 D   Perkins runs for no gain (Nitschke).

3-10-40 D   Meredith's pass intercepted by Adderley at Dallas 47, returns 15 yards.

GREEN BAY

1-10-32 D   (11:20) Wilson runs left for no gain (Jordan and Edwards).

2-10-32 D   Starr's pass blocked by Edwards.

3-10-32 D   Starr loses 10 trying to pass (Andrie).

4-10-42 D   Anderson punts to Dallas 9; ball downed by Green Bay.

DALLAS

1-10-9 D   (10:19) Perkins runs middle for 1 (Nitschke and Kostelnik).

2-9-10 D   Perkins runs left for 6 (Aldridge).

3-3-16 D   Reeves runs middle, loses 2 (Kostelnik).

4-3-14 D   Villanueva punts to Dallas 48; Brown loses 2 on return.

GREEN BAY

1-10-50   (8:11) Starr passes to Williams on right for 4 (Howley).

2-6-46 D   Wilson run loses 2 (Howley and Jordan).

3-8-48 D   Starr pass incomplete for Wilson.

4-8-48 D   Anderson punts to Dallas 32; ball rolls dead.

DALLAS

1-10-32 D   (4:09) Baynham run right loses 1 (Davis).

2-11-30 D   Perkins runs for 4 (Kostelnik and Caffey).

3-7-34 D   Meredith passes to Hayes on right for 1 (Jeter and Caffey).

4-6-35 D   Villanueva punts to Wood on Green Bay 21, returns to 31.

GREEN BAY

1-10-31 GB   (4:30) Packers penalized 5 yards for illegal procedure.

1-15-26 GB   Starr rushed, hit by Townes and fumbles ball on 19. Andrie recovers at 7 and returns for touchdown.

Packers 14, Cowboys 6.

Villanueva kicks extra point.

Packers 14, Cowboys 7.

Villanueva kicks off into Green Bay end zone; no return.

GREEN BAY

1-10-20 GB   (3:59) Williams runs right for 1 (Green and Howley).

2-9-21 GB   Starr pressured, passes incomplete to Wilson.

3-9-21 GB   Cowboys penalized 5 yards for illegal procedure.

3-4-26 GB   Starr loses 5 trying to pass (Pugh).

4-9-21 GB   Anderson punts to Hayes; fair catch on Green Bay 47.

DALLAS

1-10-47 GB   (2:30) Reeves runs left for 2 (Jordan).

2-8-45 GB   Clarke run loses 8 (Jordan).

3-16-47 D   Meredith passes incomplete to Rentzel.

4-16-47 D   Villanueva punts to Wood. Fumbled fair catch on 17; Clarke recovers for Cowboys.

DALLAS

1-10-17 GB   (1:34) Perkins runs for 3 (Nitschke).

2-7-14 GB   Meredith passes incomplete for Rentzel.

3-7-14 GB   Meredith passes to Reeves on right for 1 (Nitschke).

4-6-13 GB   Villanueva kicks 21-yard field goal.

Packers 14, Cowboys 10   (*Dallas scoring drive: 4 yards in 4 plays*)

Villanueva kicks to Weatherwax at Green Bay 41, 4 yard return.

GREEN BAY

1-10-45 GB Starr's pass blocked by Lilly.

2-10-45 GB Williams runs for 3 (Jordan).

HALFTIME SCORE: Packers 14, Cowboys 10

THIRD QUARTER

Villanueva kicks off to Caffey on Green Bay 37, returns to 44.

GREEN BAY

1-10-44 GB Anderson runs right for 3 (Lilly).

2-7-47 GB   Starr loses 4 trying to pass (Pugh).

3-11-43 GB Starr passes incomplete to Dowler on left sideline (Johnson).

4-11-43 GB Anderson punts to Rentzel. Fumbled fair catch at 21. Clarke recovers at 11.

DALLAS

1-10-11 D   (12:48) Meredith passes to Reeves for 7 (Adderley).

2-3-18 D   Perkins runs for 8, first down (Brown).

1-10-26 D   Meredith passes incomplete to Reeves in right flat.

2-10-26 D   Meredith passes to Clarke for 14; first down (Nitschke and Jeter).

1-10-40 D   Reeves runs right for 8 (Robinson).

2-2-48 D   Reeves runs right for 20 (Caffey).

1-10-32 GB Reeves runs for 3 (Brown).

2-7-29 GB   Meredith passes over middle to Rentzel for 11; first down.

1-10-18 GB Reeves runs left, loses 4 (Caffey).

2-14-22 GB Meredith passes incomplete to Rentzel on right side.

3-14-22 GB Meredith pressured, runs left for 9. Hit by Caffey and fumbles. Adderley recovers at Green Bay 13.

GREEN BAY

1-10-13 GB (7:51) Anderson runs right for 1 (Jordan).

2-9-14 GB   Anderson runs middle for 1 (Pugh).

3-8-15 GB   Starr passes to Dale on left for 12; first down.

1-10-27 GB Starr loses 16 trying to pass (Andrie).

2-26-11 GB Anderson runs right for 6 (Howley).

3-20-17 GB Anderson runs right for 9.

4-11-26 GB Anderson punts to Rentzel. Fumbled fair catch on 49, recovers at 46.

DALLAS

1-10-46 GB (4:48) Reeves runs left for 11 (Jeter and Caffey); first down.

1-10-35 GB Meredith passes to Reeves for 3 (Nitschke).

2-7-32 GB   Reeves runs right for 2 (Nitschke and Davis).

3-5-30 GB   Meredith loses 9 trying to pass (Caffey).

4-14-39 GB Villanueva's 47-yard field goal short; Wood returns from 4 to the 27.

GREEN BAY

1-10-27 GB (2:00) Anderson runs right for 5 (Lilly and Jordan).

2-5-32 GB   Anderson runs for 1 (Pugh).

3-4-33 GB   Starr loses 8 trying to pass (Edwards).

4-12-41 GB Anderson punts to Dallas 45; Hayes fair catch.

DALLAS

1-10-45 D   (:12) Perkins runs for 5 (Wood and Robinson).

END OF THIRD QUARTER: Packers 14, Cowboys 10

FOURTH QUARTER

DALLAS

2-5-50 GB   Reeves runs option left, passes to Rentzel for touchdown with :08 elapsed.

Cowboys 16, Packers 14

Villanueva kicks extra point.

Cowboys 17, Packers 14

Villanueva kicks off to Crutcher on Green Bay 31, returns to 34.

GREEN BAY

1-10-34 GB (14:43) Starr passes incomplete. Cowboys penalized for pass interference.

1-10-48 GB Mercein runs left for no gain.

2-10-48 GB Starr loses 5 trying to pass (Pugh).

3-15-43 GB Starr passes incomplete to Mercein; pass blocked by Jordan.

4-14-43 GB Anderson punts to Dallas 19; ball rolls dead.

DALLAS

1-10-19 D   (13:08) Perkins runs middle for 1 (Nitschke and Wood).

2-9-20 D   Reeves run loses 2 (Davis and Jordan).

3-11-18 D   Meredith passes incomplete long to Hayes.

4-11-18 D   Villanueva punts to Wood on Green Bay 36, no return. Cowboys penalized for facemasking.

GREEN BAY

1-10-47 GB   (11:18) Starr passes middle to Dowler for 19 (Howley).

1-10-34 D   Anderson runs middle for 1 (Pugh).

2-9-33 D   Starr pressured, pass blocked by Howley.

3-9-33 D   Starr passes incomplete to Anderson.

4-9-33 D   Chandler's 40-yard field goal short.

DALLAS

1-10-20 D   (9:44) Perkins runs for 5 (Wood).

2-5-25 D   Perkins runs for 1 (Kostelnik).

3-4-26 D   Perkins runs for 2. Packers penalized 5 yards for offsides; first down.

1-10-31 D   Reeves runs for 5 (Davis).

2-5-36 D   Reeves run loses 5 (Kostelnik).

3-10-31 D   Meredith passes on right sideline to Clarke for 16; first down.

1-10-47 D   Perkins runs for no gain (Kostelnik).

2-10-47 D   Meredith passes to Baynham in left flat for loss of 3.

3-13-44 D   Meredith passes incomplete to Rentzel in middle.

4-13-44 D   Villanueva punts to Wood on Green Bay 23, returns to 32.

GREEN BAY

1-10-32 GB   (4:54) Starr passes to Anderson in right flat for 6 (Green).

2-4-38 GB   (4:27) Mercein runs right end for 7; first down (Jordan).

1-10-45 GB   (3:57) Starr passes to Dowler in middle for 13; first down.

1-10-42 D   (3:30) Anderson runs right, loses 9 (Townes).

2-19-49 GB   (2:52) Starr passes to Anderson on right for 12 (Pugh).

3-7-39 D   (2:00) Starr passes to Anderson on right for 9.

1-10-30 D   (1:35) Starr passes to Mercein on left for 19; first down.

1-10-11 D   (1:11) Mercein runs middle for 8. Packer timeout.

2-2-3 D   (:54) Anderson runs right for 2; first down.

1-Goal-1 D   (:30) Anderson runs middle for no gain. Packer timeout.

2-Goal-1 D   (:20) Anderson runs middle, slips for no gain. Packer timeout.

3-Goal-1 D   (:16) Starr runs QB sneak to right; touchdown.

Packers 20, Cowboys 17

Chandler kicks extra point.

Packers 21, Cowboys 17 *(Green Bay scoring drive: 68 yards in 12 plays)*

Chandler kicks off into end zone; no return.

DALLAS

1-10-20 D   (:13) Meredith passes incomplete to Rentzel on right sideline; Cowboys penalized for illegal procedure.

2-15-15 D   (:07) Meredith passes incomplete to Hayes on right sideline.

FINAL SCORE: GREEN BAY 21, DALLAS 17

Cowboys Full Team Roster

1967

Player	Position	Height	Weight	Age
Andrie, George	DE	6-7	250	27
Boeke, Jim	T	6-5	260	28
Clark, Phil	S	6-2	207	21
Clarke, Frank	E	6-1	210	33
Colvin, Jim	DT	6-2	245	29
Connelly, Mike	G-T	6-3	248	31
Daniels, Dick	DB	5-9	180	22
Dial, Rice	E	6-1	185	30
Donohue, Leon	G	6-4	245	26
Edwards, Dave	LB	6-1	228	27
Gaechter, Mike	DB	6-0	190	27
Garrison, Walt	FB	6-0	205	23
Gent, Pete	E	6-4	205	25
Green, Cornell	DB	6-3	208	27
Hayes, Bob	E	5-11	185	24
Hays, Harold	LB	6-2	225	28
Howley, Chuck	LB	6-2	225	31
Johnson, Mike	DB	5-11	184	23
Jordan, Lee Roy	LB	6-1	225	26
Lilly, Bob	DT	6-5	260	28
Liscio, Tony	T	6-5	255	27
Livingston, Warren	DB	5-10	185	29
Manders, Dave	C	6-2	250	26
Meredith, Don	QB	6-3	205	29
Morton, Craig	QB	6-4	214	24
Neely, Ralph	T	6-6	265	23
Niland, John	G	6-3	245	23
Norman, Pettis	TE	6-3	225	28
Perkins, Don	FB	5-10	200	29
Pugh, Jethro	DT	6-6	260	23
Reeves, Dan	HB	6-1	200	23
Renfro, Mel	S	6-0	190	25
Rhome, Jerry	QB	6-0	185	25
Shy, Les	HB	6-1	200	23
Smith, J.D.	FB	6-1	205	35
Stokes, Sims	SE	6-1	198	23
Townes, Willie	DE	6-4	260	24
Villanueva, Danny	K-P	5-11	200	29
Walker, Malcolm	T	6-4	250	24
Wilbur, John	G	6-3	240	24

Packers Full Team Roster

1967

Player	Position	Height	Weight	Age
Adderley, Herb	CB	6-0	200	28
Aldridge, Lionel	DE	6-4	245	25
Anderson, Donny	HB-P	6-3	210	24
Bowman, Ken	C	6-3	230	24
Bratkowski, Zeke	QB	6-3	210	35
Brown, Bob	DE	6-5	260	27
Brown, Tom	S	6-1	195	26
Caffey, Lee Roy	LB	6-3	250	27
Capp, Dick	TE-LB	6-3	235	23
Chandler, Don	K	6-2	210	32
Crutcher, Tommy	LB	6-3	230	25
Dale, Carroll	FL	6-2	210	29
Davis, Willie	DE	6-3	245	34
Dowler, Boyd	SE	6-5	225	30
Flanigan, Jim	LB	6-3	240	22
Fleming, Marv	TE	6-4	245	25
Gillingham, Gale	G	6-3	255	23
Grabowski, Jim	FB	6-2	220	23
Gregg, Forrest	T	6-4	250	34
Hart, Doug	S	6-0	190	28
Horn, Don	QB	6-2	195	22
Hyland, Bob	C-G	6-5	250	22
Jeter, Bob	CB	6-1	205	29
Jordan, Henry	DT	6-3	250	32
Kostelnik, Ron	DT	6-4	260	27
Kramer, Jerry	G	6-3	245	32
Long, Bob	FL	6-3	205	26
McGee, Max	SE	6-3	210	35
Mercein, Chuck	FB	6-2	225	24
Nitschke, Ray	LB	6-3	240	31
Robinson, Dave	LB	6-3	240	26
Rowser, John	CB	6-1	180	23
Skoronski, Bob	T	6-3	245	34
Starr, Bart	QB	6-1	190	34
Thurston, Fred	T	6-1	245	34
Weatherwax, Jim	DT	6-7	260	24
Williams, Travis	HB	6-1	210	21
Wilson, Ben	FB	6-1	230	27
Wood, Willie	S	5-10	190	31
Wright, Steve	T	6-6	250	25

Individual Statistics
1967 Season Totals

Dallas

Rushing

Name	No.	Yds.	Avg.	TD
Perkins	201	823	4.1	6
Reeves	173	603	3.5	5
Garrison	24	146	6.1	0
Norman	9	91	10.1	0
Meredith	28	84	3.0	0
Clarke	4	72	18.0	1
Shy	17	58	3.5	0
Morton	15	42	2.8	0
Baynham	3	6	2.0	1
Rhome	2	−11	−5.5	0
Villanueva	1	−15	−15.0	0

Receiving

Name	No.	Yds.	Avg.	TD
Rentzel	58	906	17	8
Hayes	49	998	20	10
Reeves	39	490	13	6
Norman	20	220	11	2
Perkins	18	116	6	0
Clarke	9	119	13	1
Gent	9	88	10	1
Shy	3	36	12	0
Baynham	3	13	4	0
Garrison	2	17	9	0

Passing

Name	Att.	Comp.	%	Yds.	Yds./Att.	TD	Int.
Meredith	255	128	50	1834	7.2	16	16
Morton	137	69	50	978	7.1	10	10
Rhome	18	9	50	86	4.8	0	1
Reeves	7	4	57	195	27.9	2	1

Punt Returns

Name	No.	Yds.	Avg.	TD
Hayes	24	276	12	1
Rentzel	6	45	18	0
Renfro	3	−1	0	0

Kickoff Returns

Name	No.	Yds.	Avg.	TD
Garrison	20	366	18	0
Baynham	12	331	28	0
Renfro	5	112	22	0
Shy	5	96	19	0
Stokes	4	92	23	0
Hayes	1	17	17	0
East	1	0	0	0

Punting

Name	No.	Avg.
Villanueva	67	40.4

Kicking

Name	XP	Att.	%	FG	Att.	%
Villanueva	32	34	94	8	19	42
Deters	9	10	90	1	4	25

Interceptions

Name	No.
Green	7
Renfro	7
Johnson	5
Edwards	3
Jordan	3
Gaechter	2
Howley	1
Clark	1

Green Bay

Rushing

Name	No.	Yds.	Avg.	TD
Grabowski	120	466	3.9	2
Wilson	103	453	4.4	2
Anderson	97	402	4.1	6
Pitts	77	247	3.2	6
Willams	35	188	5.4	1
Starr	21	90	4.3	0
Mercein	14	46	4.0	1
Dale	1	9	9	0
Bratkowski	5	6	1.2	0
Horn	1	−2	−2	0

Receiving

Name	No.	Yds.	Avg.	TD
Rentzel	58	906	17	8
Dowler	54	836	15	4
Dale	35	738	21	5
Anderson	22	331	15	3
Pitts	15	210	14	0
Wilson	14	88	6	0
Grabowski	12	171	14	1
Fleming	10	126	13	1
Long	8	969	12	0
Williams	5	80	16	1
A. Brown	3	43	14	0
McGee	3	33	11	0
Mercein	1	6	6	0

Passing

Name	Att.	Comp.	%	Yds.	Yds./Att.	TD	Int.
Starr	210	115	55	1823	8.7	9	17
Bratkowski	94	53	56	724	7.7	5	9
Horn	24	12	50	171	7.1	1	1
Anderson	2	1	50	19	9.5	0	0
Pitts	1	1	100	21	21	0	0

Punt Returns

Name	No.	Yds.	Avg.	TD
Anderson	9	98	11	0
T. Brown	9	40	4	0
Pitts	9	16	2	0
Wood	12	3	0	0

Kickoff Returns

Name	No.	Yds.	Avg.	TD
Williams	18	739	41	4
Anderson	11	226	21	0
Adderley	10	207	21	0
Crutcher	3	48	16	0
A. Brown	1	13	13	0
Hart	1	8	8	0
Robinson	1	0	0	0
Wood	1	0	0	0

Punting

Name	No.	Avg.
Anderson	65	36.6
Chandler	1	31.0

Kicking

Name	XP	Att.	%	FG	Att.	%
Chandler	39	39	100	19	29	66
Mercein	2	3	67	0	1	0

Interceptions

Name	No.
Green	7
Jeter	8
Adderley	4
Robinson	4
Wood	4
Nitschke	3
Caffey	2
T. Brown	1

Team Statistics
1967 Season Totals

DALLAS	GREEN BAY		DALLAS	GREEN BAY
				OPPONENTS
		FIRST DOWNS		
261	.243	.Number	.236	.183*
109	.115	.by Rushing	64*	.98
141	.112	.by Passing	.145	.78*
11	.16	.by Penalty	.27	.7*
		RUSHING		
477	.474	.Number	339*	.443
1900	.1915	.Yards	1081*	.1926
4.0	.4.0	.Avg.	.3.2	.4.3
13	.18	.TD	.11	.7
		PASSING		
417	.331	.Attempts	.482	.337
210	.182	.Completions	.260	.155
50.4	.55.0	.Comp. %	.53.9	.46.0
3093	.2758	.Yards	.3167	.1644*
7.4	8.3*	.Yards/Attempt (Gross)	.6.6	.4.9*
14.7	.15.2	.Yards/Comp. (Gross)	.12.2	.10.6*
42	.41	.Sacked	.45	.29
294	.394	.Yards Lost Sacked	.377	.267
2799	.2364	.Net Yards	.2790	.1377*
28	.15	.TD	.21	.13
28	.27	.Interceptions	.29	.26
6.7	.8.2	.% Int.	.6.0	.7.7
		PUNTING		
67	.66	.Number	.72	.75
40.4	.36.5	.Avg.	.42.5	.41.6

Best in NFL

DALLAS	GREEN BAY		DALLAS	GREEN BAY
				OPPONENTS

PUNT RETURNS

DALLAS	GREEN BAY		DALLAS	GREEN BAY
33	.39	Number	.37	.13*
320	.157	Yards	.266	.22*
9.7	.4.0	Avg. Yards	.7.2	.1.7*
1	.0	TD	.0	.0

KICKOFF RETURNS

DALLAS	GREEN BAY		DALLAS	GREEN BAY
48	.46	Number	.59	.59
1014	.1241	Yards	.1350	.1276
21.1	.27.0*	Avg. Yards	.22.9	.21.6
0	.4*	TD	.0	.0

INTERCEPTION RETURNS

DALLAS	GREEN BAY		DALLAS	GREEN BAY
29	.26	Number	.28	.27
331	.284	Yards	.353	.370
11.4	.10.9	Avg. Yards	.12.6	.13.7
3	.2	TD	.3	.3

PENALTIES

DALLAS	GREEN BAY		DALLAS	GREEN BAY
81	.48	Number	.64	.55
785	.531	Yards	.717	.482

FUMBLES

DALLAS	GREEN BAY		DALLAS	GREEN BAY
26	.19	Number	.27	.23
14	.10	Fumbles Lost	19*	.14

SCORING

DALLAS	GREEN BAY		DALLAS	GREEN BAY
342	.332	Points	.268	.209
45	.39	XP Attempted	.35	.24
41	.39	XP Made	.34	.23
23	.29	FG Attempted	.23	.28
9	.19	FG Made	8*	.14
39.1	.65.5	% FG Made	34.8*	.50
2	.1	Safeties	.0	.0

Best in NFL

Green Bay Packers

1967 Season

17	DETROIT	17
13	CHICAGO	10
23	ATLANTA	0
27	Detroit	17
7	MINNESOTA	10
48	New York	21
31	St. Louis	23
10	Baltimore	13
55	CLEVELAND	7
13	SAN FRANCISCO	0
17	Chicago	13
30	Minnesota	27
24	Los Angeles	27
17	PITTSBURGH	24

Points Scored: 332; Allowed: 209
Regular Season Record: 9-4-1

Western Conference Playoff
28 . . . . .LOS ANGELES 7

NFL Championship Game
21 . . . . .DALLAS 17

Super Bowl II
33 . . . . .Oakland 14

Dallas Cowboys

1967 Season

21	Cleveland	14
38	NEW YORK	24
13	LOS ANGELES	35
17	Washington	14
14	NEW ORLEANS	10
24	Pittsburgh	21
14	Philadelphia	21
37	ATLANTA	7
27	New Orleans	10
20	WASHINGTON	27
46	ST. LOUIS	21
17	Baltimore	23
38	PHILADELPHIA	17
16	San Francisco	24

Points Scored: 342; Allowed: 268
Regular Season Record: 9-5

Eastern Conference Playoff
52 . . . . .CLEVELAND 14

NFL Championship Game
17 . . . . .Green Bay 21

All-Time Series
Green Bay vs. Dallas

1960	Packers	41–7	(GB)
1964	Packers	45–21	(D)
1965	Packers	13–3	(Mil)
1966	Packers	34–27	(D)*
1967	Packers	21–17	(GB)*
1968	Packers	28–17	(D)
1970	Cowboys	16–3	(D)
1972	Packers	16–13	(Mil)
1975	Packers	19–17	(D)
1978	Cowboys	42–14	(Mil)
1980	Cowboys	28–7	(Mil)
1982	Cowboys	37–26	(D)***
1984	Cowboys	20–6	(D)
1989	Packers	31–13	(GB)
1989	Packers	20–10	(D)
1991	Cowboys	20–17	(D)
1993	Cowboys	36–14	(D)
1994	Cowboys	42–31	(D)
1994	Cowboys	35–9	(D)***
1995	Cowboys	34–24	(D)
1995	Cowboys	38–27	(D)**
1996	Cowboys	21–6	(D)
1997	Packers	45–17	(GB)
1999	Cowboys	27–13	(D)
2004	Packers	41–20	(GB)

Cowboys lead series, 13–12

* *NFL Championship*
** *NFC Championship*
*** *NFC Second-round Playoff*

Packers All-Time Season Results
1960–2004

Year	Regular Season Record	Coach	Overall Finish
1960	8-4-0	Vince Lombardi	First, Western Conference
1961	11-3-0	Vince Lombardi	NFL Champions
1962	13-1-0	Vince Lombardi	NFL Champions
1963	11-2-1	Vince Lombardi	Winners, Playoff Bowl
1964	8-5-1	Vince Lombardi	Second (tie), Western Conference
1965	10-3-1	Vince Lombardi	NFL Champions
1966	12-2-0	Vince Lombardi	Super Bowl Champions
1967	9-4-1	Vince Lombardi	Super Bowl Champions
1968	6-7-1	Phil Bengston	Third, NFL Central
1969	8-6-0	Phil Bengston	Third, NFL Central
1970	6-8-0	Phil Bengston	Third (tie), NFC Central
1971	4-8-2	Dan Devine	Fourth, NFC Central
1972	10-4-0	Dan Devine	First, NFC Central
1973	5-7-2	Dan Devine	Third, NFC Central
1974	6-8-0	Dan Devine	Third, NFC Central
1975	4-10-0	Bart Starr	Third (tie), NFC Central
1976	5-9-0	Bart Starr	Fourth, NFC Central
1977	4-10-0	Bart Starr	Fourth, NFC Central
1978	8-7-1	Bart Starr	First (tie), NFC Central
1979	5-11-0	Bart Starr	Fourth, NFC Central
1980	5-10-1	Bart Starr	Fourth (tie), NFC Central
1981	8-8-0	Bart Starr	Second (tie), NFC Central
1982	5-3-1	Bart Starr	Winners, First Round, Super Bowl Tournament
1983	8-8-0	Bart Starr	Second (tie), NFC Central
1984	8-8-0	Forrest Gregg	Second, NFC Central
1985	8-8-0	Forrest Gregg	Second, NFC Central
1986	4-12-0	Forrest Gregg	Fourth, NFC Central
1987	5-9-1	Forrest Gregg	Third, NFC Central
1988	4-12-0	Lindy Infante	Fourth (tie), NFC Central
1989	10-6-0	Lindy Infante	First (tie), NFC Central
1990	6-10-0	Lindy Infante	Second (tie), NFC Central
1991	4-12-0	Lindy Infante	Fourth, NFC Central
1992	9-7-0	Mike Holmgren	Second, NFC Central
1993	9-7-0	Mike Holmgren	Winners, NFC Wild Card Playoff
1994	9-7-0	Mike Holmgren	Winners, NFC Wild Card Playoff
1995	11-5-0	Mike Holmgren	Winners, NFC Divisional Playoff
1996	13-3-0	Mike Holmgren	Super Bowl Champions
1997	13-3-0	Mike Holmgren	NFC Champions
1998	11-5-0	Mike Holmgren	Second, NFC Central (Wild-Card Qualifier)
1999	8-8-0	Ray Rhodes	Third (tie), NFC Central
2000	9-7-0	Mike Sherman	Third (tie), NFC Central
2001	12-4-0	Mike Sherman	Winners, NFC Wild-Card Playoff
2002	12-4-0	Mike Sherman	First, NFC Central
2003	10-6-0	Mike Sherman	First, NFC North
2004	10-6-0	Mike Sherman	First, NFC North

Cowboys All-Time Season Results
1960–2004

Year	Regular Season Record	Coach	Overall Finish
1960	0-11-1	Tom Landry	Seventh, Western Conference
1961	4-9-1	Tom Landry	Sixth, Eastern Conference
1962	5-8-1	Tom Landry	Fifth, Eastern Conference
1963	4-10-0	Tom Landry	Fifth, Eastern Conference
1964	5-8-1	Tom Landry	Fifth, Eastern Conference
1965	7-7-0	Tom Landry	Second, Eastern Conference
1966	10-3-1	Tom Landry	First, Eastern Conference
1967	9-5-0	Tom Landry	First, Eastern Conference
1968	12-2-0	Tom Landry	Winners, Playoff Bowl
1969	11-2-1	Tom Landry	First, Capitol Division
1970	10-4-0	Tom Landry	NFC Champions
1971	11-3-0	Tom Landry	Super Bowl Champions
1972	10-4-0	Tom Landry	Winners, NFC Divisional Playoff
1973	10-4-0	Tom Landry	Winners, NFC Divisional Playoff
1974	8-6-0	Tom Landry	Third, NFC East
1975	10-4-0	Tom Landry	NFC Champions
1976	11-3-0	Tom Landry	First, NFC East
1977	12-2-0	Tom Landry	Super Bowl Champions
1978	12-4-0	Tom Landry	NFC Champions
1979	11-5-0	Tom Landry	First, NFC East
1980	12-4-0	Tom Landry	Winners, NFC Divisional Playoff
1981	12-4-0	Tom Landry	Winners, NFC Divisional Playoff
1982	6-3-0	Tom Landry	Winners, Second Round, Super Bowl Tournament
1983	12-4-0	Tom Landry	Second, NFC East
1984	9-7-0	Tom Landry	Fourth, NFC East
1985	10-6-0	Tom Landry	First, NFC East
1986	7-9-0	Tom Landry	Third, NFC East
1987	7-8-0	Tom Landry	Second, NFC East
1988	3-13-0	Tom Landry	Fifth, NFC East
1989	1-15-0	Jimmy Johnson	Fifth, NFC East
1990	7-9-0	Jimmy Johnson	Fourth, NFC East
1991	11-5-0	Jimmy Johnson	Winners, First Round Playoffs
1992	13-3-0	Jimmy Johnson	Super Bowl Champions
1993	12-4-0	Jimmy Johnson	Super Bowl Champions
1994	12-4-0	Barry Switzer	Winners, NFC Divisional Playoff
1995	12-4-0	Barry Switzer	Super Bowl Champions
1996	10-6-0	Barry Switzer	First (tie), NFC East
1997	6–10–0	Barry Switzer	Fourth, NFC East
1998	10–6–0	Chan Gailey	First, NFC East
1999	8–8–0	Chan Gailey	Second, NFC East (Wild-Card Qualifier)
2000	5–11–0	Dave Campo	Fourth, NFC East
2001	5–11–0	Dave Campo	Fifth, NFC East
2002	5–11–0	Dave Campo	Fourth, NFC East
2003	10–6–0	Bill Parcells	Second, NFC East
2004	6–10–0	Bill Parcells	Second (tie), NFC East

Index

A

Adderley, Herb, 26, 101, 181
  in Ice Bowl, 139, 158, 177
Alabama, University of, 106, 191
Albans, Dick, 65
Aldridge, Lionel, 151
All-American Football Conference
  (AAFC), 49–50
Allen, Ermal, 135, 222
Allen, George, 112
  1967 NFL playoffs, 116–121,
  125
Ameche, Alan "The Horse," 73,
  208–209
American Football League (AFL),
  89–90
  television and, 32–33
Anderson, Donny, 105, 141–142
  in Ice Bowl, 141, 143–144,
  149, 173, 190–194, 198,
  199–203
  possible touchdown of,
  199–200, 226
Andrie, George, 84–85, 219
  game day weather and, 15
  in Ice Bowl, 131, 143,
  151–152, 158–159, 181, 192,
  198, 198
Arkansas, University of, 57
Atlanta Constitution, 27
Atlanta Falcons, 27, 89, 102,
  114, 230
Austin, Bill, 67

B

Baltimore Colts, 31, 50, 75, 110,
  120
  in Super Bowls, 32, 223
  versus New York Giants, 53,
  65–66, 73, 208
Bass, Dick, 82, 117
Baughan, Maxie, 117–118, 121,
  127
Baynham, Craig, 128–129

Behrend, Ken, 23
Bengston, Phil, 20–21, 101, 136,
  180, 230
Bergey, Bill, 100
Bettis, Tom, 101
Bible, Dana X., 48
Biever, John, 139, 209, 213
Biever, Vernon, 139, 209
Blaik, Earl "Red," 38, 66, 67
Blair, Sam, 42, 219, 224–225
Boeke, Jim, 172
Bourgeois, Viola, 47
Bowman, Ken, 30, 141, 142,
  227–228
  in Ice Bowl, 151–152, 154,
  173, 207, 213
  on Starr's quarterback sneak,
  219–220
Boyd, Bob, 55
Bradshaw, Terry, 137
Braisher, Dad, 20
Brandt, Gil, 172, 176
Bratkowski, Zeke, 105
Brito, Gene, 119
Brodie, John, 121
Brooklyn Eagles, 37
Brookshier, Tom
  on Dailey, 148
  on game day weather, 11, 12,
  14
  at Ice Bowl, 21, 148,
  149–150, 159–160, 219–220
  on Verna, 147
Brown, Jim, 71, 73, 83, 88,
  127–128
Brown, Paul, 34, 49, 65, 68, 128
Brown, Roger, 120
Brown, Rosey, 63–65, 67, 122
Brown, Timmy, 82
Brown, Tom
  in 1966 NFL championship
  game, 87, 88, 205
  in 1967 NFL playoffs, 124

  in Ice Bowl, 185
Bryant, Paul "Bear," 44, 191
Buck, Jack, 12, 14, 139, 148,
  158–159, 170
Burns, Jerry, 183

C

Caffey, Lee Roy, 177–176
  in Ice Bowl, 136, 170,
  176–177, 180–181
Campbell, Marion, 118
Carroll, Dr. Gerry, 36
Cartwright, Gary, 40, 59
Casey, Bernie, 117, 124
CBS, 33
  coverage of 1966 NFL cham-
  pionship game, 86–88
  coverage of Ice Bowl, 11, 12,
  16, 18, 23–24, 146–150,
  206–207, 215–216, 223–224
Chandler, Don, 24
  in Ice Bowl, 130, 132, 154,
  180, 186, 216
  as New York Giant, 53–54
Chicago Bears, 37, 51, 102, 111,
  117
Christiansen, Jack, 61
Clark, Phil, 159
Clarke, Frank, 87–88, 96–97, 176
Cleveland Browns, 34, 110, 223
  in 1950s, 31, 44–45, 50, 65,
  72–73, 83
  1967 NFL playoff, 127–129
Cohane, Tim, 33–34, 36
Collier, Blanton, 128
Collins, Gary, 128
Colorado, University of, 144, 154
Conerly, Charlie, 62–65, 66
Connell, Joe, 134
Connelly, Mike, 113, 135
Cosell, Howard, 35
Creasy, Bill, 23–24, 148, 206,
  219, 223

Crowley, Jim, 49, 66, 80
Curry, Bill, 26, 29–30, 101, 188

D

Dailey, Bob, 23–24, 148, 219, 220
Dale, Carroll, 21
    in 1966 NFL championship game, 87
    in 1967 NFL playoffs, 124, 127
    in Ice Bowl, 143, 194–195
Daley, Art, 27, 123, 133
    at Ice Bowl, 143, 209, 219–223
Dallas Cowboys, 11–13
    1966 NFL championship game, 85–88
    1967 season, 91–92, 111, 114–115
        individual stats, 242
        playoff game, 127–129
        record, 246
        team roster, 240
        team stats, 244–245
        see also Ice Bowl
    flex defense of, 44–45, 82–85
        diagram, 83
    record of, 1960–2002, 249
    record of, versus Green Bay, 247
    scouting efforts of, 172
    shifting I-formation of, 137
        diagram, 138
    uniforms of, 21
Dallas Texans, 89
Daly, Dan, 227
Davis, Willie, 11, 91, 101, 124, 181
Dawson, Len, 99
Detroit Lions, 61, 98, 102
Devenport, Dave, 23
Donnelly, Joe, 39
Donohue, Paul, 176
Donovan, Artie, 65–66
Dowler, Boyd, 21, 124, 154–155
    in 1966 NFL championship game, 87

in Ice Bowl, 143–145, 153–156, 192–193, 198, 207, 216
Dowling, Tom, 39

E

Edwards, Dave, 153, 158, 181, 192, 195, 222
Effrat, Louis, 31
Elizabeth City State Teachers College, 172
Elsberger, Cy, 14
Esquire, 27–29, 34
Ewbank, Weeb, 68

F

Favre, Bret, 228
Fitts, Bill, 146, 148, 149
Fleming, Marvin, 105, 124, 127, 143
Flynn, George L., 225
Fordham University, 36–38, 66, 80
Frederickson, Tucker, 82

G

Gabriel, Roman, 117, 124–126
Gaechter, Mike, 143
George, Bill, 108
Gifford, Frank
    game day weather and, 12, 14
    at Ice Bowl, 24, 139, 146, 148, 185, 206, 223–224
    on Lombardi, 62
    as player, 31, 56–58, 62–65, 67, 76
Gillingham, Gale
    in 1967 NFL playoffs, 125, 126
    in Ice Bowl, 141, 173–172, 192, 197–199
Gillman, Sid, 68
Gossett, Bruce, 124
Grabowski, Jim, 87, 105, 126
Graf, Fritz, 215
Graham, Otto, 31, 44, 49–50, 61
Green, Cornell, 42, 129, 192

Green, Ernie, 127
Green Bay Packers, 11–13
    1966 NFL championship game, 86–88
    1967 season, 91, 98–99, 102, 103–105, 109–111
        individual stats, 243
        playoff game 116–117, 121–127
        record, 246
        team roster, 241
        team stats, 244–245
        see also Ice Bowl
    conditioning of, 29–30
    fans of, 15, 17–18, 19, 25–26, 123, 132–133, 171
    Lombardi's arrival at, 75–78
    power sweep of, 13, 79–81
        diagram, 79
    record of, 1960–2002, 248
    record of, versus Dallas Cowboys, 247
    65 Give influence play of, 196–198
        diagram, 199
    31 Wedge play of, 203–204, 207–208, 213–215
        diagram, 214
    uniforms of, 20
Gregg, Forrest, 91, 121–122, 181
    in 1967 NFL playoffs, 127
    in Ice Bowl, 141, 159, 198, 225
    on Nitschke, 101
Grier, Rosey, 31, 44, 56, 57–58, 69–70, 72
    Los Angeles Rams and, 118, 119
Groza, Lou, 73

H

Halas, George, 90
Hanburger, Chris, 180
Harrington, John, 19
Hart, Jim, 114
Hayes, Bob, 85, 92, 129, 173
    in 1966 NFL championship game, 87–88
    in Ice Bowl, 216

Hecker, Norb, 27

Heinrich, Don, 58, 63

Heinz, W.C., 28

Hickerson, Gene, 128

Hirsch, Elroy "Crazy Legs," 61

Hornung, Paul, 14, 27, 33, 75–77, 198

  at Ice Bowl, 159–160, 185

  power sweep and, 80–81

  retirement of, 91, 98, 108

Houston Oilers, 18, 141

Howell, Jim Lee, 38, 51, 52–56, 66–67, 74

  on coaching, 57

  on Landry, 54, 56, 60

  on Lombardi, 54, 60

Howley, Chuck, 84

  in 1966 NFL championship game, 87

  in 1967 NFL playoffs, 129

  in Ice Bowl, 190–191, 193–194, 199, 213, 222

Huff, Sam

  as New York Giant, 31, 44, 53–54, 57–59, 70–72

  as Washington Redskin, 94, 97

Hunt, Lamar, 90

Hyland, Bob, 132, 141, 142

I

Ice Bowl

  by quarter

    first, 24, 130–145

    second, 150–160

    third, 171–177, 179–186

    fourth, 187–216

  play-by-play, 234–239

  starting line-ups, 232

  statistics, 233

  weather, 11–24, 130–131, 157–158, 187

Illinois, University of, 100–101

Instant Replay (Kramer), 122, 219, 227

Izenberg, Jerry, 27–28, 34–35, 133

J

Jeter, Bob, 87, 180, 183–185

Johnson, Charley, 114

Johnson, Chuck, 27, 160, 170, 198

Johnson, Marie, 23

Johnson, Mike, 144–145, 155

Jones, David "Deacon," 117–120, 181

  in 1967 NFL playoffs, 124, 127

Jordan, Henry, 20, 101, 105, 125

Jordan, Lee Roy, 84, 114, 191, 230

  in 1966 NFL championship game, 87

  in Ice Bowl, 141, 191, 195–196, 199, 200, 222

Josephson, Les, 124

Jurgensen, Sonny, 32, 106

K

Kaine, Elinor, 92, 108

Kansas City Chiefs, 13, 88, 99

Kapp, Joe, 137

Karras, Alex, 98, 143, 157

Katcavage, Jim, 72

Kavanaugh, Ken, 64

Kelly, Leroy, 127–129

Kensil, Jim, 18

Kolman, Ed, 53, 64, 66–67

Kostelnik, Ron, 137

Kramer, Jerry, 76, 81, 105, 219, 230

  1967 NFL playoffs, 122, 125

  game day weather and, 15–16, 20

  in Ice Bowl, 141, 158, 172–173, 188, 192–193, 199–200, 212–213, 215

    possible offside of, 215, 225–227

  on Lombardi, 35, 78, 220

  New York press and, 103–104

  on Olsen, 122–123

  on Starr, 108

Kriwanek, Russ, 23

Kuechle, Oliver, 27

L

Lambeau, Earl "Curly," 16

Lambeau Field, 16–17, 228–229

  practice fields, 26–27

  underground heating system, 12–14, 17, 18, 130, 218

Lamson, Chuck, 124

Landry, Alicia Wiggs, 22, 49, 55

Landry, Robert, 47

Landry, Tom

  1966 NFL championship game, 85–88

  1967 season, 92, 129

  coaching style of, 40–41, 59–60

  death of, 230

  flex defense of, 44–45, 82–85

    diagram, 83

  4-3-4-defense of, 44, 69

    diagram, 45

  at Ice Bowl, 22, 134, 140, 156, 160, 205–206, 212, 219–222

  on Lilly, 112

  on Lombardi, 59, 68

  Meredith and, 93–98

  New York Giants and, 43–44, 50, 55–60, 68–74

  New York Yankees (football) and, 48–50

  offensive strategy of, 13, 46, 92

  religion and, 46–47

  on Starr's quarterback sneak, 222

  at University of Texas, 47, 48–49

  World War II and, 43, 47–48

Landry (St. John), 47–48

Lane, Chuck, 18–19

Lavelli, Dante, 44

Layne, Bobby, 47

Lea, Bud, 27

LeBaron, Eddie, 95

Lilly, Bob, 84–85, 111–114, 229

  family of, 114

  on game day weather, 12–13, 15, 130, 157–158

in Ice Bowl, 134, 141, 143, 173, 190, 197–199, 203–204, 207–208, 222, 228

on Landry, 42–43

on Packers, 134, 142

on Starr, 156

Lindsey, Dale, 128

Liscio, Tony, 176

Lombardi, Harry, 35

Lombardi, Marie Planitz, 36–37

Lombardi, Matilda, 34

Lombardi, Vince, 11, 20, 75–82

1966 NFL championship game, 86–88

1967 season, 102, 104–105, 116–117, 121–127

coaching career before NFL, 37–38

coaching style of, 13, 25–29, 34, 38, 61–68

death of, 39, 230

on Gregg, 121

halfback sweep of, 63–65

diagram, 64

at Ice bowl, 12–14, 17–18, 21, 22, 205, 208–209, 212, 215, 215–218

Lambeau Field heating system and, 12–14, 17, 18, 130, 218

Mercein and, 126–127

New York Giants and, 38–39, 53–68

power sweep of, 13, 79–81

diagram, 79

press and, 27–30, 33–35, 116–117, 215

religion and, 39, 116–117

Starr and, 106–108

on Starr's quarterback sneak, 204–205

at Super Bowl II, 225

Wright and, 150–151

Look, 33

Los Angeles Rams, 55, 111

1967 NFL playoffs, 116–117, 120–121, 125–127

Luksa, Frank, 22

Lundy, Lamar, 118, 120

M

McAfee, Ken, 67

McGee, Max, 78, 192

McHan, Lamar, 106

Mack, Tom, 125

McLean, Ray "Scooter," 77

Madden, John, 228

Manders, Dave, 135

Mara, Wellington, 38, 59–60, 69, 126, 131

Marchetti, Gino, 66

Matisi, Tony, 36

Maule, Tex, 219

Meador, Eddie, 117–118, 126

Melotte, Joe, 23

Mercein, Chuck, 105, 126–127, 219

on game day weather, 15, 130, 131

in Ice Bowl, 141, 143, 189, 191, 194–198, 203, 207–209, 214–215

Meredith, Don, 13, 85, 92–98

1966 NFL championship game, 86–88, 205

in Ice Bowl, 134, 136–139, 150, 157–158, 173, 176–177, 180–181, 183–186, 216, 222–224

Miami Dolphins, 223

Miller, Glenn, 27

Miller, Tom, 23

Minnesota Vikings, 89, 102, 111

Mitchell, Bobby, 119

Modzelewski, Dick, 69–70

Moore, Jerry, 34, 35

Moore, Ted, 14, 171–170

Ice Bowl play-by-play of, 136, 144, 145, 153–154, 160, 185, 190, 191, 192, 193, 194, 195, 196, 198–199, 213, 215, 216

Morin, Milt, 129

Morrall, Earl, 70

Morton, Craig, 94, 96, 114, 173

Motley, Marion, 49

Murchison, Clint, 135

Murray, Jim, 35

Myers, Jim, 135, 160

Myhra, Steve, 73

N

National Football League (NFL), 50

1956 championship game, 51, 68

1958 championship game, 31, 73, 208

1966 championship game, 85–88, 132, 205

1967 playoffs

Eastern Conference, 127–129

Western Conference, 116–117, 123–127

1967 championship game, *see* Ice Bowl

divisions created, 89–90

television and, 31–33

National Football League: The First Fifty Years, 31

Neely, Ralph, 85, 92, 188, 230

on Davis, 181

game day weather and, 15, 22, 157

in Ice Bowl, 135–136, 138, 176, 181

on Meredith, 97

on Packers' defense, 101–102

New Orleans Saints, 89, 91, 98, 111, 114

New York Yankees (football), 48–50

New York Giants, 31, 41, 50–51, 110, 208

4-3-4 defense of, 44, 69

diagram, 45

halfback sweep of, 63–65

diagram, 64

Landry at, 43–44, 50, 55–56, 68–74

Lombardi at, 38–39, 53–68

offensive/defensive rivalry of, 55–57

play numbering system of, 67

New York Jets, 32

New York Post, 29

NFL Films, 22, 32, 145

Niland, John, 147, 176

Nitschke, Ray, 11, 26, 98–102, 105, 177, 179, 220–221, 229, 230 in 1966 NFL championship game, 86–87

in 1967 NFL playoffs, 117, 124, 125–126

family of, 100

on game day weather, 21

in Ice Bowl, 135–138, 177, 180, 182, 189, 194, 209–212, 215–218

Nobis, Tommy, 100, 105

Nolan, Dick, 41–42, 134

Norman, Pettis, 88, 114, 172

Notre Dame, University of, 54, 66, 80

O

Oakland Raiders, 18, 225

O'Donnel, Bob, 227

Olsen, Merlin, 93, 117–118, 120, 124–125

Owen, Steve, 68

at New York Giants, 38, 44, 50, 70–71

at Philadelphia Eagles, 65

P

Palau, Andy, 37

Paquin, Leo, 37

Parilli, Babe, 106

Parker, Buddy, 70

Parker, Jim, 122, 125

Patton, Jimmy, 72

Pearson, Preston, 99–100, 137

Perkins, Don, 87, 92, 129, 173, 182, 220

in Ice Bowl, 135, 173, 182

Perkins, Steve, 221, 223

Peterson, Orvell, 23

Philadelphia Eagles, 65, 111, 176, 183, 209

Pitts, Elijah, 87, 105, 126

Pittsburgh, University of, 80

Pittsburgh Steelers, 65, 70, 102, 111, 114, 137

Press

at Ice Bowl, 11–23, 139, 143

Lombardi and, 27–30, 33–35, 116–117, 215

in New York, 103–104

See also CBS; Moore, Ted

Pro Football 1967 (Zanger), 91

Pro Football Chronicle, The (Daly and O'Donnel), 227

Pro Football Illustrated, 91–92

Proski, Johnny, 18–20

Pugh, Jethro, 85, 172, 230

in Ice Bowl, 22, 172–173, 181, 188, 199, 203–204, 207, 212, 215, 225–227

Putnam, William, 23

R

Reeves, Dan, 92, 98, 114, 128, 173–176, 230

in Ice Bowl, 136, 138, 150, 173–177, 180–185

option pass of, 183

diagram, 182

on Starr's quarterback sneak, 226

Remmel, Lee, 14, 27, 223, 228

Renfro, Mel, 42, 85, 87, 176

in Ice Bowl, 153–156, 194, 198, 199

Rentzel, Lance, 92, 93, 114

on game day weather, 15, 21–22

in Ice Bowl, 139, 150, 157, 176–177, 181–185, 187, 206, 212, 216

Rhome, Jerry, 94, 175

Riffenburgh, Beau, 125

Ringo, Jim, 176

Robb, Joe, 122

Robinson, Dave, 88, 124, 177, 206

Robustelli, Andy, 31, 44, 72

Rockne, Knute, 66, 80

Roland, Johnny, 114

Rote, Kyle, 52–53, 57–58, 61

Rowe, Harmon, 49

Rozelle, Pete, 18, 90

Run To Daylight (Lombardi and Heinz), 28, 35, 107

Ryan, Frank, 128–129

S

St. Cecilia High School, 37–38

St. John, Bob, 23, 47–48, 212, 221

St. Louis Cardinals, 110, 114

San Francisco 49ers, 42, 50, 121

Schaap, Dick, 219

Schachter, Norm, 16, 134, 203, 205, 210

Schafrath, Dick, 128

Schnelker, Bob, 65, 160

Schramm, Tex, 88, 94–95

Scott, Ray, 88

at Ice Bowl, 139, 148, 170, 216

Shapiro, Milton, 127

Shaw, Buck, 49

Shecter, Leonard, 27, 28–29, 34

Sheppard, Bob, 58, 72

Sherman, Allie, 126

Sherrod, Blackie, 218, 221, 224

Shula, Don, 65

Skoronski, Bob, 221

in Ice Bowl, 150, 151, 198, 200, 210

Smith, Don, 55

Smith, Red, 35, 39, 116–117, 126

Snow, Jack, 117

Snyder, Cameron, 23

South Carolina State College, 118

Southern Methodist University, 92–93, 94

Speedie, Mac, 44, 49–50

Spieller, Art, 145, 209

Starr, Bart, 11, 21, 25, 76, 77, 98, 105–111, 179, 229

in 1966 NFL championship game, 86–87

in 1967 NFL playoffs, 120–121, 124, 127

in Ice Bowl, 141–144, 150–159, 173–174, 181, 187–216, 218–219, 225–226

injuries of, 27, 98, 105–106, 109–110

on Jones, 121

second quarter pass, 154

diagram, 155

Starr, Cherry, 107
Stautner, Ernie, 83–84, 131, 174, 191, 193
  on Lilly, 112–113
Stokes, Sims, 24, 92, 130, 132
Stram, Hank, 13, 89
Summerall, Pat, 59, 73, 150, 206, 216
Super Bowl, 90
  I, 11, 13, 88, 90, 99, 108
  II, 90, 225
  III, 32
  V, 223
  VI, 223
Sutherland, Jock, 80
Svare, Harland, 56, 70
Svoboda, Bill, 70
Swiacki, Bill, 63

T

Tarkenton, Fran, 119
Taylor, Jim, 27, 71, 80–81, 152
  in 1966 NFL championship game, 87
  move to Saints, 91, 98, 108
Television, 31–33. *See also* CBS
Texas, University of, 47, 48–49
Texas A&M University, 178
Texas Christian University, 112, 113
Texas Technological University, 141
Thurston, Fred "Fuzzy," 17–18, 122, 217
Thurston, Mark, 17–18
Tinglehoff, Mick, 137
Tittle, Y.A., 49
Torgeson, Torgy, 118
Townes, Willie, 85, 192–193
  in Ice Bowl, 143, 159, 192, 208, 213
Triplett, Mel, 65
Tubbs, Jerry, 196
Tulsa, University of, 193
Tunnell, Emlen, 62, 72

U

Unitas, John, 31, 73, 106, 120, 188, 206, 216
U.S. Military Academy (West Point), 38, 66
Utah State University, 118

V

Verna, Tony, 23–24, 146–148, 149, 206, 215, 219
Villanueva, Danny, 140, 150, 159, 171, 171, 181, 186
Vince Lombardi on Football (Flynn), 225
"Violent World of Sam Huff, The," 71

W

Wagner, Len, 14, 217
Wagner College, 52
Wallace, William N., 33
Ward, Arch, 49
Warfield, Paul, 128
Washington Redskins, 65, 70, 94, 98, 111, 114
Webster, Alex, 65, 67
"What's My Line?", 99
White, Ed, 112
White, Jack, 48–49
Wietecha, Ray, 160
Wiggins, Bill, 48
Willard, Ken, 82
Williams, Travis, 105, 110–111, 124–125, 127, 230
  in Ice Bowl, 150, 152, 200
Wilson, Ben, 105, 150, 153, 158
Wisconsin State University of La Crosse Marching Chiefs, 19, 159
Woessner, Bob, 22, 153, 154
Wolf, Ron, 228–229
Wood, Willie, 26, 87, 101, 125
  in Ice Bowl, 140, 159, 160, 183–185, 193
Wright, Rayfield, 92
Wright, Steve, 150–152
WTMJ radio. See Moore, Ted

Y

Yale University, 126
Yelvington, Dick, 67
Young, Buddy, 49

Z

Zanger, Jack, 91, 92
Zima, Jim, 22–23, 221